S0-BSK-010

ST. MARY'S COLLEGE OF MARYLAND
ST. MARY'S CITY, MARYLAND 20686

Sense of Place: Mississippi

Sense of Place: Mississippi

EDITED BY
Peggy W. Prenshaw
and Jesse O. McKee

UNIVERSITY PRESS OF MISSISSIPPI • *Jackson*

Copyright© 1979 by
THE SOUTHERN QUARTERLY
Manufactured in the United States of America

Cover design by Bob Luke

Second printing, 1980,

Library of Congress Cataloging in Publication Data
Main entry under title:

Sense of place: Mississippi.

    Papers presented at a symposium held at the University
of Southern Mississippi, Hattiesburg on Oct. 5-6, 1978.
    Appears also in the Southern quarterly, v. 17, no. 3 & 4.
    Includes bibliographical references and index.
    1.   Mississippi—Civilization—Congresses.
I.   Prenshaw, Peggy Whitman.   II.   McKee, Jesse O.
F341.S4   976.2   79-26098
ISBN 0-87805-110-4
ISBN 0-87805-111-2 pbk.

Contents

Introduction

Most Americans feel a special attachment to a specific geographical area within the United States; that is, they have a "sense of place." The factors which contribute to the development of one's sense of place (or topophilia) are numerous and varied. Typically, family ties, landscape features (mountains, streams, plants and trees), types of food, architectural styles, and a host of other cultural and environmental traits help people to identify with a specific geographical place.

Mississippi is a state with a rich cultural heritage. In many respects it shares traits with the other forty-nine states, and yet it also possesses a unique history, a specific landscape, and its own individuality. What, then, makes the place *Mississippi* different and what causes many Mississippians, whether they presently reside within the state or live outside, to develop an affective bond with their state?

In October 1978, with the aid of a grant from the Mississippi Committee for the Humanities and the cooperation of administrative and staff personnel at the University of Southern Mississippi, we assembled a group of scholars and public officials for a two-day symposium on the campus at Hattiesburg to identify and discuss what is distinctive about Mississippi, its land, its people and culture. A specific aim was to explore the factors which have contributed to the development of a Mississippian's sense of place. In addition, the symposium participants sought to examine the values for the individual and the community that come from having a strong sense of place, and to consider policies and actions of the media, governmental agencies, and businesses that promote or threaten a citizen's bond with his or her environment.

Persons invited to speak at the symposium represented such diverse disciplines as literature, music, art, religion, folklore, architecture, anthropology, archeology, social history, journalism, community and regional planning, and cultural-historical geography. Their presentations ranged from keynote addresses to forums and focus papers. In addition, the symposium celebrated the sense of place through musical performances, multi-media presentations, folklife displays, films, and arts and crafts exhibits. The more than 250 persons who attended the symposium represented a cross section of Mississippians.

In March 1979 we were informed that the symposium had been selected for a national award, the 1979 Creative Programming Award, given annually by the Conferences and Institutes Executive Committee of the National University Extension Association. We wish to thank all of the participants who contributed to the success of the symposium and thus to our receiving this award.

We are pleased to offer the following papers from the symposium in a special issue of the *Southern Quarterly* and as a separate volume for the participants and others interested in the topics raised here. Included are the four keynote addresses, the combined papers from each of the three forums, and six focus papers from the concurrent sessions. A copy of the symposium agenda is placed at the conclusion.

The publication of these papers represents the final stage of our endeavor to address the important issues involved in understanding what a sense of place is and how it is experienced in Mississippi. We regard these issues as representative of those encountered by any person or society seeking to understand the relation of human beings to their special places. These papers take up the particular case of Mississippi, but we trust they do so in ways that will suggest to citizens and scholars everywhere what is involved in the vital connection that links a man or woman to this world, the connection that defines one's sense of place.

Peggy W. Prenshaw, Project Coordinator
Jesse O. McKee, Project Director

A Sense of Place
and the Americanization
of Mississippi

WILLIE MORRIS

When I was running *Harper's Magazine,* an irascible friend from New Orleans who had been living in New York City for a long time used to come to the bar on Madison Avenue and 34th Street where we'd congregate with our writers after work. One afternoon there were a couple of people there from Mississippi, and we were talking about change in our native state. After listening to a little of this, my friend from New Orleans launched into this tirade: "You fellows are writers, and you have the gall to say you want to change Mississippi? You must be insane. Here you are from a place that's produced the best damned writers in America . . . that's always had the courage of the most noble fools . . . and the most haunting landscape in all the United States . . . and a spoken word that would make a drunk Irishman envious . . . and miscegenation that's the envy of Brazil . . . and a sense of the histrionic that would pale the Old Testament . . . and a past so contorted that it embarrasses the people of Scarsdale . . . and you say you want to *change* Mississippi?" He finished with an exultant flourish: "Why if I were you, I'd put up big green signs at every point of entry into Mississippi which said, 'Posted. No Trespassing.' "

I will admit something in the brooding Celtic side of me responded to my friend's wild injunction. I described something of this scene in a book I once wrote, and I received two dozen letters from Mississippi people saying my friend was absolutely right. Three of the correspondents said they would put up the signs themselves. I am a writer, and everyone I ever knew from Mississippi who has used the written word knows in his deepest heart that Mississippi is different, that there is something almost indefinable in our chemistry which makes

3

us so, that there is a resonance in the very word *Mississippi* which demands the attention of the spirit, that, black and white, we are obsessed with the slow mournful passing of the seasons and the stories we tell on each other and the things our people were and did, the peculiar quality of our humor and the opposition of our good-mannered civility and our rebelliousness, and the dark shadows of our past that, in combination, make us unique among our contemporary Americans. I see this every time I return home, such as now, and I see it too every time I'm in the company of Mississippians in Northern places. When Mississippians meet by chance far away, is it not something to behold? The swapping of tales about family and places, the talk of mutual friends down here—and we always know someone in common in Itta Bena or Iuka or Tchula or Osyka—the stories about football or fishing or some long-vanished preacher—are signs of an extraordinary mutuality. I have met black Mississippians in the North who were much more similar to me in background and preferences than the Yankee Wasps I worked with every day. If I were forced to distill, to isolate from all this, some common denominator to our curious distinctiveness, I would say it had to do with an *awareness of community,* a profound feeling for communal origins. When William Faulkner said in the opening paragraph of his essay "Mississippi" that "Mississippi begins in the lobby of a Memphis, Tennessee, hotel and extends south to the Gulf of Mexico," we knew in our hearts the heroically strange kingdom which lay in between.

Yet this, of course, is only part of the broader question before us, for in the Deep South, and I think especially in Mississippi, the American twentieth century arrived much later, and with infinitely more frenzy and destructiveness, than it did in other sections of the United States. There are reasons for this that would fill volumes of history, and indeed have. As the century progressed, Faulkner himself spent more time on the Snopeses than on the Compsons. In Mississippi, as in much of the lower South, the old warring impulses to be both Southern and American have created their own special tension, and I think no more so than today, when the communal heritage of our native land is threatened by that relentless urge to mobility and homogeneity which I fear is the hallmark of the greater society.

Mississippi, as God help us we all know, has often given itself to extremes, and through the years two of the greatest ones have been the desire, on the one hand, to dwell forever with all the myths and trimmings of a vanished culture which may never have truly existed in the first place, certainly not the way we wished it to, and the frantic compulsion, on the other, to reforge ourselves as an appendage of the capitalistic, go-getting entrepreneurial North. The quest of the Yankee dollar, in the pejorative meaning, has never been far from the better angels of our nature. Between these two extremes there have been complex lights and shadings, and considerable ambivalence and suffering. And until quite recently one constant has been the Northern view of the South—and especially of Mississippi as the most Southern of the South—as a kind of crucible of the national guilt, a playing ground for the nation's oscillating guilts about itself. It was not too many years ago that D.W. Brogan, who was a British historian but who might just as well have been speaking for much of Northern sentiment, called Mississippi, for instance, "the most savage and backward of all the forty-eight American commonwealths."

Yet one of the many ironies of our history is that even in dire moments we Mississippians considered ourselves intensely American. All through our early history Mississippians were warriors for nationalistic causes, for continental expansion, for laying to rest the specter of European domination. Even the rhetoric of secession was couched in language that was deeply Americanistic—the constitutional ideals of the founders. Throughout the 1850s my great great uncle Henry S. Foote, United States senator and then governor of Mississippi, spoke—as did others—of "the good old Union, sage fruit of our immortal ancestors." In his first inaugural Lincoln was wise in appealing to "the mystic chords of memory" which might hold the Union together, those chords were strong in Mississippi, but the sound of the distant drummer prevailed, to what staggering costs. L.Q.C. Lamar; a Mississippian, was instrumental in bringing North and South together again after the bloodiest war mankind had ever known. In two world wars Mississippians were noted for their devotion to the flag. In Yazoo City as a boy I played taps over the graves of many Mississippi boys of both races brought home from Korea. The

Americanization of Mississippi began before Mississippi was even admitted to the Union. And on election night of 1976, it was the electoral votes of Mississippi which swung the balance to the first Southern President of the United States in well over one hundred years. Given our complicated, disparate, ethnic American society, I believe the United States has a reservoir of good will and understanding among ourselves and a tradition of making our system work—the most monumental of our failures being the Civil War—that is unmatched by any other nation in the world. And Mississippi both partakes of this rare human achievement and contributes to it. Few Mississippians can better testify to the importance of being most Mississippian and American than my friend Turner Catledge, who brought to his direction of the greatest newspaper in the world, the *New York Times,* his love for both.

For black Mississippians the urge toward being American was at once more complex and more straightforward. Never have there been more splendid Americans than the black Mississippians who through the decades had the courage to demand justice and equality under the American ideals they shared. The oldest and the most incorrigible of all the hyphenate-Americans, C. Vann Woodward wrote in his *Burden of Southern History*, were the white Southerners and their ancient contemporaries, the Southern blacks. America, the finer instincts of it, are in the very soul of Mississippi, and always have been, and that is something not to be forgotten, nor taken lightly.

Now we are witnessing, I think, three peculiar transformations in our life which have surfaced so recently—in a generation or perhaps even less—that, although as Mississippians and Americans we may pay lip service to their presence, we may not yet be wholly aware of their long-range consequences.

One is the patent fact that the North, or the non-South, has become heir to many of the problems of a society such as Mississippi. The exodus of black Southerners to the great cities of the East and the North surely constitutes the largest and most dramatic migration of a people in the history of the human race. The triumph of Allis-Chambers in rural Mississippi and elsewhere in the South has become more and more complete. Brother Will Campbell, God bless him, driving through the Mississippi Delta one recent afternoon with our mutual friend, the writer Marshall Frady, looked out into a cotton field and claimed he saw a tractor going up and down the furrows all by itself, without a driver. And as time went on, as the blacks arrived in the North, they found that their traditional advocates, the white Northern liberals, were leaving for Westchester County. The tormenting social problems of school integration, inadequate living conditions, and all the rest which the North might have prepared itself for—it certainly preached to Mississippi about them long enough—seemed to rise full born there in the acute urban context. The collapse of civil order in one Northern city after another, continuing now in the mayhem of the streets, is no cause for rejoicing among Mississippians; it should be a source of the deepest human sorrow.

Second, in these years we are seeing a Mississippi that is catching up to the older social ideals and values of the more pristine America. Nowhere, of course, has this been more evident in Mississippi than in the massive integration of the public schools. This has brought dislocations, and up to a point a drift to private academies, and we have a long, long way to go. Yet, who twenty years ago would have foreseen the day to day manifestations of this vast social change? Who, in 1961 when Meredith was admitted to Ole Miss, would have predicted it? The emerging biracialism of Mississippi can be seen everywhere—in the newspapers, television, parent-teacher meetings, in a courtesy and politeness between the races in public places. Perhaps it takes someone who does not live here year round to feel this true sense of change—and to me all this is less a result of the Americanization of Mississippi, although the federal presence certainly was the catalyst to the process, as Mississippi itself responding to its own genuine heritage: whites and blacks living together.

I was watching an Ole Miss-Alabama football game on national television not too long ago with some Northern friends in New York. The game was being played in the stadium in Jackson. There were Confederate flags everywhere. The Ole Miss band broke into *Dixie* about once every five minutes. Meanwhile, down on the field, the Ole Miss and Alabama cheerleaders were black and white, so were the bands—and so, of course, were the football teams. An Ole Miss halfback, a black from Meridian, scored on a long touchdown run. Black and white Ole Miss players embraced each other and exchanged the soul slap. The Confederate flags waved in the stands. The band played an energetic *Dixie* for the twentieth time. One of my Northern friends watching the game said: "*What the hell's going on down there?*"

Ben Williams, the first black to play football for the Yazoo Indians, was also among the first blacks to play for Ole Miss. In his senior year at Ole Miss, Ben Williams—now with the Buffalo Bills—a black boy from Yazoo County—was elected Colonel Rebel.

"What the hell's going on," indeed? Certainly not perfection—nothing in the human race in Mississippi or elsewhere is perfect—but dramatic moments are revealing of more subtle, and perhaps more everlasting realities.

My third point is that we are also seeing a Mississippi that threatens to be severely damaged—one hopes not inundated—by the rampant commercialism which the Europeans of the 1950s called with much hostility "Americanization," and which may very well be more than we ever bargained for.

Not too long ago a Northern literary critic called me "the youngest of the established Deep Southern writers who lived in the South of pre-suburbia." That is quite an intoxicating phrase. True or not, I can assure you that when I was growing up, the closest thing Yazoo City had to suburbia was the hamlet called Little Yazoo, which consisted of a general store which never had anything you ever needed, a bootlegger in the back of a dilapidated garage, a Negro undertaker who was the richest man in town, and a precarious unpainted establishment with a sign in front saying: "Roaches, minnows, worms, and hot dogs."

All this was before the television culture, before the neighborhood shopping centers and supermarkets and the new federal expressway swooping down out of Jackson through the lush green hills of kudzu toward my beloved Yazoo. My growing up then was the Mississippi many of us know and remember. That was back when the only device protecting Republicans, as the saying went, was the game laws. It was a lazy town, stretched out on its hills and its flat places in a summer sun, lethargic and dreamy. People sat out on the front porch in wisteria nights with the grass wet in dew. We were forever playing tricks on everybody. And it seemed we were always listening to older people telling stories, their voices blending into the nights, about the Great

Flood of '27, or about the owner of the funeral parlor who walked down main street and killed one of the newspaper editors with a pistol, then came back to his funeral parlor and lay down in a coffin and shot himself through the head. Always the stories being told! About the eccentricities of certain ancient ladies of a generation before, about the big funeral of 1929 of a military hero from an old family and how the monoplanes flew over the grave and dropped flowers, about love affairs never consummated and rivalries which sometimes never ended in bloodshed, about old gentlemen in starched high collars and tobacco stains on their whiskers. We were so isolated then. Time seemed to stand still for us when we wished it to, although I think we wanted it to move on, to hurry up toward something—young fools that we were.

The beauty of the Mississippi land engulfed us—the smell of it in springtime, the katydids in the trees, the dark wetness of the shadows. The black people were everywhere, moving up and down the streets, the sounds of their music and laughter wafting over from the next block—the town would have been ghostly and bereft without them. On one of these nights a big passenger plane mistook the few lights of the dirt airport for Jackson, circled around Yazoo and finally came to a skidding halt in the mud. Everyone who heard the motors drove out to the airport before the plane landed, and a representative of the chamber of commerce put up a stepladder and said to each frightened passenger climbing down, "Welcome to Yazoo." In those days the presence of inevitable natural death was everywhere, the eternal passing of the generations, and people talked of those who had died years before. In the cemetery under its elms and oaks and magnolias I would touch with my hand the burial stones I know to this day by heart:

> My husband with thee departed all my hopes.
> Asleep in Jesus, Blessed Thought.
> God's finger touched him, and he slept.
> Remembered in life, lamented in death.

And I remember the political barbeques in the park or in some dusty clearing in the woods, the politicians sweating in the sun and blaming everything on the black people, the patent medicine posters on the sides of barns and stores, the vast flat countryside drowsing in the heat of July.

I recall Jackson in those years as if time has stood still for me, visiting my grandparents on North Jefferson Street across from the Jitney-Jungle—the long walks at twilight through forests of crepe myrtles, the old ladies on the galleries exchanging pleasantries, "Come in and have some ice-tea, you heah?" Then on to look for foreign stamps on the letters in the trashbin at the state capitol. Jackson was a sleepy state capital town then, with broad boulevards of houses faintly ruined, and over it all an aura of containment.

Now all my own people are dead. My grandparents and great aunts and uncles lie in the crumbled old section of the cemetery in Raymond, only a few yards from a rusty wrought-iron fence enclosing fifty unidentified Confederate dead. When my mother died last year I had to close down the house where I grew up in Yazoo and put it up for sale—the trial of finding family things in the back corners of closets: a program for my mother's piano recital in 1916, a faded photograph of my father in a baseball uniform in front of the Standard Oil Building on State Street in Jackson in 1922, another of my great grandmother holding a parasol in 1885, yellowed clippings from high school. The moment came that I stood alone in the empty house. Did I know then how it would grow to haunt my dreams and nightmares? In the gloom of it that day I strained to hear my mother's music on the piano again, my father's footsteps on the porch, the echoes of boys playing basketball in the backyard, the barks and whines of Tony, Sam, Jimbo, Duke, and Old Skip. When I left the house I locked the front door and did not look behind me.

These are *Mississippi* things I describe. They are common, are they not, to all of us.

Now Jackson from Highway 55 looms before one like a city devastated by some alien intrusion. It all seemed to have happened so quickly: the parking lots, motels, franchise stores, pizza parlors, all those accoutrements out at the edge of the great American schizophrenia, a whole beautiful terrain wiped out and vanished. The view could have been of Cleveland, Ohio. And down in those older sections whole neighborhoods likewise seemed to have disappeared—North State Street a thoroughfare for barter and commerce, of one duplex after another, and chrome and asphalt and concrete where venerable landmarks had been. My grandparents' house torn down for a parking lot for a shopping center. A solitary magnolia stands in a plot of grass near where the house had been. Not long ago I found my name in the bark of the tree, carved there by me when I was ten years old.

Surely all this, too, is common to us. Mississippians drive everyday from suburbias to work through urban sprawls identical to any Eastern or Midwestern city. My neighbor on Long Island, Craig Claiborne of Indianola, whose writings in the *New York Times* and elsewhere have made him the country's foremost writer on food, was telling me just the other day that even the Mississippi recipes he is getting nowadays have a certain national uniformity. "Yankee recipes from Mississippi?" I asked my friend Craig. "No, but kind of Yankee-ized," Craig said. A new air of acquisitiveness envelops the whole South. At a recent conference Dean Faulkner Wells, the niece of William Faulkner, told me the sidewalks were gradually being demolished in Oxford and that at the new McDonald's near the Ole Miss campus the proprietors had put up a photograph of Mr. Faulkner near a poster advertising the quarter-pound cheeseburger. What would Major de Spain think of that—or Uncle Isaac McCaslin?

Robert Penn Warren was speaking of his native southern Kentucky when he said in an interview: "I began to look for a place down there, but suddenly I saw it was a different world. The people aren't the same people. Oh, more prosperous and all that, but not the kind I had known—with a certain personal worth. So we are stuck with a new world. With certain virtues I'd be the first to grant, but perhaps some fatal defects." A bit extreme, perhaps, but most of us must have had similar thoughts of late.

Benjamin Forkner and Patrick Samway may have been speaking of Mississippi just as of the South as a whole when they wrote in their introduction to *Stories of the Modern South*: "Certainly the post-World War II South offers little to allay the fears of the 1920s and '30s. The New South of commerce, speculation, and industrial growth has become a permanent reality. Of course no one would argue that the rapid development of the South and of Mississippi in the twentieth century has been without its advantages. Southern universities have prospered. And many of the negative legacies of the past, the oppressive poverty, the vicious sharecropping system, the rural isolation and illiteracy, the crimes of segregation, are gradually disappearing. But the necessary changes have brought their modern plagues, and no Southerner, no matter how enthusiastic he may be about progress and the new wealth, would deny that the face of the land has lost something of its old character."

My feeling for Mississippi as a physical place today is like a montage: old men in front of a country cafe in Belzoni, watching big cars speed by; the ghastly descent on the main road into Vicksburg with the rootless franchise stores, and so close to that haunted battlefield where thousands of boys died; a whitewashed Negro church out in the red hills with Negro children climbing a tree beside it; the bar of a Holiday Inn in Jackson at midnight, country people in town for the day juxtaposed with executives from Chicago, all getting drunk to the strains of Willie Nelson; land ripped raw for some new development near Port Gibson within sight of the Presbyterian hand on the church pointing to the Lord; the eternal quiet of a crossroads hamlet in the Delta where time has not moved.

In a class of young writers here at the university yesterday a student asked me whether in the face of all these changes Mississippi can retain those qualities of the spirit that have made it unique. I told him I did not know. I went on to suggest to the young student, however, that the preservation of those qualities must derive, in the future of Mississippi, from those old impulses of the imagination which have made the literature of Mississippi the most powerful in twentieth century America. It is no accident, I said, that Mississippi produced Faulkner, the greatest of all the American novelists, and perhaps the greatest of all novelists, and Eudora Welty, and Walker Percy, and Shelby Foote, and the distinguished others. I must add that I, as a younger writer, am proud to be part of this remarkable heritage.

These impulses of the imagination that gave us our literature were an expression of many things:

—the act of speech, of stories handed down, where a distinctive language—which still exists in Mississippi—vivid, concrete, sly, dramatic, is deeply honored

—the language of music, the rich evocation of real, sensual things, which also remains strong and vital here

—the love of a place—where individual human beings, relation-ships, family histories, the link with generations gone, not only mat-tered, but buttressed the everyday life

—the ineluctable perception of a common past: a past of guilt and tragedy and suffering, but also of courage and nobility and caring

—and at the very base of all this was that rarest and most indispen-sable sustenance for literature: and that is memory.

The young people of Mississippi must learn to remember who they are, and where they come from. They must be encouraged to re-member; there is a message to be carried.

At the Delta Arts Festival in Greenwood last spring, a member of the Chamber of Commerce asked me: "What can we do to improve Mississippi's image?" I replied that we let the people of the Bronx, or Boston, or Detroit worry about Mississippi's image as much as they desired—but that Mississippians should concern themselves with their image among one another.

This conference in itself is an undying memento that Mississippi's sense of place is still cherished.

On looking over these notes this morning I found myself curiously disappointed in them. There was so much to be said on a subject I feel to be at the soul not just of Mississippi, but of the America of which it is a part. But after a while, I decided the hope for belonging, for belief in a people's better nature, for steadfastness against all that is hollow or crass or rootless or destructive, is as old as mankind itself and cannot be encompassed in some formula, or credo, or statement, or rationale. Wherever we live, we Americans who call ourselves Mississippians will find a way to remember.

Staying Home or Leaving

WILL D. CAMPBELL

Well, I am supposed to make a speech—I had not written my speech, and when I got here and saw that Willie Morris had such a dandy little speech all prepared I had to go back to the motel and put something down. I had only an hour, and I sat for the first forty-five minutes looking at this yellow sheet of paper. After forty-five minutes I had three words—*dream on Mississippi!*

Dream of the little backwoods country store with old men sitting idly on the porch. But don't forget that the old men sitting there are not mannequins; they are not props for you to drive by and look at—they are real people. They are sitting there because they have nothing else to do. Their time has gone by. They feel useless because they are useless. They feel lonely and alone because they are lonely and alone. They are just waiting to die. Maybe it isn't such a pretty picture after all.

Dream of the pastoral scene as you drive from Hattiesburg to Gulfport; dream of seeing the small herds of Jersey cows standing in the moss-covered live oaks at dusk, the indistinguishable bovine smell drifting into the windows and settling on your windshield and on your double-knit suit. But don't forget that two feet, old at forty-five, hit the floor at 3:30 this morning, and the farmer made his way to the barn to relieve the pressure of the udders by hand, or perhaps with an antiquated milking machine. He had done more work before you got up than you will do all day, and his day had just begun.

Dream of the fields of the new mown hay—their smell like nothing other. But don't forget that it's 115 degrees out there and the straw sticks to the sweat as it flies down the back of the field hand's duckhead overalls, and it stings and itches and burns. The bales are heavy and get heavier as he has to lift them and throw them higher and higher onto the wagon or the bobtail truck.

Dream of following the '57 pickup truck down Highway 49 piled high with lightered stumps and snags and scraps of wood from the slaughtered forests on their way to the Hercules Company. But don't forget what those forests looked like one hundred years ago and what they look like today. And don't forget the smelly, sweaty old black men, with the dynamite caps and the fuses and the deafening thunder they endure to get the stumps and snags out of the ground. And don't forget how little they reap from their labors.

Dream of football games on Saturday afternoon. Yes, dream of the black and white cheerleaders and halfbacks and marching bands. But don't forget Medger Evers and Mickey Schwerner and Andy Goodman and James Chaney—all rotting in their graves before black people could be on that field of play.

Yes, dream on Mississippi. But dare not forget the nightmare. In short, let's not turn this conference into a symposium of nostalgia freaks. No one—not one—in this room loves Mississippi more than the one who stands before you. Of that I am certain. And he has given the better part of his adult life to trying to make it a better, a more democratic, a more just place to live. No one—not one—in this room feels more keenly than I do a deep and abiding sense of place when the name Mississippi is heard. No family in this nation is closer and more protective and loving to one another than my own. But that closeness—that protectiveness, that love, that sense of place—has been forged on the altar of our common suffering much more than on some romantic notion of ease, contentment and tranquility.

I remember my childhood. But it is hard to romanticize walking barefoot through the frost to milk the cows at daybreak before going to school, the cow's tail heavy with matted cockleburs, slapping you beside the head, your near-frozen ear aching as it begins to thaw with the rising of the sun. Then, just about the time your bucket is full, the old cow kicks at a fly. Her foot—with an abundance of her waste—lands right in the middle of the bucket. (My wife still can't understand, after all these years, why I leave about an inch and half of milk in the bottom of a glass.)

It is hard to romanticize digging potatoes with a seven inch Oliver chill and an old mule, the rosin from the potatoes sticking to your hands as you pick them up, put them in piles, bank them and put on pine straw and pine bark and old boards to keep them from freezing so you will have something to eat and take to school in the winter. It is hard to romanticize your father's being sick and you and your nine year old brother making the entire crop. It is hard to romanticize being embarrassed when your Sears Roebuck shoes didn't come in time for the first day of school and having to go barefooted in front of your girlfriend. It is hard to romanticize the lady who ran the lunch-room—we called it the soup kitchen during the Depression. There were three categories of people, and she would come every day and take the headcount. Now you could buy your lunch for four cents. Those who did—the rich children—were the ones whose daddies were in the First World War, and they got a government pension of $46.97 a month. Rich! And so when she asked, "All those buying their lunch?" little fellows couldn't get their hands high enough. Or, you could trade commodities for your lunch, take a ham or soup stock or something—corn meal. And then, at the end, she would say in the most saccharine and patronizing voice and manner, "And now all the little relief children, hold up your hands." And the prettiest girl in any fourth grade class in the world sat behind me, and my hand did not go quite so high.

I do not wish to dampen the spirit of this beautiful occasion, but I must say that before one can understand what the term "sense of place" means, he must first understand the nature of tragedy. Mississippi does have a deep sense of place because Mississippi has a history of tragedy and suffering. Before one can be truly happy, he must have known heartbreak; otherwise, he won't recognize happiness when it comes.

We are, to say the least, losing the sense of place. I won't place any judgment on the loss one way or the other, except to say that in my opinion, as the sense of place is lost, there is also a rapid increase in loss of freedom. I have known for a long time that I am less free than my father, who made a living as best he could on a hard scrabble farm in Amite county. He was and is less free than his daddy. And my children are less free than I and their children are going to be less free than they are. Now sure, you say, but look at all the choices they can make that you couldn't make, so how can they be unfree? They can make *choices*, but they can't make decisions, and there is a difference. They can choose whether or not to get married. I couldn't choose that. You get twenty-one and you're not married, and there is something the matter with you. Go get married. They can choose whether or not to have babies. We couldn't choose that. My daddy couldn't and my granddaddy couldn't. The young today can even choose what sex they want to be. But those choices are really not *decisions*. The demonic part of it, in my opinion, is that it all came about—this loss of freedom—under the guise of progress.

Our second-born daughter early in her years said that your loss of freedom begins when you get a social security card, and therefore, she reasoned, "I will not get a social security card and I will be free." Well, that lasted until she went to get a job. Then she got a social security card. Now one would be utterly mad to stand before such a gathering as this and denounce the Social Security system. I remember when that legislation was passed, and I remember seeing a big editorial statement which ran in all the Hearst newspapers saying on the eve of the passage of the legislation, "If this legislation passes, then in your lifetime there will be a file on you that will record how many times you have been married, how many times you have been divorced, where you go to church, where you work, how much you make, and so on and so on." Even the most conservative of the American press denounced this as yellow journalism. But who would not settle for so little in our files today?

The various and sundry agricultural programs which were passed when I was a child, and God knows they were welcome—I was mighty happy when we got that first little check for not planting cotton—those programs which were designed one by one to keep people like my people, small one-family farms, on the land were in less than a generation appropriated by the gentry and the landed. They were used to run my people off the land so that instead of a sixty-acre cotton farm's being able to provide a living for six people, a well-known senator is paid $257,000—or some such amount—not to do something he didn't intend to do anyway. Namely, plant cotton. I was mighty, mighty glad, when that first incandescent bulb dropped down out of the kitchen ceiling. We didn't have to use coal oil any more. And we didn't have to bury twenty-five pounds of ice in a sawdust pit to put in our chocolate milk on weekends, if we could afford the chocolate or the twenty-five pounds of ice.

One would be a lunatic to argue against progress of industry, of comfort, of enjoyment, which the Tennessee Valley Authority brought into our region. And yet, coming along with it have been dehumanizing and demeaning effects—land often appropriated which nobody needed for anything except for people who make $35,000 and above to drag their boats around on, throw their beer cans out on. I attended a meeting in Kentucky where they said they were going to build a Camp-O-Port. Well, I didn't know what a Camp-O-Port was. This gentleman who was with me enlightened me and said that it was where you fly your jet airplane in and pitch your tent along the side of the runway. But it's for the people. Well, I don't know many of the people on food stamps who run around in jet airplanes.

I think this loss of freedom goes back to the loss of sense of place and the importance of what we are trying to talk about—and I'm not trying to talk about some romantic, pristine era when everybody was cruising down the river on a Sunday afternoon. The maintaining of sense of place is terribly, terribly important. I think it is important, if for no other reason, for the reason that crazy Frenchman Jacques Ellul, a lawyer and one-time political figure (still political scientist and theologian), layman at the University of Bordeau, gave in his important books *The Political Illusion* and *The Technological Society*. He says that the new environment, the environment in which we live today, is not nature, is not history; it is technique. There is a technique for doing everything, whether it's teaching school, being a doctor, or running a road grader. We are a generation of technicians. There is a way to run government, and that is the way governments are run. I was impatient during the recent unpleasantness called the Vietnam War when some of my young friends, and some not so young, would despair or become disgruntled with the stars and stripes—a war which I very much opposed, by the way. But then, they would unfurl the banner of Hanoi or Peking or Moscow or Havana, as if anything any different was happening there. There is a technique for running government and that's what runs it. So I don't vote any more.

When our people came to these counties, this part of Mississippi from Virginia, the Carolinas and Georgia, and started stopping along the way—those who were not hardy enough to make it on to Amite County—they had to battle the environment in which they found themselves. Nature is what they had to deal with: forests which they couldn't farm, swamps, cottonmouths, frost, hot sun, droughts, mosquitoes, snakes, floods—nature. Now all these are virtually conquered. We can and do drain the swamps when we have need of them, push down the forests when we need to or want to, irrigate when it dries up, build canals for the floods, pour tons of malathion in the air to kill the mosquitoes. There is no nature left. After the Civil War our people, my people and yours, the environment—all—were history. We were constantly devising and designing ways to react to our recent history and our defeat. Did pretty well at it. But now, there is not that history. Now, it's technique. So what we are talking about, I think, when we talk about a sense of place is how do we fit it in? What we are talking about really is survival. And so when we come together and talk, at least in my judgment, about sense of place, we are not talking some romantic nonsense. We are talking something very realistic and very hardnose. We are talking about survival in a technological and post-technological era.

We are not going to get back to the basics of Lukenbach, Texas, that Waylon Jennings sings about. But we can tell the stories like Willie Morris is doing here, in the manner of Judah and Israel, and they mean something. The stories we tell to our children are important. If not, I have wasted an awful lot of time. But they are important provided we don't lie, provided the stories are true. I guess about this time you are wondering what all this has to do with the subject that is on the program, "Staying Home or Leaving." Well, I will be very candid with you. It has nothing to do with it. I will also tell you how that subject came about. Jesse McKee called me one day. He was getting a little impatient, as the academic types tend to do, and he said, "We need a title for your speech." Well, I didn't have a speech so how could I name it? Don't name a baby before you see what it's going to look like. But he pressed me, and he said, "Well, never mind the speech. We've got to get this to the printer." Words to a country song had been running through my head that morning, words a friend of mine from down here south of Poplarville wrote—can't get much south of Poplarville and still be in Mississippi. I say south of Poplarville because I want to keep him in Mississippi because what I am going to say in the next few minutes has to do with Mississippi songwriters and performers. Red Lane is his name. The song begins:

> It's like trying to throw a rope around the wind.
> It's like trying to keep a snowflake from melting in your hand.
> Trying to find a reason for staying home or leaving
> Is like trying to find a raindrop in the sand.[1]

That's sense of place for you. After I gave this speech that name I figured I've got to write something around that subject. It occurred to me that wasn't such a bad idea; in fact it might have been a revelation.

If you are going to talk in terms of sense of place in the South, what better way than to talk about its music? I am a purist on the subject of music. If it's not country, I don't like it. I'm not talking about folk music—that's something else. I think—and I believe I can document this, at least to my own satisfaction—that country music is the only true American art form. I know you have heard that said about jazz. Jazz has its roots in Africa. Folk music has its roots in Britain and the continent of Europe. But country music—well maybe the truth is nobody but Americans could have thought up anything that bad—but its ours, and it is authentic and I like it. "Trying to find a reason for staying home or leaving." It's hard to do. Jesse Winchester—that name mean anything to you?—country songwriter from Mississippi. During the war he went to Canada because he had a thing about killing folks. He wrote a song which became a hit, strangely enough. It was recorded, the hit version, by a black man named Stoney Edwards. I would like to read some of the lyrics to the song. You apply it yourself to the subject we are talking about. Notice that he doesn't say if it's a good or bad place, he just says that its *his* place.

I think I see a wagon rutted road,
    with the weeds growing tall between the tracks.

---

[1]From the song THROW A ROPE AROUND THE WIND by Red Lane and Larry Henley © 1971 Tree Publishing Co., Inc. and Hastings Music Corp. Used by permission of the publisher.

And along one side runs a rusty barbed wire fence
　　and beyond that sits an old tar-paper shack.

Mississippi, you're on my mind.
Mississippi, you're on my mind.

I think I hear a noisy Old John Deere
　　in the fields specked with dirty cotton lint.
And below the field runs a little shady creek.
Down there you will find the cool, green leaves of mint.

I think I smell a honeysuckle vine,
　　the heavy sweetness like to make me sick.
And the dogs, my god, they hungry all the time,
　　and the snakes are sleeping where the weeds are thick.

Mississippi, Mississippi, you're on my mind.[2]

Tragic song written in a tragic era by a tragic human being expressing his deepest emotions, and what should have been the deepest
emotions of us all. I live in Tennessee now, and I had to make the
decision to stay home or leave, with some help, I might add, at the
time.

I got a letter during that same period when Jesse Winchester was
writing songs from a young man and his mother. I didn't know them,
but somewhere they had heard of me so they wrote me this joint letter.
The mother said that the two of them had gone from not too far from
here to the Michigan-Canadian border. The boy—twenty years
old—had made his last appeal to the draft board. If it were denied, she
was going with him to Canada. She said when her boy was ten years
old he used to follow the hunters and rescue wounded game and take
them back to his room and put splints on their legs and bandage their
wings, and when they were well release them in the fields and forests
again. The county seat newspaper ran an article about him—put his
picture in the paper for being so humane; his Sunday School class
gave him a little plaque to go on his wall, and his Cub Scout den gave
him a merit award for being humane. She said, "Now just ten years

　　[2]From the song MISSISSIPPI, YOU'RE ON MY MIND © 1970 Fourth Floor
Music Convention. Used by permission.

later they can't understand why my boy won't shoulder the gun to shed his brother's blood." I told a friend of mine about that letter and he wrote a song called "I Wonder if Canada Is Cold" with lines like "kill or be killed," "just ain't much of a future," "one last look at home Mom," "I'll be back someday if I can," and so on and so on. Music and songs about staying home or leaving, leaving because the causes won't let you stay, and yet having your guts torn out because you are there and not where you came from, knowing you aren't there because they wouldn't let you stay. But always, as in the case of Jesse Winchester, they pass no judgment on whether the place is good or bad. It's just "my place." "That's where I came from." "That's where my daddy hunted: that's where my people are."

Charley Pride from over here at Sledge, Mississippi, sings about a "Mississippi Cotton Pickin' Delta Town":

> Down in the Delta where I was born,
> All we raised was cotton, potatoes and corn.
> I picked cotton 'til my fingers hurt,
> Dragging a sack through that Delta dirt.
> I worked hard the whole week long,
> Picking my fingers to the blood and bone.
> Ain't a whole lot of money in a cotton bale,
> At least when you try to sell
> In a Mississippi Cotton picking Delta town.
> One dusty street to walk up and down,
> Nothing much to see but a starving hound
> In a Mississippi cotton picking Delta town.[3]

Then again, he sings a very popular and I think good song, and very telling song, that relates to our subject this afternoon, "I Wonder Could I Live There Any More."

> Have you ever been awakened by the crowing of a rooster
> While the night's dew is heavy on the ground?
> And the voice of Uncle Ben seems to break the morning's silence
> Bringing light to windows all around.

[3]MISSISSIPPI COTTON PICKIN' DELTA TOWN © 1974 Hall-Clement Publications. International copyright secured. All rights reserved. Used by permission.

It's time to rise and shine
To start another hard work day.
Get the cows in; start the milking chores.
It's nice to think about it,
Maybe even visit,
But I wonder could I live there any more?[4]

Maybe not. I couldn't. I followed the rules, I thought. They said we need educated preachers. So I went; I worked hard. Went to some good schools, they said. Took me a while to get over it but I finally did, I think. But I couldn't quite get over it. Because I couldn't live there any more. I had the very thing they had said you have got to have, that education, that alleged sophistication. But when it's over, "He's not like he was when he left. He can't preach with the same fire and fervor that he could when he was a boy. He doesn't pray like he used to." They were dead right. Dead right. Wonder could I live there any more? No. Probably not. But it's very important that it's there.

[4]WONDER COULD I LIVE THERE ANYMORE © 1969 Jack and Bill Music Company. International copyright secured. All rights reserved. Used by permission.

Defining a Sense of Place

PEIRCE LEWIS

The Southern land has always evoked special emotions in its own people. A sense of place is something that comes with the territory. But the South has its adopted offspring as well, and I am one of them—a foster child of the South, tied by emotion, if not by blood. When Willie Morris of Yazoo City, Mississippi, talks about going "*North* toward home," I recognize the sentiments, for I have long had similar feelings; only my compass directions are reversed. It was almost fifty years ago when I first saw the highway signs that read US 1-South, but my heart still leaps up when I see them, just as it did then. It is not a subject for rational discourse, but something that lies deep in the vitals. I cannot help thinking that there must be a good many more Northerners who feel the same way.

In a visitor with such feelings, changes in the South over the last half-century inevitably provoke very mixed emotions. On the one hand, there are changes for *good* which are so powerful that they are cause for incredulous rejoicing. The matter of race is the most obvious, the most important, and the most gladdening. For all practical purposes, Jim Crow is dead, or at least moribund, and the South's peculiar tragedy seems finally to be playing itself out. Thus, for the first time a black can dwell almost anywhere in the South without fear of being humiliated or emasculated. We are all the richer for it, black and white alike, for the South has shown us all that human progress is more than a catchy phrase, but may in fact occur anywhere if decent people work together with patience and intelligence and good will.

Economic and political conditions have changed too, and mostly for the good. To be sure, economic levels in many parts could stand

24

improvement, but the Census no longer can automatically report that Alabama, Louisiana, and Mississippi occupy the bottom three positions on any national register of income or education or nutrition. The improvement in politics sometimes seems only relative; excesses in the Baton Rouge statehouse may only appear less lurid when compared with recent triumphs of rascality in Harrisburg and Boston. But Southern politics really are better than they used to be, or at least it seems so to me. It is hardly possible any longer for some semi-literate mountebank in a rotten borough to get himself elected in perpetuity by chewing the right kind of plug, snapping the right color of galluses, and hollering Nigger at predetermined intervals. I very much doubt if a Theodore Bilbo, for example, could get himself elected senator from Mississippi today, and when one can say that, one knows the South has come a long way. In the course of time, it seems entirely plausible to imagine a graduate of Tuskeegee sitting in the governor's chair in Montgomery or Jackson, elected with no special fuss by a coalition of voters from both races.

If a Southerner feels euphoric when he has finished making such a list of achievements, he has every right to do so. Behind the world's back, the American South has fought and won a quiet revolution that will, I think, be recorded in future history books as one of the most important and heartening events of the twentieth century.

But there is another, gloomier side to this story of revolutionary success, and it is not surprising, for revolutions are seldom tidy affairs. To my way of thinking—and to that of many other observers also—there are unmistakable signs that the South, in its race to "catch up with the rest of the country," is losing many of the qualities that long made it a beloved place—not just for Southerners, but for uncounted other Americans. For all the evils of the old South, we knew that Southerners had done what most Americans had conspicuously failed to do in their own bailiwicks—to work out, over a long long time a life of gentility and humanity that can spring only from a special people who are deeply rooted in a special place. For all its sins, the South had defined a sense of place in clearer and more satisfactory terms than any other part of the United States. Today, however, in what its boosters please to call the New South, that sense of place seems blurred and eroded, much as the geographic boundaries of the South seem blurred, as one looks for them, driving southward along US 1. That sense of place, once so clearly understood and quite unnecessary to define, now seems urgently in need of definition. I do not mean that we need a dictionary definition, for they are seldom very useful when we want to talk about important, elusive ideas. I merely mean that we need to grapple once more with the subtle but vital relationship between human beings and the places they inhabit.

Genius Loci in American Places

But can we, in fact, talk sense about a "sense of place"? Does it really exist, apart from a rather trendy phrase that seems to be on everyone's lips these days? And if it does, how much effort are we willing to expend in trying to preserve it where it now thrives, to invigorate it where it seems to be languishing? Can it, in the long run, be preserved at all in a world where a new generation of Snopses bestride the land, alight with the Atlanta Spirit, their carpetbags now made indestructible by Samsonite, their bib overalls discarded in favor of double-knit leisure suits, and the moonshine they once drank from Mason jars disdained for dry Martinis, sipped in air-cooled bars that revolve eternally above the canyons of Peachtree Street? The new Snopses are easy to talk about and easy to disparage because we can see them and they look just like the Snopses of New York and Los Angeles—their Northern and Western kin. In such a world, the idea of a sense of place seems fuzzy and elusive. Can we talk about it at all?

It is not an easy job. Southerners or not, we are all Americans, and Americans have seldom been comfortable talking about abstract ideas. For better or worse, we are better mechanics than we are philosophers, better equipped to repair a faulty vacuum cleaner than to discuss ideas like a "sense of place."

More traditional societies in past time had no such difficulties. Even the practical Romans had a phrase for it. They talked about *genius loci*, and they meant it quite literally. To the Romans, it seemed quite reasonable to believe that living spirits inhabited certain places which were peculiarly theirs, and those spirits naturally protected those places against enemies.

Modern Americans, of course, have no time for such talk. We do not rely on spirits to protect our cities: the local planning commission will do the job, or in dire emergency we call in the police to restrain those who threaten public safety. But even though we reject the Roman theology, we recognize the idea that there is something intangible in certain places—a kind of quality that makes certain places special and worth defending.

Our literature and our institutions make it plain that the linkage of particular people with particular places is taken seriously, and it's been so as long as history records. It was no accident that British (and other) nobility took the name of their home places as part of their personal names, and invoked those place names in time of personal trial. Listen, as Shakespeare's young Harry, the future Henry V, throws down the gauntlet to his enemy Thomas Mowbray in the first act of *Richard II*. It is a terrible and moving moment, as the future king of England dares his enemy to come forward, and puts in jeopardy all he holds dear: his name, his honor, but first of all, his *place*. "Harry of Hereford, Lancaster, and Derby, stands here for God, his sovereign, and himself, on pain to be found false and recreant," and goes on to challenge Mowbray to mortal combat. This callow young man is somehow more than an adolescent brawler named Harry; he is the man of Hereford, Lancaster, and Derby; he is defending not only his good name, the name his parents gave him, but the names of the places that give him privilege and identity. He carries those place names like proud badges, and throws them like a gauntlet in the face of his enemy.

Again, we Americans know the feeling, even though we find Shakespeare's language quaint or archaic. One can catch the spirit of place, for example, in our most basic institutions. There is nothing in the Constitution that says so, but everybody knows that the Senate of the United States is the *upper* house of the Congress, the house which represents not mere people, but the places we call states. No reasonable person, surely, can be expected to know the name of the representative from the 5th District of Mississippi, but anyone who pays attention to American institutions knows who Senator Stennis and Senator Eastland are. We may not know very much about those senators as persons, and we may or may not approve of their political views, but we know their names, just as we know Harry of Hereford. And both men are considerably larger than life, for they are more than simply members of the U. S. Congress. They are the gentlemen from Mississippi, and one is never allowed to forget it.

These examples suggest several things about the spirit of place. First of all, it is often easier to see its results in human behavior than to define it in precise terms. Second, the spirit of place is not a one-way proposition: what we might call "placefulness" is a complicated symbiotic relationship between a locus on the earth and the people who inhabit or perceive that locus, and that relationship is very largely aesthetic. Finally—and a matter of some importance—having a sense of place may not be an unmixed blessing.

Examples are better than definitions. Texas is a Place with a capital P, and if you doubt it, walk into a Houston bar with a Yankee accent and start making Texas jokes. Texans can do it, but Yankees would be well-advised to refrain. Obviously, there is nothing inherent to the soil of Texas which predestined it to be a Place (although I understand one can buy a bag of Texas dirt at souvenir stands at the Dallas-Fort Worth Airport), and Texas would not be a Place without Texans. To be sure, it is quite possible to deplore Texan behavior, and I know a good many Easterners to whom the sound of a Texas accent is equivalent to drawing one's fingernails down a blackboard. All that is beside the point. Texan turf is important to a Texan, and there is a pantheon of dead Texans to prove it.

So I am not claiming that a sense of place will produce undiluted virtue. Obviously, there is nothing particularly admirable about a bellicose drunk in a Houston saloon. The same is true, of course, when street gangs in Harlem try to kill each other in defense of a certain patch of asphalt turf. Surely, one can argue, Harlem's genius loci must be very malevolent indeed, and the sin of cutting your enemy's throat with a switch-blade is not less heinous because you have a "sense of place."

The problem here is more apparent than real. Having a "sense of place" does not guarantee virtue—no more in a Texas bar than on Lennox Avenue in Harlem. But reverse the reasoning and ask the question again: what happens when a sense of place is absent? Again, examples are better than speculation.

Consider the case of New Jersey, a state so conspicuously lacking in a sense of place that most residents would think the phrase bizarre. Benjamin Franklin is supposed to have remarked that New Jersey served as part of a digestive tract that stretched between New York and Philadelphia, although he disclaimed knowledge about which end was which. In Pennsylvania, where I teach, university professors know that taking cheap shots at New Jersey is an infallible way to make students laugh. (A friend of mine, a geologist, alludes to the Coastal Plain of southern New Jersey as an area "where the sea withdrew in disgust." Such wisecracks seldom fail to bring the house down, especially if the house contains a fair number of sophomores.)

To be sure, there are Texas-jokes too, and we all routinely laugh at them. But there is a mordant quality to those New Jersey jokes, just as there is a mordant quality to much of New Jersey itself. We laugh *with* the Texans, for we secretly envy them their pride. We laugh *at* New Jersey and pity her, but who would dare to pity Texas? In sum, an overblown sense of place does not necessarily make Texas or Texans lovable, but the absence of a sense of place—the absence of a benevolent genius loci—is a near guarantee of trouble. One can love or hate Texas. It is hard even to detest New Jersey.

The conclusion, then, seems inescapable. To have a sense of place—to sense the spirit of a place—one's own place—is as indispensable to the human experience as our basic urges for food, or for sex. Indeed, we even use similar words to describe our emotions. We speak of "hunger" to return home, just as we speak of hungering for food. Our affection for certain beloved places is as intense, perhaps, as our affection for people we love. To be sure, one can overindulge one's hunger for food: that is gluttony. One can overindulge one's sexual urge, and that is debauchery. So also, one can overindulge a love of place, and more than a few wars have been fought "in defense of homeland, or fatherland," or what have you, and they were murderous wars indeed. But I do not think that one can survive as a humane creature on this earth without special attachments to special places.

A good many Americans, of course, recognize this basic need for association with place. At a superficial level this need is reflected in the recent popularity of Alex Haley's *Roots*. At another level, there is growing popular demand that big corporations and big government stay out of local affairs so that local people can adjust their affairs to meet particular local needs—in our terms here, to find and define their own peculiar genius loci. Our current binge for antiques and kindred nostalgic memorabilia reflects that same urge to seek attachment to something solid, something permanent, something valuable, and something very particular. One need not look far to find other straws, flying in the same wind.

To be sure, Americans are not unique in this need for a sense of place: we are, after all, members of the human race, and we share basic human needs with people of all nations. But I would suggest that Americans have seldom done a very good job of creating genuine places, much less of preserving them. Our national sins are more commonly those of New Jersey than those of Texas; we suffer from too little sense of place—not too much. We have paid, I think, a high price for our failure, and we will continue to pay a high price until we set about to mend our ways. By that, I mean that we must learn to recognize genius loci, to nurture it when we find it, and, if we are lucky, even discover ways of inculcating a sense of place where it does not now exist.

At best, however, that will be very difficult, perhaps impossible. But if we are to succeed at all, I think we need to recognize that America's failure to create an environment where a sense of place develops easily, is not accidental. The failure is based on some deep-seated habits, and those habits will be very hard to kick—even if we wish to kick them, and it may very well be that we do not. Let me explain.

Mobility and a Sense of American Place

We are, we Americans, an unprecedented people, in an unprecedented country, doing unprecedented things. I do not say these things easily, for they have the ring of cheap jingoism, and I do not mean them that way. But consider what we have done. In a little over two centuries the American nation grew from a thin band of displaced Europeans, about a million and a half people strung out along a few hundred miles of the Atlantic coast between Georgia and New Hampshire, and effectively settled more than three million square miles of territory, while meantime setting free whole nations of immigrants from overseas. It was the fastest act of voluntary large-scale settlement that the world has ever seen. Both within the country and from overseas, the American experience saw the largest migration in human history, and—with the lamentable exception of African slaves—that migration took place in an environment of unprecedented human freedom. To be sure, we made mistakes, and they were not small mistakes, either. I will not stand before an intelligent audience and defend our treatment of Indians, much less the way we cut our forests and ravaged agricultural fields. I will not defend the egregious waste that accompanied the American experience. But we conquered a continent, and we set free millions and millions of men and women in the process. The American experience was absolutely and literally without precedent: nobody had ever done anything like it before. It is quite beside the point that we are not perfect, but we are better than most, for when we make mistakes, we persistently try to correct those mistakes. If anyone doubts that statement, he need only pick up any major foreign newspaper and read about our failures. When we fail, the world press cries out in alarm and indignation, and the reason is plain: no other nation in the world is held in such esteem—no other nation holds such hope. For most of our history, the American dream has been the world's dream—of economic plenty, of political freedom, of human dignity.

The reasons for the American success story, of course, are complex, and whole armies of historians have spent their lives working out the details. But none of it could have happened without *mobility*, without incessant migration of people. Consider, after all: only the mobile Europeans came to America in the first place; only the mobile Americans moved west across the Appalachians, across the Midwest, across the Great Plains, spilling finally across the Sierra to California, the golden coast, the most mobile place of all. It was no good reproaching Americans because they moved around so much and so aimlessly. Quite simply, mobility worked. At an elementary level, it was the key to political freedom, and European feudalism simply disintegrated when peasants began walking off their wretched little plots, abandoning their fields, and abandoning their allegiance to local lord or baron to go places like Ohio and Texas and Oregon. Small wonder that those lords often tried to stem the migratory tide, for they saw—as tyrants often have—that one can't enslave a person who is free to move. Thus, the Fugitive Slave Laws enraged Northern abolitionists, just as the repeal of those laws enraged Southern slave-owners. Plainly, slavery was impossible if a slave could walk off a field at will, and to those who opposed slavery, any obstacle to mobility represented interference with the basic American right to seek economic and political freedom wherever it was to be found.

It was the same, of course, with social freedom. The ancient European expression, "He knows his place," can be taken both figuratively and literally. If you know your place and are stuck there, you cannot aspire to better things, either in terms of social status or in terms of physical location. Small wonder that the rigid English class system was built on the philosophy of that phrase, and small wonder that most Americans see a violent shade of red when anyone tells them that they *should* know their place. The idea simply goes counter to our whole national history and geography.

Above all, mobility gave Americans an incredible freedom to experiment with new ways of doing things, and if the experiment didn't work, we could abandon the project and move on. Cut too many trees in northern Michigan? No problem—move on. Slums developing around our central cities? No problem—move to the suburbs. Northeastern machinery wearing out? Never mind—abandon the old factories of New England and the old industrial belt from Boston to Chicago—and move if you like to Georgia, or Texas, or California.

Mobility was multi-dimensional. As we moved in space, we also moved in time. "Things aren't working today? Never mind. Things'll be better tomorrow. It's been true right along, hasn't it?"

And it has, of course. Just as movement west has worked better than movement east, movement forward in time—toward the future—has worked better than retrogressive backward movements. It is quite natural for Americans to be "future-oriented" and to use the word "reactionary" as a dirty word. After all, what has the past ever done for you?

Thus mobility became a national habit—among the young, a fetish. Mobility not only brought freedom, it became the symbol of freedom. The American language is full of familiar expressions that make the point: "Where are you going on your vacation?" (The assumption is that if you have free time, that you'll go somewhere). For many adolescents, getting a driver's license is an important part of the rite of passage into adulthood, and teen-agers "cruise the block" as a symbol of sexual maturity. As the child grows up, movement ceases to be a privilege and becomes a right, to be flaunted proudly in the face of one's juniors. Machines of movement, whether automobiles, motor-cycles, airplanes or all-terrain vehicles, are not mere machines—they are instruments of freedom, and potent symbols. It is easy to see why the police have trouble controlling dirt bikes, or good-buddies driving Mack trucks.

But the price of mobility has been fearsome. The physical effects are bad enough—our rapacious treatment of land, based on the childlike belief that there would always be more. Like birds who foul their nests, we could always move on—and on. The psychological costs are just as great, and Americans have known that for a long time too. The greatest of America's tragic novels deal not so much with interpersonal rivalries or struggles between man and God, but with uprooted wan-dering people, striving to come to terms with themselves and with a land so new they could not properly call it home. Paradoxically, the greatest of those novels possess an extraordinary sense of place: Mark Twain's descriptions of the Mississippi River and John Steinbeck's evocations of California display some of the grandest geographic imagery in the English tongue. But it is no paradox that the pro-tagonists of these novels—Huck and Jim on that Mississippi raft—the Joads driving their jalopy across those endless miles toward the green valley of California—are seeking freedom through mobility. Some critics read *The Grapes of Wrath* as a story of human triumph over adversity, but to me, it is the blackest tragedy. The Joads tragic flaw is being American, for they set out on that long agonizing journey in the belief that they will find a new place, and with it a new freedom. Instead, they find that California has been taken by others, and the Joads are pursued mindlessly from one anonymous migrant camp to another. Steinbeck leaves us with no hope that the Joads will ever find a place which they can call their own. They belong nowhere, the ultimate tragedy of golden California, and America at large.

Does it matter? Well, Thomas Wolfe thought it mattered, and his cry, "You can't go home again," is a cry of mortal torment. Oscar Handlin and Daniel Boorstin both thought so too. Handlin calls our ancestors "The Uprooted," and Boorstin laments that we are a "nation of Bedouins." And most Americans, I believe, think it matters too. One of CBS's most sensitive reporters, Charles Kurault, is "On the Road," eternally searching . . . for what? For places and people that are solid, that are out of the mainstream of place and of time—gandy-dancers on a small Southern railroad—fiddle-makers in isolated Appalachian valleys. In a sense, Kurault's search is every American's search—for reassurance that there are places, however remote, that will survive our frenetic passion for mobility, places where we can go and find the genius loci, alive, healthy, and benevolent. What makes Kurault's reporting so unbearably poignant, I think, is not simply Kurault's basic decency and sensitivity as a reporter of the human condition, but what he is showing us: that these people with their profound sense of place are old people, discarded people—discarded like that Southern railroad, and ultimately doomed. In their attachment to place, Kurault's people are genuinely unAmerican. And Kurault's *places* are endangered species. I am sure we have all had the feeling, after watching one of his superb reports, that we should cry out, "Kurault! Don't tell us where it is! Don't let us come and spoil it!"

So, we know that the loss of placefulness is more than a "social problem," in the chill lexicon of social psychology. The lack of a sense of place means a lack of responsibility to place, and the consequences are horrendous. We find the country littered with plundered, abandoned places—not merely buildings, but entire cities, entire regions. We abandoned the old Cotton Belt, and we abandoned the High Plains, and the migrations that followed the abandonment rank high on our list of national disasters. We abandoned Newark and Detroit and the south side of Chicago, and the results were riots, unprecedented in American history. Today, we are in the process of abandoning the whole industrial belt of the urban Northeast on grounds that the factories are obsolete, and besides, the "Sun Belt" is a nicer place to live. I live near that region of abandonment in central Pennsylvania, and I know the human costs of that abandonment: a residue of discouraged, demoralized, pessimistic people, who curse their fate, but have no idea of what to do about it. Inevitably, some public or private charity will find a way to put these people on the dole—the Appalachia program is just one of many—but such programs are merely cosmetic and ultimately hopeless. The problem of the Northeast is the problem that has plagued Detroit and Mississippi and the whole United States: we have no experience to help us cope with old geography, no cultural habits to inculcate a sense of place which would demand of the inhabitants that they find some other solution to their problems than panic-stricken flight. Americans, as geographic physicians, are better pediatricians than they are gerontologists.

The question, of course, is how to deal with that problem, the national abandonment of places. And if my argument is correct, that problem will never be solved unless we can somehow find a way to inculcate Americans with a sense of place—to inculcate places with a genius loci that will make Americans want to take responsibility for their care.

Preserving Places: the Options

There are, I think, three different directions we can go. We can look to the future, manipulate it, and try to make it better than the present. That has been the way of conventional city and regional planning, and I think it has not worked very well. We can look to the past and try to preserve its monuments, as a basis for improving the present. That is the way of conventional historical preservation, but I don't think that has worked very well either.

Or, we can look to the present, and try to discover places where a genuine genius loci is alive and well, and try to discover the environment in which it thrives. That strikes me as the most sensible way. But before elaborating, let me explain why I think that both conventional planning and conventional preservation are dead-end paths if we hope to preserve or to implant a sense of place in late twentieth century America.

Consider planning first. When I say that planning has been unsuccessful, I don't mean that we should stop looking ahead and trying to figure out what to do about our future problems. Any sensible person or society does that, routinely, and so it should. I mean, instead, that conventional planning, as traditionally practiced in the United States by one government agency after another, has failed miserably to inculcate, much less to preserve, the geographic attributes which are necessary if a spirit of place is to flourish.

The case is not hard to make, for the evidence is laid out in city after city, region after region across the United States. The hard facts are these: most traditional American planning has either been ineffectual, or, worse, it has been grossly destructive. If you want to see the ineffectiveness of most civic planning departments, visit one of them, and ask to see a copy of their "master plan." (They are sure to have one.) Then go outdoors and compare the plan with reality. Again and again, one can find gorgeous plans—carefully drawn, beautifully colored, expensively printed, often dating from the 1960s, the '50s, even back to the '20s—which have lain dormant in map drawers, without the least hope of being turned into reality. Alabaster cities gleam only on paper, and their plans are stained with the tears of rebuffed senior planners. I should be very surprised, indeed, if Hattiesburg, Mississippi, does not have such a plan, drawn up some time in the 1920s, showing great boulevards, classical buildings, with happy pedestrians strolling beneath fine trees—and I should be equally surprised if present-day Hattiesburg bears more than passing resemblance to that plan.

If it does, then Hattiesburg has been luckier than many other cities. Every now and then, the traditional planners had their way, in places like Detroit and Saint Louis and Buffalo, and there the result was mass devastation, courtesy of the Urban Renewal Program. Renewal, indeed! To look at downtown Buffalo, one would think the Germans had won World War II, and that the Luftwaffe had taken revenge for the bombing of Dresden. The same thing happened to my hometown of Detroit. Back in the 1930s, Detroit was a rough town, but it had a healthy sense of place. Detroit had more than a few defects, but I think the worst ones could have been cured with a little tender loving care. By the time the planners were finished, however, most of the central city was devastated, and the surroundings were slashed to ribbons by interstate highways, also laid out by the best planners of the time. By 1967, a demoralized population raged through what was left of many neighborhoods and tried to burn them up.

But lamenting the fate of Detroit will do us little good unless we learn from Detroit's mistakes and not repeat them in New Orleans or in Hattiesburg. Where did Detroit go wrong?

The answers are not hard to find, I think, because they are devastatingly simple. The Detroit planners of the 1950s made the assumption that old things were bad things and eagerly tore down almost everything that dated from the nineteenth century. Those same planners, looking to the example of T.V.A., worked on a second assumption: that large-scale changes were better than small-scale changes, and that they should strike while the iron was hot. (After all, who could tell when federal funds for urban renewal would run out?) But beneath those ideas was a more general, and very utopian, philosophy that if we only wiped the slate clean, we could build again, from scratch. If Detroit contained dark satanic mills, then we would tear them down, and make room for a new Zion. People who opposed those views— and there were precious few of them in Detroit in the 1950s—were dismissed as reactionary, and a good share of the city was destroyed.

Herbert Gans and Jane Jacobs had already predicted what would happen if you did such things, and they were right.[1] As the old houses were torn down, the people fled, and as the old monuments were leveled, there was less and less reason for native Detroiters to return to the city of their birth. The town was scarcely recognizable. As for the delicate tissue of streets and buildings and trees and people, it had simply been torn to shreds.

I need not bludgeon the point, I think. Both urban renewal and the interstate highway programs, two of the most disastrous pieces of legislation to pass the United States Congress, have (thank God) run low on money, and I may be overly sanguine in thinking that the 1950s and 1960s version of urban renewal is pretty thoroughly discredited. Before we rush to judgment, however, we need to remember that planners were not evil or malicious people. They were simply Ameri-

[1]Gans's most influential work is *The Urban Villagers* (New York: Macmillan, 1962); Jacobs's is *The Death and Life of Great American Cities* (New York: Random House, 1961).

cans like us, with utopian ideas, an inclination to think big, with very little patience, and more than a little arrogance. (More than incidentally, those planners talked—and still talk—of "Pilot Programs," supposedly experimental. They were not experimental at all, of course, simply because nobody waited to find out what the results were. After all, it would take twenty-five years to discover what interstate highways would do to St. Louis, and federal programs don't last that long. Well, we know now, but it's too late to help Detroit—much less Buffalo or Harrisburg or St. Louis or a host of other hapless placeless towns.)

So the future didn't work, we said. The alternative, then, was the past, and that meant historic preservation. But we look around us to see where preservation has worked, and the story is very much the same as that in planning—only in reverse. Instead of doing too much, we have done too little. Here and there we find buildings saved, labeled "historical," commonly isolated from the outside world with a white picket fence. Admission to this historical world is one dollar, children under twelve are free. Meantime, "historic districts" are created—in the West called "Old Town," where student archaeologists solemnly dig up the ruins of Chinese grocery stores, and state historic markers demark the place from which the pony express departed. Meantime, down the street, somebody has started a wax museum, somebody else is selling antique license plates, and employees of the local Holiday Inn are dressed up to look like colonial soldiers or Betsy Ross, depending on their gender. On the edge of the historic district, somebody has built a "Frontier Fort," where one can buy souvenirs, and lollipops made by Mennonites in Lancaster, Pennsylvania.

Criticizing such behavior, alas, is like shooting fish in a rain-barrel. We all deplore such places (Donald Meinig, a very perceptive geographer from Syracuse University, calls them "fake places"), yet they continue to flourish, even as we splutter about them. If we look for plausible pieces of historic preservation, we find them rare indeed. The reason is not hard to find. We have treated history as an item, which can be fenced off from the "real world." We have encouraged people to think of certain places as "historical," and thus worth saving, while other places are not historical and thus belong to another category. But history is not a thing, to be bought and sold. History is a dimension, and we are part of it. C. S. Forester spoke truthfully of "the river of time," like a stream which flows—sometimes furiously over rocks and falls—sometimes in quiet little pools—but always moving.

Not long ago, a journalist, L. Thomas Frye, wrote a column in the *Sacramento Bee*, in which he complained, "My history is missing."[2] Frye, it seems, had been a boy in the old part of Sacramento—now converted to "Old Town"—once again "fashionable and respectable with smart shops, good restaurants and watering spots." Old Town, it seems, is a monument of California's Gold Rush history, and everything else has been removed. In Frye's words, "Old Town's 20th-Century history has been eradicated as systematically as possible. The successive layers of the buildings have been peeled back and thrown away, leaving no evidence of their varied use as rooming houses, bars, wholesalers, pawnshops, and labor headquarters. These middle years are not represented in the restoration. . . . Something is missing," he says. "My history is missing. It wasn't like this. I am a stranger here." Frye's lament is familiar: Old Town Sacramento looks wonderful, but the spirit of the place has flown.

Well, we all recognize the pattern. It is the Rockefeller's Williamsburg, only in nineteenth century western garb, instead of eighteenth century British colonial costume. We can admire such places, perhaps learn from them, but neither Williamsburg nor Old Town Sacramento is part of our lives. They are something else, something apart. Compared to the river of time, they are like bottled water: harmless, perhaps useful, but not very nourishing.

It may seem as if I am dismissing both planning and historic preservation as worthless or damaging institutions, but that is not so. (For what it is worth, I am a member of our town's planning commission, and I am a paid-up member of the National Trust for Historic Preservation.) Both planning and preservation have made major contributions to the quality of our lives. Zoning ordinances, prepared by planning commissions across the country, have prevented uncounted miles of highways from becoming billboard alleys. Without the tireless work of a few preservationists, heaven knows how many beautiful old buildings would not lie buried in ruins under some asphalt parking

[2]L. Thomas Frye, "Old Sacramento Looks Fine—But Something Is Missing," *Sacramento Bee*, Forum, 17 July 1977, p. 5.

lot. What we need to realize, however, is that the great *successes* of both planning and preservation are negative successes. A successful zoning ordinance says "NO" in stern language to people and buildings that we want to keep away from us. A successful preservationist is one who stands firm and says "NO," even as the bulldozer approaches. (There is more to it than that, usually. Preservation usually involves some kind of rehabilitation too. But you can't rehabilitate something if it's lying in wreckage at your feet.) We should get over the idea that being negative is bad and realize that a good strong "NO!" may be one of the most constructive words in the English language. We cannot preserve a sense of place unless some very tough people are prepared to say "NO" many many times. But saying "NO" will not create a sense of place, even though it may help to preserve one.

Preservation in the Present Tense

Which brings me to my last point: The failures of planning and of conventional preservation suggest that we should look elsewhere. If we genuinely want to preserve a sense of place or to inculcate a sense of place where one is weak or non-existent, we should look around and see where the spirit of place is vigorous, and try to find out why.

And, mirabile dictu, such places do exist. Over the last half-dozen years I have been singularly lucky, for I have had a chance to live for a while in a few of them. New Orleans is one of those places. Montreal is another. Berkeley, California, is a third. And, I have spent enough time in Boston and San Francisco and Charleston, South Carolina, over the years to recognize at least three more. Most of us could make our own private list, and many places in rural America would surely qualify.

What do these places have in common? What magic qualities have combined to bestow that priceless quality: a sense of place? The artist Alan Gussow remarks that *place* is "a piece of the whole environment which has been claimed by feelings."[3] Plainly, if we adopt Gussow's terms, we are talking about a subjective thing, and it is quite useless to try measuring it, at least as social scientists try to measure indices of the "quality of life." There is no point in measuring the bacterial count

[3] Alan Gussow. *A Sense of Place: The Artist and the American Land* (San Francisco: Friends of the Earth, 1971), p. 27.

of the water supply or even per capita income: New Orleans would fail dismally on both counts. There is no point in counting the number of divorces or purse-snatchings or muggings: San Francisco would do badly on such a scale as that.

Political stability is not the measure, although the degree of political activity by ordinary citizens might very well be: as witness the frenetic political activity of people in all places that I have mentioned. And even if we could somehow measure moral virtue, I doubt very much if either San Francisco or Paris would score very high. No, what we are talking about is a place that can be directly experienced, intimately known, and passionately loved by its inhabitants. ("Love" is not a term that lends itself well to the cold hands of mensuration—Masters and Johnson to the contrary, notwithstanding.)

Let me, then, suggest a kind of laundry list of things that I perceive in all of these magic places. I do not suggest that the list is complete. Indeed, I know it is not, and I would be very glad to have the list corrected, or amended, or simply lengthened. Above all, I would like to see the list shared with other people of like mind. If there are any magic ingredients, any essential elements, we should all know about them.

All of these places, no matter what else they have, have *a sense of shared experience*. And, very often, that experience is NOT shared by other folk who do not inhabit that particular place. That simple idea has several important corollaries.

People in these places are constantly reminded of these experiences by the presence of tangible objects. Sometimes, those objects are monumental totems—like Berkeley's Campanile on the University of California campus, or the Golden Gate Bridge in San Francisco, or St. Louis Cathedral in New Orleans, the steeples of St. Phillip's and St. Michael's in Charleston, or Mount Royal looming above the city of Montreal. But that is not enough, and besides, not many places are lucky enough to have a Golden Gate Bridge. Many towns, however, have parks with a bit of statuary. The little stone cherub in Louisburg Square in Boston is a tiny object, but pound for pound it has done more to give Beacon Hill a sense of place than any item one could imagine. Those statues and church steeples are important because they remind us where and who we are. Who can forget MacCauley's Horatio standing at the bridge, facing his enemy and certain death "for the ashes of his fathers, and the temples of his gods?"

But monumental things, however important, are not enough. To have a sense of place, there must be common things, vernacular things, easily recognized as peculiar to the place, and the object of general affection. One of the best examples of this sort of thing is the preservation of common old houses: the miles and miles of Victorian houses of San Francisco serve that function nicely there, or the red-wood bungalows of Berkeley by Maybeck and his imitators, the shot-gun houses and camelback oddities of New Orleans or those hundreds of curious porticoed houses peculiar to Charleston, South Carolina, and its immediate environs. Those common vernacular houses, pecul-iar to a particular place, give distinctiveness to the place, and help tie its present to the shared experience of a common past. The implica-tions for historic preservation are obvious: we have set our sights too low. Instead of preserving single houses, or single monuments—ultimately a futile business—we should be identifying and insisting on the preservation of those things that give a place particularity. We should be prepared to refuse to issue demolition permits over whole counties, if necessary, and the legal penalities for illicit demolitions should be sure, swift, and fierce.

But it is not enough to preserve houses, even though we preserve a lot of them. We must know why we are doing it, and that takes education. One of the greatest gaps in American public education is the teaching of plausible local history, which explains to the residents of particular places why their place is important.

It is easy to misunderstand that remark. I am not urging some kind of foolish boosterism, which is basically implausible and self-defeating. I am suggesting that most places don't care much about themselves because they don't know very much about themselves. Nor is it easy to find out. How often, after all, can one find a local history book, which is written gracefully, well-illustrated, based on careful and honest re-search, and which—above all—shows how the particular place fits into the larger context of national and even world history? I know of very few, although Michael Lesy's *Wisconsin Death Trip* comes closer than most—as does the wonderful little guidebook about Pierce County, Wisconsin, called *St. Croix Border Country*, written by two geographers from the University of Minnesota, Harry Swain and Cotton Mather. But it is no coincidence that one can walk into any local bookstore in New Orleans, or in San Francisco, or in Charleston, or in Montreal, and pick up a pretty good local history book.

There are other ways to remind ourselves of those common local experiences. Newspaper columns, such as Herb Caen's acerbic column in the San Francisco *Chronicle*, are seized by San Franciscans, who read Caen's in-jokes in the private knowledge that they, and only they, will understand them because *they* are San Franciscans. Caen's writing is often catty and exaggerated, and that is one reason that San Franciscans read him, but Caen's writing is honest—to the degree, at least, that he makes no effort to sugar-coat the defects in the city he obviously loves so passionately. Good local journalism is critical to a sense of place, as Ralph McGill and William Allen White have shown us, in different places, and at different scales. Conversely, nothing is more dangerous to a sense of place than the creeping syndicates that buy up small town newspapers, and turn them into thinly disguised versions of a Long Island shopping guide, studded with cheerful hints for housewives, and canned editorials written by grey gnomes at the wrong end of the AP wire.

It is equally important, I think, to make common things visible, in any way that one can. Joseph Pennell's pencil sketches of New Orleans's back streets in the 1890s did more to preserve the French Quarter and its sense of place than any federal grant that I know about. Elizabeth O'Neill Verner did the same thing for Charleston for more than half a century. Victor Steinbrueck's naive sketches of Seattle's Pike Street Market are brutally honest, including telephone poles, winos, prostitutes, and "adult" moviehouses, yet Steinbrueck's *Market Sketchbook* helped make the people of Seattle aware that the Pike Street Market, for all of its blemishes, was an irreplaceable treasure. The result was the saving of the smelly, dogeared, wonderful market, and the understanding that Seattle was not going to have its genius loci monkeyed with!

Peculiar celebrations, peculiar institutions, and particular gathering spots fall into the same category, of course. What would New Orleans be without Mardi Gras, Creole food, and Jackson Square? Conversely, what will happen to downtown Philadelphia when the city fathers stand by helplessly and watch the closing of the old Reading Terminal Market where generations of Philadelphians have gathered to celebrate good eating and good conversation? I think I know, because I know what happened when the Bellvue-Stratford closed. The prospect is unpleasant. Both the Reading Market and the Bellvue-Stratford were places where Philadelphians routinely gathered to share common, but particularly Philadelphian, experiences. Philadelphia is frantically building little "parklets," and turning streets into "pedestrian malls," but they look like everybody else's parklets and malls. The old Philadelphia may have been dirty, but it was a special place, and people gathered there for exactly that reason.

What I am advocating, of course, is very ad hoc. For Americans, who are fond of formulae, it may sound discouraging. But I myself am not discouraged, for I see something happening all over the country that heartens me greatly. That "something" is a rise of local organizations in small places—small towns, small neighborhoods in large cities (like that which has emerged along Summit Avenue in Saint Paul), groups of people who are saying repeatedly: this is our place, and we are going to define it. Such organizations, increasingly, are insisting that places are very particular, and particular local decisions and definitions be made locally. In my opinion, that is an almost unmixed blessing.

I do not mean that local organizations should shut their doors to outsiders, nor that we engage in some neo-Know Nothing brand of anti-federalism. Quite the contrary. The wise community will keep its collective ears and eyes open to what is going on in other places, and the wisest community of all will deliberately go afield to discover what is happening elsewhere, what is *working*. There is no need, after all, for every town across the United States individually to have to rediscover the wheel. Among other things we need to invent some easy ways for these local organizations to keep in touch with each other, if only to exchange information. Above all, we need to know about places—and know the truth about them.

One final example will make the point. In most parts of the country, tourists are viewed with mixed emotions. They are valued because they bring money, but detested because of their gauche behavior. But what would happen to a place if it could entice intelligent, sensitive tourists who came to visit because they wanted to learn about the special qualities of that place, not because they were seeking some kind of warmed-over Disneyland? That's pretty far-fetched, you say? Is it because the intelligent tourist is such a rare bird? Is it because the average tourist goes to Holiday Inn for the best surprise which is no surprise, and goes to 7-11 stores from Portland, Maine, to Portland, Oregon, because he knows where to find the milk? (4th shelf back, dairy section on the right.)

Well, there are a lot of people like that, but this is a big country, and there are also lots of intelligent, curious, sensitive people who might very well visit an otherwise unheralded place and do it tactfully, if they knew what to look for. What would happen if our hypothetical tourist could come to an ordinary Southern county with the expectation that he could find a well-written, well-illustrated, honest guide to the county, a handbook that might cost a couple of dollars, and would guide him through the streets of the county seat and the countryside around it, explaining what he is seeing—a book that was strong on truth and context, but light on magnolias and Tupelo honey? I can't help thinking that the respect for place would be buoyed immeasurably, not only by the visitors, but by local residents who watched those intelligent visitors as they walked the streets of their town with affection and understanding.

I know. Right now that image is a pipe-dream. Such guidebooks for intelligent laymen are rare as hens' teeth. But if they did exist, imagine what would happen to the spirit of place in community after community across the South, and indeed across the whole United States!

The South could use some guidebooks like that, and, although the Southern landscape is perhaps more subtle and intricate than any other in the country, I think it might be easier for Southerners to write such books than for people in most other regions of America. I'm talking about detailed books, about small areas, about the size of a county—and Southerners have always been comfortable with their counties. Nor should it be hard to find literate local people who know the turf and have a sense of language. But there ought to be lots of these guides—enough that tourists aren't tempted to descend in droves on one particular county "because it has that simply divine guidebook, y'know?" (It's hard to preserve a sense of place if the exhaust fumes from the tour buses are killing off your magnolias.)

One can imagine doing such things in the South, however, only because there is still a little time left—time, that precious commodity. If the rural and small-town South still possesses a sense of place, it is not because of any special inherent virtue but mainly because the great bland placeless world has not yet elbowed its way in.

But that's not going to last long. Those new Snopeses are surely coming, and they will bring the Atlanta spirit, and what passes in the New Atlanta for a sense of place. You will know them by their words and deeds. They don't talk about the South; they call it the Sun Belt, and they think "regional development" is just fine. They come bearing cable TV and Holiday Inns and low-cal barbeque and hamburger helper and malls with Muzak and canned editorials in your local newspaper, and you can put it all on your Master Charge. You'll pay later, but it's already later than you think.

I don't know whether those new Snopses can be stopped or even discouraged, although I confess to being less than optimistic. But I do know this: they can only be stopped in places where intelligent, dedicated people are cudgeling their brains to find ways to preserve and instill a sense of pride in local places, a pride based on very specific knowledge of those places and dedicated to telling the truth about those very specific places. We don't hear that kind of talk very often from planners and policymakers, or from scholars either. But perhaps it is time we did.

Mississippi:
A Personal View of Its Past
and a Hope for its Future

T. D. YOUNG

When I grew up in the 1930s in east Mississippi, I was not aware that the state of my birth was depraved, nor did I in my innocence feel deprived. True, we didn't have much money, but neither did any of our neighbors because the whole country was undergoing what I later learned was the Great Depression. But we did have a way of life which I in my ignorance thought was of pretty high quality. We knew who we were and where we were from without having to think about it, and if we could believe the visiting evangelist at our annual revival, and most of us did, we were paralyzed with horror when we thought of our inevitable destiny. Most of us were Baptists and Methodists and we sat quietly—and some even contritely—as the awful truth was revealed to us. Some of our friends and neighbors, however, were of different faiths and during these moments of crisis, they were moved to ecstasy and shouted and spoke in unknown tongues. Our attitude toward these good people can be best illustrated, I believe, by a story an uncle of mine used to tell of how a friend of his controlled an unruly mule. (I have heard this story from many other sources.) Each time before my uncle's friend gave his mule a command, he would go around in front of her and whack her across the nose with a well-seasoned ax handle. "That's to get her attention," my uncle's friend always said. Everytime he hit the mule he knocked her to her knees. Then when she got up, she did exactly as she was told. Although my uncle did not approve of the way his friend controlled his mule, he too made his living looking at the wrong end of one of these arrogant, headstrong animals, and he thought a mule ought to be taught to mind. He always concluded his story: if a thing is worth doing, there is more

47

than one way to do it. We always felt that attracting the attention of the Lord was mighty important business, and any way a body could get this job done we heartily approved of. If shouting was the best way, we deeply envied the man who could yell loudest.

The church was undoubtedly the center of our lives—religious, educational, and social. In addition to the regular services and the revival, there were always the all-day singings and memorial days, the latter two inevitably including dinner on the ground. If everything we did was clearly in the sight of God, we were not as sure that all of our actions met with His absolute approval. For every church occasion gave us the opportunity to express our approval of and our lasting affection for the young lady who happened to catch our fancy at the moment.

After church came the school. My high school was very small; only eight in the graduating class. I doubt if the professional educator would rank it very high on his evaluative scale of a school's quality, for there was a highly restricted curriculum. In fact we had only one curricular choice to make during high school. After the tenth grade we chose either the college preparatory course or the vocational course. If we chose the college preparatory course, we took Latin. If we thought we were going to enter the labor force without benefit of college, we took agriculture. (The girls who thought they immediately were going to become homemakers enrolled in home economics.) All the other courses were the same in both curricula. But I had the same English teacher from the seventh grade through the twelfth. She knew she did not have to tolerate a subject-verb disagreement from me after the 9th grade, and she didn't. Despite my cleverness in trying to find a pun in its title, she also knew I was wasting my time trying to report on *The Camp Fire Girls' Trip up the River* in the 10th grade; therefore she required me to read *David Copperfield, Vanity Fair, Pride and Prejudice, Jane Eyre,* and *Oliver Twist.* As a consequence I found when I went to college that I had already "covered" much of the material included in freshman English and some of that studied in sophomore literature. What I really had was a sensitive, conscientious tutor who was very much interested in my educational development. I wonder if one gets the same kind of devoted personal attention in the so-called comprehensive high school of today.

Even before church and school was family. In addition to my brothers and sisters, of which there were five, I lived within walking distance of seven aunts and uncles with equally large families, and someone was always visiting one place or the other. Every one of the meals we had then seems to me now a ceremonious occasion. These visits, added to social affairs—dances, box suppers, ball games, birthday parties—kept us so fully engaged that, as I said in the beginning, we hardly had time to realize how deprived we were.

College was quite a revelation to me. I learned, from a study conducted by two sociologists at the University of North Carolina, that the "plane of living" in Mississippi was the lowest among the forty-eight states in the union. The two eminent social scientists based their conclusion on many facts, including the following: we spent less money on books, magazines and newspapers than the citizens of any other state, as we did on libraries, museums, and public education. We also had fewer automobiles and telephones and less indoor plumbing. These misleading, half-true derogatory remarks could be continued almost endlessly, but I want to repeat only two more of them because they contribute to a point I wish to make. A waggish New York publisher said that Mississippi must have the most unusual educational system in the history of civilization, that surely almost everyone down there must be able to write but few apparently could read, because each year the number of unpublished novel manuscripts he received from Mississippi was far greater than the number of finished books he sold in the state. Finally, and this is my last example, a reviewer in the *New Yorker* said of Faulkner's *Absalom, Absalom!*— now considered by many to be Faulkner's masterpiece and one of the greatest novels in American literature—"There is nothing wrong with this book," Mr. Clifton Fadiman wrote, "except it was obviously written by a crazy man and only a crazy man could understand it."

As might be expected, Mississippi soon became a journalistic whipping boy. Much of the press seemed to think that most of the evils of an imperfect social order were concentrated in Mississippi. No so-called civilized people anywhere at any time had ever possessed such an overt sense of racial injustice. (Now, surely not due to any astounding spiritual transformation on our part, this undeniably serious epidemic has spread and now exists in Boston, Louisville, Cleveland and as far away as Great Britain and South Africa.) Too, we were the most naive political people ever given the power of franchise, for we nearly always concluded our one-party elections by placing in the highest office of the state a political demogogue, who, like Willie Stark of *All the King's Men,* would divert as much of the state's resources to his own uses as he needed. Indeed, we seemed, in the eyes of some, to be trying mighty hard to earn the epithet by which we were sometimes referred—the worst state in the union.

I give these last allusions because they introduce a topic that perplexed many literary scholars of the time. I remember reading a few years after I had left college an essay with the shocking title, "Why Mississippi for God's Sake?" The essay first made a statement that to me at the time was not only startling but so pleasing I almost forgot all those unpleasant charges against my home state. After periods in which New York, Boston, and Chicago had been the centers of literary activity in the country, this writer said, the pendulum had swung and now it pointed South. A disproportionate number of literary awards between 1925 and 1950, he wrote, had gone to Southerners. Writers of the most distinguished books appearing in the last two decades, he continued, were from the South and the most important writer of the period was from Mississippi. The truth of the matter, he concluded, is that literary renaissance is occurring in the section where one would least expect such a development. Thus his question: "Why Mississippi for God's Sake?" Why did Mississippi—and not New York, California, Wisconsin or Massachusetts—produce William Faulkner, Eudora Welty, Richard Wright, and a score of other important writers? The truth of the matter is that Mississippi for no apparent reason had suddenly become a nest of singing birds; literary activity was flourishing in the region that H. L. Mencken a few years before had called "the Sahara of the Beaux Arts."

Much has been written about the reasons for this Southern Renaissance, and I think it would be helpful if we would review a few of these explanations. Donald Davidson in his essay "Why the Modern South Has a Great Literature" suggests some reasons why the renaissance in Southern Literature occurred. To view the Southern society as backward, he writes, is to make a "misleading assumption": "In number and size of cities, in number of factories, in number of farmhouses with modern plumbing, the South may be 'backward,' [but] that does not mean that Mississippi or any other state is, for that reason, socially, culturally, intellectually backward. . . . I can easily argue the contrary and assert that Southern society in the 1920's and 1930's was the most "advanced" in the United States." The quality of its literary output during this period, he continues, makes it very advanced indeed.

Most significant for our purposes here, I think, is Davidson's description of the kind of society that existed in Mississippi and in many other parts of the South in the three decades between the two great wars. It was, he insists, "a traditional society which had arrived at a moment of self-consciousness favorable to the production of great literary works." His definition of a traditional society is essential to our understanding of the kind of place Mississippi was in the immediate past, the time when it was receiving the undisguised scorn of much of the rest of the nation. "A traditional society," Davidson writes, "is a society that is stable, religious, more rural than urban, and politically conservative. Family, blood-kinship, clanship, folkways, custom, community, in such a society, supply the needs that in a non-traditional or progressive society are supplied at great cost by artificial devices like . . . government agencies."

Davidson and his friends realized that the society of their region was undergoing rapid and dramatic change. The agrarian order was giving way to an industrial one. Surely no one could do anything to alter the movement of progress; no one could make time stand still. An urbanized society was inevitable, but Davidson and some of his fellow artists thought they should do everything within their power to help shape the order of the new society. It was man's responsibility, they felt, to maintain contact with the natural world, to retain his awareness of aesthetic and religious reality, to avoid the inevitable brutalization that always accompanies a life lived solely for material values. In other words, Davidson argues, man should attempt to control, insofar as he can, the kind of world in which he has to live.

Allen Tate states this awareness of the physical place in which one lives and works in a slightly different manner. About 1920, he wrote many years ago, the modern Southern writer entered the contemporary world. He realized for the first time that all the evil in the world was not the wicked machinations of the damn yankees. At the same time he strode into modernity, however, he glanced back into the past out of which he had emerged. It was this act of seeing the "past in the present," this double focus, that allowed the Southern writer of Tate's generation to transcend "time's monotone," to break out of the "new provincialism," a conviction which holds that the only reality is the present moment.

This ability to see the past in the present—to realize the past is not dead, as Faulkner said, it's not even past—permitted the Southern writer of a generation ago to feel a sense of belonging to a specific geographic location and of sharing its history, its communicable tradition and idiom. This awareness of place as more than merely a location where things happen, to know it as a concrete phenomenon that allows an interrelationship between personal and cultural history, permitted the writer to attach values to precise local places. A quotation from Eudora Welty's brilliant essay "Place in Fiction," illuminates the point I am trying to make: "Place in fiction is the named, identified, concrete, exact and exacting, and therefore credible, gathering spot of all that has been felt, is about to be experienced, in the novel's progress. Location pertains to feeling; feeling profoundly pertains to place; place in history partakes of feeling, as feeling about history partakes of place."

If the function of literature is, as John Crowe Ransom asserts, the reconstitution of experience, its nature is profoundly affected by this feeling of a separate individual living in a specific concrete place. A much different form of literary expression comes from the man who regards himself, as one of Walker Percy's characters laments, as an anyone living anywhere. One reason, therefore, for the renaissance in Southern letters between 1925 and 1950, despite the backwardness of the region, is the fact that the section is one rich in natural detail; and the Southern writer did not feel alienated from his region in the way writers from other sections of the country did. The important Southern writers, including Faulkner and Welty, were not expatriates, instead they were searching for means through which they could become more acutely aware of their native traditions. This search for awareness brought them closer to their traditional heritage. It instilled within them a sense of belonging to a place, to a society however imperfect. Theirs was not the search of their younger colleagues who sought meaning in an absurd universe.

We realize, I hope, that no writer of the stature of William Faulkner can be created in a social and cultural vacuum. The kind of social order he grows up in will determine in part the kind of writer he will become. The sociologist is much too pragmatic to believe, I am sure, that the way to create writers like William Faulkner and Eudora Welty is to place them in a society with a "plane of living" as low as that existing in Mississippi during their formative years. There must be other causative factors that affect their literary careers and some of these I have been trying to suggest.

Another point I hope I have made. There is a great difference between what the sociologists mean by "plane of living" and what a humanist might call "quality of life." In fact it appears that often the quality of life deteriorates as the plane of living rises. This phenomenon, I take it, is something we should all hope to avoid; in fact one of the purposes of this conference is to find a way to prevent a decrease in the quality of life we may enjoy as the plane of living increases. Some of the writers who participated in the Southern renaissance were concerned about the uncontrolled growth of unselected industry. They took a very dim view of the useless destruction of our wilderness, for they said that "nature controlled and converted to man's uses" was a distorted and partial view of nature. Nature, they argued, should be regarded as a force inscrutable and contingent because it is such a concept that propagates man's belief in God. They were seriously concerned about what would happen to man's basic humanity if he were destined to turn tap 316 three quarters of a round 10,000 times a day for his entire working life. Surely all pleasure would be removed from the work itself; all that would be left would be the weekly paycheck and the material necessities and pleasures it would obtain. Many of the writers involved in the literary renaissance found the promises of such a life less inviting than the life they were giving up. They were as nostalgic about their early lives as I am about mine. Anyone who has visited the bedroom communities across the Hudson from New York City, the innercity slums of Jersey City, N.J., Gary, Indiana, Akron, Ohio, Youngstown, Ohio—and the list could be continued almost endlessly—knows the result of short sighted public policy, and the disastrous mistakes these cities made, we must make an honest attempt to avoid.

There seems to be widespread agreement that the South will indeed rise again. All economic indicators point, as both *Newsweek* and *Time* reported recently, to the Sun Belt as an area marked for unprecedented economic development during the next two decades, and those of us who live here would like to experience this transformation of our way of life with fewer damaging wounds to our psyches than our neighbors to the north and east have suffered. Despite the old adage that one learns from experience, it seems that seldom, to repeat another aphorism, do we profit from another's mistakes. Recently I participated in a discussion with a group of scientists who had planned a perfect community 100,000,000 miles in space. This community would include 10,000 people of all ages who would enjoy a temperature that stayed always at 72 degrees; they would breathe pure air made on the site from animal and human waste. In an environment free of bacterial and viral infections, they could expect to live for at least two hundred years, a perfect society, a new Jerusalem on a hill, this one 100,000,000 miles high. I was told that technology for the project had been done by physicists, mathematicians, and engineers. When it became clear that man had enough technical skill to launch the platform and maintain it in space, a couple of social planners were called in to deal with the problems created by so many people living together in absolute isolation. What I thought was a glaring deficiency in the planning procedure for this space community was the absence of a humanist: someone concerned that ten thousand people live as human beings and not as animals; someone who would insist that those people living completely to themselves would develop aesthetic forms as well as economic forms in the society that would evolve.

John Crowe Ransom—poet, essayist, social, literary, and cultural critic—insisted that it was important that a society develop both economic forms and aesthetic forms. In the first stage of its development a society must concentrate on its economic forms—the ways of earning a living with as little loss of energy as possible, the means of protecting itself against its natural enemies, be they nature, wild Indians or a foreign power; development of the acquisitive urge so that one could collect a sufficient quantity of the world's goods to protect himself and his family from need even in a time of emergency or catastrophe. Along with these economic forms a society, in a later stage, should begin to develop aesthetic forms—myths, religion, poetry, customs, a code of manners and morals, accepted patterns of behavior, for it is through these aesthetic forms that barbaric man is converted into civilized man. Let me give you one example of what I mean. Only human beings are capable of the kind of affection that the great renaissance writers—Sidney, Daniel and Spenser—defined with precise exactness as human love. Like all other animals the human feels lust, but this basic passion is elevated to the much more complex emotion called love through a series of carefully regulated social conventions. At a certain level of society is, first of all, the coming out party or the debutantes' ball, the official announcement of the family that the daughter is prepared to receive serious attention from the young men of the community. These occasions are followed, ideally, by an active period of dating so that the young people can get better acquainted. (Some dating has occurred, of course, before the coming out party but presumably it was not of the same intensity or seriousness as that following the ball.) Gradually the number of suitors decreases until only one is left and then comes a formal engagement, followed by another series of parties and finally the wedding, the formal reception, and the honeymoon. What this series of rigidly controlled social convention proposes to effect is to refine animal passion into human love. Man begins with a natural attraction for all women, any woman, as the male animal for the bitch; but by following the pattern of activities outlined above, this attraction, though it loses none of its force, becomes much richer and is directed not toward *any* woman but toward *one* woman. Thus we have a monogamous marriage, children, and a family. And the family is the basic unit of modern society.

I explain this process at some length because I believe the aesthetic forms are as important in any society as its economic forms. Any social planning regardless of its kind, any public policy, that fails to nurture with great care its aesthetic forms does so, I think, with a great chance of dismal failure. One wise man has said that no great society has ever existed without a poetry and we should not expect ours to be an exception. By "poetry" I think he also means the other aesthetic forms I have mentioned. *Lady* and *Gentleman*, *Yes, Sir* and *Yes, Mam* still mean something in the South. One who walks around in downtown Atlanta and sees the tallest hotel in the world, passageways over the street forty stories in the air, and the sidewalks so crowded with people that he can hardly move, might think he is in New York, Chicago, or Boston. But if he walks into one of the stores and talks to a clerk or gets a taxicab to the airport, he will quickly perceive a difference. The difference is more than the mere fact that the natives of Atlanta are able to speak American English in a manner practiced in the national capital; there is a feeling of mutual concern, a willingness to be of service, a natural display of appropriate mannerliness—in short, a demonstration of how one human being should treat another. What I am trying to suggest briefly is that we have certain attitudes, feelings, customs and patterns of behavior in the South that we should retain, regardless of what other changes we may make, or should make, in our social order. (These attitudes still exist despite Walker Percy's observations that there are more Cleveland-like suburbs in Atlanta or Nashville than there are in Cleveland.) When I meet a person and he asks me where I'm from, I say "Winston County"; if his next question is, "Are you related to the Dr. Young who used to live there?"—I know that's one person whom I don't have to try to convert. He already has the Southern attitude toward important matters. He knows I am *someone* from *somewhere*.

As you can see, I'm really leaving the technical discussions of specific kinds of public policy to you experts. I would like, however, to end as I began with a personal reference. Some time ago I spent a year in England. On this sojourn I was accompanied by my wife and our youngest son. All of us dreaded the year abroad, I think, because my work, visiting professor at the University of Leeds, would require that we live in a city of approximately one million people, almost completely industrialized. We were all convinced that it would be a most undesirable place to live. I am happy to report, however, that because of the enactment of wise public policies regarding land use we were pleasantly surprised. We felt as much at ease there as anywhere we have ever lived. In the immediate vicinity of our house—just across the street in fact—were business establishments to satisfy our ordinary needs—butcher, post office, bakery, grocery, green grocer, bank, TV shop, hair dresser, and service station. Within two or three minutes from our house was a four-mile wide green belt—complete with walking trails, bicycling and jogging paths, picnic grounds, overnight camping sites, and even wilderness. One result of these zoning laws, allowing each neighborhood to have its own small business establishments, and of this green belt on which no commercial establishments were allowed, was to discourage suburban shopping centers. This fact and the presence of cheap dependable public transportation to the center of town fostered the establishment of downtown shopping malls and prevented the abandonment and decay of the innercity so characteristic of many American cities. I know Leeds has slum areas, but its citizens were able to conceal them much better than we have been. Any one who drives through many of our Delta towns and villages knows exactly what is meant by environmental blight.

Images and Impressions of Mississippi and the Sense of Place:
Native View/Outside View

DAVID J. BODENHAMER

Most people define a society from the perspective of their position in that society. So, it is not surprising that the view of Mississippi held by natives of the state contrasts sharply with the image held by those people who live outside the state. This session examined the images of the state from the perspective of both groups—natives and outsiders—and attempted to explain the reasons for those images.

While each of the discussants presented his own perception of the state's image, there was more agreement between them than one might have expected. Perhaps this consensus reflects the fact that each panelist had experienced life in Mississippi firsthand, while each had also lived outside the state. Three men—Hudson, Young and Catledge—are native Mississippians who received their post-secondary education outside Mississippi; Hudson, however, was the only one of the three to return to live as an adult. McMillen reversed the pattern of his fellow panelists. Born in Michigan, he came to Mississippi for his undergraduate education and returned to the state to pursue his career.

In their formal remarks the speakers addressed three major themes—the negative image of Mississippi's past, the state's continuing racial problem, and the idea of a "New Mississippi." The panelists agreed that events of the past thirty years had caused people outside the state to portray Mississippi as the most backward, poverty-stricken, and racist part of the nation. As Young noted, "To some, Mississippi was synonymous with the KKK, lynching, superstition, religious fundamentalism, back-looking and past-loving."

Mississippians reacted defensively to such descriptions. Myths of moonlight, magnolias and a genteel life were among the images raised to counteract the negative perceptions of outsiders. But neither the benighted Mississippi nor the backward Mississippi were accurate portraits of the state.

Perhaps more than anything else, Mississippi's negative image, and the source of much of its shame, stemmed from the history of race relations in the state. But each speaker also acknowledged the progress that Mississippians had made in this area. To Young, this progress was the major reason for a changed attitude toward Mississippi by the rest of the nation, while McMillen believed that the change in the racial climate had enabled the state to shed the burden of backwardness and to embrace the idea of a "New Mississippi." Both men also suggested that Mississippi's image changed when it became apparent that racism was a national problem.

No panelist was willing, however, to advance more than a cautious optimism that past injustices were over. Catledge remarked that "race is still our greatest problem," and Hudson's comments served to underscore that reminder. To Hudson, the only black on the panel, the failures of blacks to achieve any major statewide office, the sight of Klansmen marching openly, and the existence of "segregation" academies made it difficult to gauge whether or not real change had occurred. Yet most discussants were convinced that the 1960s had marked a watershed in the history of race relations in Mississippi. And at least one speaker suggested that Mississippi could now set an example in racial harmony for the rest of the nation.

Each speaker noted that a new, more positive image of Mississippi was replacing the state's older, negative image. As defined by national journalists and the state's own leaders, this "New Mississippi" has "tremendous potential" in human and natural resources. The future offers unlimited material advancement and continued improvement in race relations. According to its advocates, the "New Mississippi" has become a part of the "New South," an area that has redeemed its past and is now ready to rejoin the nation.

The panelists were not willing to grant this new image of Mississippi much more validity, however, than the old one. Problems of poverty, unemployment and lack of educational opportunities still remain. Mississippi continues to rank fiftieth among the states in many of the categories which social scientists use to measure the quality of life. For some of the discussants the "New Mississippi" will not come until it solves the basic social and economic problems that consign Mississippi to its low rank. Everyone agreed that merely to embrace a new myth will not solve these problems.

Even in the "New Mississippi," panelists suggested, race would continue to be a problem. Blacks and whites view the future in different ways. For whites the state's new image offers the promise of material prosperity, but for blacks the future is more uncertain. Mississippi has been legally desegregated, but the races remain separated by culture and circumstance, if not by choice. Questions of when and how this situation would change, or indeed if it would change, make blacks approach the future more cautiously.

The few questions asked after the formal presentations had ended revealed that the audience was also concerned with Mississippi's racial problems. When asked about the "sense of place" held by young black Mississippians, Hudson replied that black youths now face the task of working in a dominant white culture while maintaining their ethnic identity. To him, the question of whether to remain ethnically identifiable or whether to subordinate ethnicity to participation in a broader white society is the central question that black Mississippians must answer before they can gain a true "sense of place." Young agreed with this assessment. He noted that for many of the state's citizens the problem of race had ceased to be one of desegregation but rather how to maintain individual and ethnic differences while pursuing the goal of equal opportunity for everyone.

Summary of Remarks by
Turner Catledge

After brief introductory comments, Turner Catledge proposed the following song to Will Campbell, an earlier speaker at the symposium: "Mississippi, you never knew how much we love you; Mississippi, you've never known before how much we care." But, he quickly continued, "We love you, Mississippi, not because of your virtues but despite your faults." This is the test of any love.

As one raised in the "isolated and insulated" community of Philadelphia, Catledge claimed that he did not address the audience as an ex-Mississippian, even though he had lived most of his adult life outside the state. He always meant to return, and he had never left Mississippi in spirit. So he welcomed with great anticipation the invitation to attend the symposium. This was his opportunity to witness for himself the changes in Mississippi and to hear about those changes from others who loved the state.

But Catledge acknowledged that he returned also because of his obligation in past years "to cast a searching eye on Mississippi and to explain ourselves to the rest of the country, to the readers of the *New York Times*." As executive editor of that newspaper it was his lot to direct coverage of events "which constituted the most sordid chapter in the history of the state." The story of Mississippi's racial turmoil was an unhappy one personally because some of the most tragic events of the period occurred in or near his hometown of Philadelphia. Catledge spoke of his dedication to objective reporting of the incidents, but even so, he admitted, "my heart was near breaking."

Now, Catledge remarked, "a proud Mississippi has redeemed itself to a great extent and is now prepared to offer an example in human relations to the rest of the nation." This redemption, which came through community consciousness and federal law, has answered the state's deep yearning for a better image. And the change has been fundamental: "No cosmetics could cure that image; it had to come from inside." Still, he warned, race is "our greatest problem." It is a problem, moreover, that Mississippians cannot avoid, even if there are no quick solutions to it. He cautioned that perhaps "there are times when we must accept tolerable non-solutions [to the race problem]." But that does not change the state's mission to the rest of the nation and the world to help promote harmonious living among different peoples. This, Catledge concluded, is Mississippi's true heritage.

Mississippi:
A Native View

ROY HUDSON

Most of us define social institutions from the perspective of our positions in those institutions. In fairness to my audience and to myself, therefore, I find it necessary to assert that, although my views originate from my position as a native Mississippian, they also originate from my position as a black, educated, socially sophisticated, politically confused middle class, Mississippi person.

I claim no great profundity of insight into this place we call Mississippi. I feel that I, as well as most other Mississippians, fall far short of having Robert Burns's desired gift, "to see ourselves as others see us." I must admit also that my views on Mississippi vary significantly, depending on where I am and to whom I'm revealing those views at any particular time. When conversing with outsiders who direct condescending or self-aggrandizing expressions toward Mississippi, I tend to take a defensive posture; yet when involved in exchanges among my compatriots, I tend to express views very similar to those of the outside critics. I rush to explain, however, that when I take a defensive posture toward outside critics I tend to do so from the position that they are as bad as we are, rather than from the position that we are as good as they are. This stance, perhaps, reveals something about my feelings toward the general order of American society.

For many years I used my views of Mississippi as a point of reference from which I set my political allegiance. Simply put, my position was that whatever was good for Mississippi was bad for me and, conversely, whatever was bad for Mississippi was good for me. In this context I am defining Mississippi as such controlling structures as those of state government, the white voting majority and the economic power establishment. In deciding which candidate to vote for in a political election, I drew the conclusion that if Mississippi was for him I'd better be against him, and that if Mississippi was against him it would serve me well to be for him. As a result of taking such a position,

I never voted for a winning candidate who carried Mississippi or my local voting precinct until the election of Jimmy Carter as president in 1976. I cannot say that my views of Mississippi have changed significantly as a result of voting with the majority for Jimmy Carter. Frankly, I believe that in some recent elections many of the regular white voting majority were confused by the weird state of affairs of post-Watergate politics and voted along with blacks to help elect state and national politicians.

I believe, however, that there is a strong commitment on the part of many voters and politicians to see that blacks cannot again lay claim to putting a major candidate in office. I feel that for a significant time to come race will still be the underlying determiner in Mississippi politics. I acknowledge the fact that the exhortation of racial bigotry no longer sets the tone for Mississippi politics, but the race issue still exists in more subtle tones.

While acknowledging the progress that Mississippi has made in race relations, we must not close our eyes to the vestiges of a darker past that still rears its ugly head. As much as I want to identify with the "New Mississippi," I still find myself distressed by the physical evidence that many of the problems still remain. When I see robed Klansmen openly and defiantly flaunt their symbolism of hate and aggression, I find it difficult to see the "New Mississippi." When I see private "segregation academies" rise in acclamation of a perpetual desire for segregated schools, I find it difficult to see the "New Mississippi." When I see Mississippi continuously hold to fiftieth place on almost all of the economic indicators, I find it difficult to see the "New Mississippi." For these reasons the "New Mississippi" is still to come.

My despair with the negative characteristics of the state is compounded by my view that, more and more, Mississippi mirrors a national trend toward greater social stratification and a wild rush toward self advancement. I sincerely feel that the real sense of place will be defined when we deal with the hard element of a new generation of young people who do not have the hope and vision I had when I was coming of age in the 1960s. When a whole generation of young people, and black people in particular, see greater restrictions in employment opportunities, more barriers in their quest to become educated, they become frustrated, desperate and lose faith in those values they have learned to accept. When unemployment among young blacks rises to thirty-three percent and when thousands of young blacks are denied entrances to our state institutions of higher learning and the general mood of our social institutions becomes insensitive to their needs, we create a mass of people who are without hope. Maybe we wish that they would just go away, but they won't. Just like our magnolias and ante-bellum mansions, they are the legacy of a social system whose injustices were of such magnitude that we must strive even harder now to rectify the damage it inflicted upon a race of people.

The final impression I want to make is that you are not seeing the real Mississippi in this audience here today, nor are you seeing it in Roy Hudson standing here in a pin-striped suit speaking the language of his Ivy League education. The real Mississippi lies out there in the hearts and minds of many whites who still cherish the old way and in the faces of many blacks who have yet to see the "New Mississippi."

Let those of us who have insight into the realities of the past and the progress of the future commit ourselves to helping bring about one common view of hope and prosperity for all Mississippians.

Mississippi:
Two Views from the Outside

T. D. YOUNG

Since I am a native of Mississippi, it may seem unusual that I have been asked to view my state as an outsider. The truth, as some of you know, is that I have spent much of my adult life outside the state, although all of that time I have regarded myself as a sojourner who would return home as soon as circumstances would permit. Situated, then, away from home, I have always been acutely aware of how my state was regarded by my friends, acquaintances, and colleagues. It seems to me that during the past half-century there have been two separate and largely contradictory attitudes toward the Magnolia State.

The first of these, which originated in the gloomy days immediately following the Civil War, was given its most authoritative statement by

Howard W. Odum and Harry E. Moore in a compendious study entitled *American Regionalism: A Cultural-Historical Approach to National Integration*. These two eminent sociologists were attempting, among other other things, to determine the "plane of living" in each of the forty-eight states by measuring income per capita; the percentage of homes having telephones, radios, automobiles, indoor plumbing; the amount of money spent on public education, symphony orchestras, and public libraries, the number and kind of newspapers and magazines subscribed to; and many other phenomena. As you would suspect, when the data from these sources were compiled, the South was the most backward section of the country and Mississippi was the most backward state in the South. (Donald Davidson once remarked, after having studied Odum and Moore's conclusions, that he didn't see how Faulkner was able to live, much less write, during the time he was composing *The Sound and the Fury, Light in August, Absalom, Absalom!* and his other great novels.) It is true that if one confines his study to this one source, he will easily be convinced that Mississippi lacked everything that made New York, Massachusetts, or Wisconsin great—educational facilities, museums, libraries, hospitals, theaters, and the like. The "plane of living" in Mississippi was without the slightest doubt the lowest in the nation.

Journalists, especially those working for periodicals published in the Northeast, were quick to divert Messrs. Odum and Moore's data to their own purposes. A writer in *The Saturday Review of Literature* labelled Mississippi the land of the three B's—Bilboism, Bigotry, and Backwardness. A second-rate novelist writing in *Harper's* proclaimed that after much thought and soul searching he had concluded that "Mississippi is the state the nation can best afford to do without." An Arkansas politician began one of his best known speeches with the exclamation, "Thank God for Mississippi," for only the presence of my home state kept his from the bottom of all the statistical tables. When confronted with the fact that the South had dominated the American literary scene from 1925 to 1950 and that the most important Southern writer of the period had come from Mississippi, one scholar expressed his exasperation with the question: "Why Mississippi, for God's sake?"

Such examples could be multiplied, but I hope I have made my point. Between the early thirties and the middle sixties the adjectives most often used to describe Mississippi by those living outside the state were "intolerant," "reactionary," "ignorant," "red-neck," "uncivilized." To some, Mississippi was synonymous with the KKK, lynching, superstition, religious fundamentalism, backward-looking, and past-loving.

By the middle or late sixties, however, the attitude toward Mississippi and the South generally seemed to be undergoing a transformation. Some national columnists found that we were undertaking to solve our racial problems with a seriousness of purpose that was completely unexpected and that in some areas our progress was easily detectable. Then with the election of Jimmy Carter one widely read journalist declared Reconstruction officially over and the South, including Mississippi, a member in good standing of the federal Union. So great has been the shift of opinion in recent years that a few months ago both *Time* and *Newsweek* announced to the world that the Sun Belt, a region from Carolina to Florida, from Texas to Kentucky, was fast becoming the financial and economic center of the country. In the view of one economist, by 1990 there will be two centers of economic power in this land of almost unlimited potential: Atlanta and Houston. Mississippi was placed in the area that would help Atlanta become the kind of metropolis in which one would expect to find the tallest hotel in the world. Now our state is described as one of "great promise," "tremendous potential," "abundant undeveloped resources," and the like. No longer, apparently, to use one of John Crowe Ransom's phrases, need we retain our Southern heritage merely as "a gardenia" to "stick in our buttonholes" on our infrequent trips to New York. We are no longer second-class citizens.

In my view both of these attitudes are distorted. The appraisal of the South based on Odum and Moore's "plane of living" includes only a partial view because it failed to take into consideration those characteristics of a social order I would surely include under the phrase "quality of life." The Odum-Moore formula for measuring the level of a society was based almost exclusively upon those phenomena that serve the principle of utility. These are those which Ransom would classify as economic forms, "forms of intense practicality . . . recipes of maximum efficiency, short routes to 'success,' to welfare, to the attainment of national satisfactions and comforts." A more nearly accurate measure of the "quality of living" available in a social order would include not only these "economic forms" but also those that Ransom calls "aesthetic forms"—art, manners, religion, rites, rituals, customs, and ceremonies. The South, including Mississippi, has always had these aesthetic forms in abundance, providing a far richer, more satisfying and fulfilling life than the paucity of economic opportunities would suggest.

The other view—the one labelling the region as possessing almost unlimited potentiality—fails to give appropriate attention to those factors Odum and Moore include in "plane of living." The Odum-Moore study was recently brought up to date, and we are no longer forty-eighth. Now we are fiftieth. There are plenty of problems all around us now that will take all of our industry, ingenuity, and resources to solve. To abandon them for the promise of a rosy, utopian future would be very foolish indeed.

Images of Mississippi

CHARLES SALLIS

For most Americans, the South has been viewed as a place apart, with customs and mores and a history all its own. Outsiders and, for that matter, Southerners, too, knew that the South was once a section distinguished by plantations and slavery, that it attempted to break away from the Union, that it used violence and terror to prevent the acquisition of equality by its black citizens during and after Reconstruction, and that since then it had been a land of discrimination, poverty and national scorn.

Yet, within the past few years a remarkable transformation has taken place. Whether for good or ill, one hears of Northern business flooding southward into the so-called Southern Rim or Sun Belt, extending from the Carolinas across the Deep South to Arizona and California. Eighty-five percent of the population growth in the nation since 1970 has occurred here. Southern cities are becoming like those elsewhere in the nation. And the Deep South has its first president since Zachary Taylor of Louisiana was elected on the Whig ticket in 1848. National magazines have recently had special sections on the South, and they all have said that the role of the South has very important implications for the future of America. And Mississippi is part of that future.

"Nothing in all history had ever succeeded like America, and every American knew it," wrote Henry Steele Commager just a few years ago. Indeed, America has been imbued with a sense of destiny for success that has permeated her national character. Most Americans believed that nothing in the world was beyond their power to accomplish. And, until very recently, the fates seemed to verify that conviction. As it turned out, it was a myth.

Along with the myth of success, America also conceived of herself as the epitome of innocence. From the beginning, the New World was seen as a new chance for a tired Old World. The blessings of nature and successful endeavors reinforced this feeling.

These myths of success and innocence influenced the nation's view of the South, for the South was neither successful nor innocent. The national attitudes in turn affected the attitudes of Southerners toward themselves; we became paranoid and defensive and apologetic for our frustrations and guilt.

In recent years, however, America's blind optimism has begun to show signs of erosion. The nation's confidence in itself began to slip in the 1960s and 1970s. The assassinations of the Kennedys and King, the urban riots, the alienation of youth, the loss of an unpopular war, Watergate, and the dishonorable resignations of a president and a vice-president—all these had a tremendous impact upon the national psyche.

Concurrent with this national mood of disillusionment, there occurred a renewed interest in the South. Somehow, suddenly, the South was no longer viewed as the "backyard of the nation." There were riots and demonstrations in the North for several hot and long summers. Riots over school integration were occurring in Boston, not Little Rock or Birmingham! Racial strife was no longer a "Southern problem" exclusively; it was a national concern.

Just as significant, there was a realization in America during this time that "progress" was not always desirable; many Americans were becoming weary of the complexities and tensions of industrialized society, of polluted air and water, traffic jams, urban crime and indifference. Now, many began to say, perhaps there was something desirable about a more relaxed lifestyle—the way it "used to be," the way it still was in much of the South. Thus, the South became more a part of the nation at just the time when national longings were turning toward virtues long associated with the South (at least in myth): closeness to nature, love of the land, simplicity, rootedness, stability, family, small towns, intimacy.

In 1958 James McBride Dabbs in *The Southern Heritage* called upon Southerners—both blacks and whites—to preserve the best of their heritage, to retain and nurture the good and to discard the unworthy. Others, including David Donald, a native of Goodman, Mississippi, and now Professor of History at Harvard, have developed this theme further. In his Commencement Address to the Millsaps College graduating class in May, 1976, he said:

> All of us know that there is not one South; there are at least two. One of these Souths is a land of violence and hatred. This is the South where whites kept blacks in slavery for more than two centuries and then held them in segregated serfdom, in some ways more degrading than slavery, for another hundred years. This is the South where the farmers raped the land, the factory owners squeezed their mill operators, and the planters cheated their tenants. This is the South that is thin in culture, suspicious in outlook, and bigoted in ideas. . . .
>
> But there is another South. I do not invoke images of magnolia-shaded plantations, where young gallants rode to the foxes, cheered on by damsels in hoops and crinolines, and where happy pickaninnies divided their time between eating watermelons and serving mint juleps to the Old Massa. That South never existed outside of fiction. But there is, and there always has been, a real South of basic goodness and decency, whose inhabitants, black as well as white, have a deep sense of attachment to place, a strong feeling of kinship, and a profound belief in their God. This is the South that is a land of frankness and openness, a land of generosity and courtesy.

The South, including Mississippi, seems to me to be at a kind of crossroads. We live in an age in which nationally there appears to be a loss of purpose, an erosion of confidence and a decline in the feeling of sense of community. Southerners of all races seem to have a unique sense of time and place, of belonging, of community, no matter how tough the times have been. Perhaps we can lead the nation in finding its lost purpose and restoring its confidence and sense of community. Perhaps that is our mission and our purpose. Perhaps that is Mississippi's role in the nation. Maybe the prodigal daughter can lead the way.

Preserving, Creating, and Destroying the Sense of Place:
Public Policy and Decision Making

GRAHAM HALES

This forum was focused upon public policy as it influences the destruction, creation, and preservation of a sense of place in Mississippi. The discussants explored the basic problem of how to balance desired economic development with an environment in which a sense of place is fostered. The difficulty of finding a satisfactory public policy for this area of human concern stems partly from the multiplicity of factors that shape a sense of place.

Mississippi is enthusiastically committed to economic growth. This comparatively recent commitment has both positive and negative aspects. Negatively, our state finds itself at or near the bottom of most lists of economic accomplishment. Positively, we can develop our economic policies in light of mistakes made in other areas of our nation. The failure of other sections to preserve a sense of place in their rush toward technological and economic success may be avoided here.

Robert Wales discussed sense of place as an identifiable object or event of our environment and examined some current policy problems involved in maintaining a quality environment. Patti Black examined the role of the Mississippi State Historical Society in preserving our historic record. She briefly sketched the history of the Society and its preservation efforts through the archives, archaeology, historic structures, and museum divisions. She also noted avenues open to citizens and communities desiring legal and financial aid in preservation efforts. Robert Thorne strongly urged the public's education concerning the urgent need to protect non-renewable resources. Economic development advocacy should be balanced by an assessment of possible destruction of archaeological sites. Thorne also commented on the problems raised by private ownership of historic sites. Volney Cissna discussed zoning as one way communities can secure areas of historical value, with special attention to historic buildings and properties. He reviewed recent legislation affecting historic preservation. Frank E. Smith concluded the forum with the observation that sense-of-place sentiment can mask negative as well as positive goals. He reminded the audience that economic stagnation and poverty were and are part of Mississippi's sense of place and he called for a balanced approach in our effort to preserve a sense of place.

Several focus questions concerning the preservation and destruction of a sense of place emerged from the overall comments of the panelists. In particular, the speakers focused on several dilemmas inherent in balancing competing values: How does society balance progress with preservation? Faced with "now or never" opportunities to safeguard special sites and artifacts for future study, how does one use limited funds and/or public policy to seize these opportunities? To what extent do romantic ideals of Mississippi's sense of place mask realistic economic, social and cultural poverties of significant segments of Mississippi's population?

The panel raised questions that citizens must face in planning policy. The complexities and political antipathies inherent in various options were honestly addressed. There were no simple solutions presented that would be satisfactory to the various interest groups in our state, but awareness of the problems and of the parameters of possible solutions was heightened.

Environment, A Sense of Place and Public Policy

ROBERT W. WALES

An intelligent public dialogue is a starting point for the development of public policy which will shape the future of Mississippi. As a policy goal, a sense of place involves many dimensions that remain inchoate, diverse, and overlapping. Many facts are not known, and most of the alternative growth choices we face and will be facing have not been developed. Nevertheless, from time to time it is necessary to consider where we are and where we have been in order to decide more wisely where we should be going.

The ideas I will be dealing with in this paper come partly out of my educational and research interest in environmental planning and partly out of a more recent exercise in tying environmental planning to the sense-of-place concept. Specifically, I attempt to explore the relationships between environment, environmental quality, and a sense of place so as to suggest the implications of these terms for future policy decisions in Mississippi.

Environment, Environmental Quality and A Sense of Place

Webster's Third International Dictionary (1963) defines *environment* as the "aggregate of all the external conditions and influences affecting the life and development of an organism."Environment, then, is considered not only in terms of physical configurations, location and space, but also in terms of direct experiential and sensory surroundings as a primary source of living experience and as a primary conditioner of physical and psychological development for each individual human being.

It is difficult to conceive of an environment in any but holistic terms; but our pragmatic philosophy—the scientific mind—rejects the concept of "wholeness" on the grounds that we cannot be masters of all things. In practical terms we have come to understand environment through a description of its parts. Thus we talk of political, economic, social, cultural, psychological, artificial, natural, and visual environments.

The concept of environmental quality is generally understood as a state of the environment expressed in terms of preferences rated on a scale of desirability versus undesirability. Even though qualities may exist without man, it is man who makes the judgments that define qualities—both individual and consensus. An individual may attach some value or measure of quality to an environment, and the "group," a similar or somewhat different value to the same environment. Quality, then, is a separate reality for each individual but may contain universals for a great many individuals.

Attempts to measure environmental quality have been undertaken by several major disciplines, notably economics, psychology, architecture, sociology, geography, and the environmental sciences. Methodological approaches and the objects of measurement differ among the disciplines to the extent that each has developed its own understanding of how ideals and values should be defined and are manifested in laws, norms, and sanctions of society.

The objective elements of an environment are empirical, reproducible and easy to measure. Absolute scales can be applied: census data and economic indicators deal with the objective. Environmental quality indicators, on the other hand, go beyond the objective to include the subjective. These conditions or factors are not reproducible with certainty. They measure the feelings and attitudes that indicate the condition and conditioning or "state of mind" of citizens and society. There are no costs, prices, or incomes to which most subjective variables can be converted.

The difficulty of coping with the subjective is readily apparent in a consideration of the visual environment. Peter Coltman has identified the following elements as composing the whole of a visual environment:[1]

Uniqueness—the element or combination of elements which sets an environment apart from people or places.

Character—an enlarged scale of uniqueness: the southern coastal softwood belt or the riverine hardwoods of the Mississippi Delta.

Completeness—nothing more is needed to complete the response. Sounds, smell, and feel are evident; a missing element would not result in a complete environment.

Scale—the environment may be as grand as Niagara Falls, or as small as a courtyard, but both can be complete environments.

Participation—similar to scale but with the additional dimension of offering engagement, both mental and physical. Some environments are to be seen, others experienced.

[1] Peter Coltman, "Thoughts on Environment," *Kansas Engineer*, March 1968, p. 14.

Suitability—each feature of the visual environment provides a satisfying experience or response. Elements invoking a negative response (litter, smog, polluted water) are unsuitable characteristics of an environment.

Compatibility—When each element of the natural or artificial landscape balances the other or sets up dynamic relationships (even in contrast), then compatibility can be said to exist.

As used here, sense of place refers to the character and personality of the state and to the special aura that surrounds a particular place, including the affective bond or feeling people have for a place or geographical area. The concept also involves, I think, environments or events which at one time or another were designated as rare in the experience of an individual or a society. To be rare in this sense one environment or event must be distinguishable from another. The basis for the distinction is not always clear, however. One may take a realist's view of rarity. For the realist, an object or event is unique within a purview: given a certain boundary, there exists few or more like it. For the idealist, a rare object is one that is archetypal: it is the most typical of all the objects it represents, having the most nearly perfect form.[2]

A waterfall, natural area, botanical garden, and specimens in museums are the usual natural objects of rarity. But it is also possible to regard other kinds of environments or events as rare. One's birth city or state, for example, can be distinguished as rare in the sense that an individual can value a place of birth and thus value the characteristics of the place. The ability to distinguish oneself as having been born in Mississippi becomes more meaningful since it establishes a degree of individual or group identity not possible when speaking more generally of being born in the United States or the world.

It is possible to identify and relate oneself to a nested set of environments, or spaces, by type of use or activity. At the smallest scale, for example, there exists the home with its numerous subenvironments; then come the neighborhood, city, and state. That environment, whatever the scale, in which man operates and is aware of is the perceptual or cognitive environment. Awareness may be derived from physical

---

[2]Martin H. Krieger, "What's Wrong with Plastic Trees?" *Science*, 179 (2 February 1973), 148.

sensitivity to environmental stimuli or from experience or learning.

The most important element of an identified environment is its "edge" or boundary. Within the boundaries people "learn" a set of expectations appropriate for specific actions.[3] Any given environment may stimulate an entire scale of value responses ranging from desirable to undesirable. Those qualities which invoke a sense of security, of familiarity, and of habit—of belonging—can, I think, be said to be sense-of-place qualities. Such qualities, when perceived from within, always involve positive responses. Neutral or negative qualities may exist, but these are not valued as sense-of-place qualities.

When individuals or groups encounter unfamiliar environments which do not immediately fit a preconceived scheme of order, responses assigned to the environmental setting may be negative. Perhaps the most common occurrence of negative response is the "passing-by" view of a given environment. A New Yorker, for example, may have little place in his universe of discourse for assigning positive meanings to elements of a Mississippi environment that do not fit his experience. The same may also hold true for a Biloxian traveling through an unfamiliar Delta setting.

Negative responses are also experienced in greater frequency from "within." Such responses are exemplified by concern shown at this symposium that Mississippians are losing their sense of place. This concern is valid, I think, although it is not uniquely Mississippian in occurrence. We are today living in an environment of a technologically advanced country in which technical and economic factors have come to dominate our cultural, historic and aesthetic features. The rapidity with which we are manipulating, modifying and introducing incompatibilities into our environment has outreached our ability to come to terms with these newly evolved structures and systems.

Destroying, Creating and Preserving
Our Sense of Place

In less complicated technological times man was, in general, at terms

[3]For an excellent account of bounded environments and cognitive awareness see Robert G. Lee, "The Social Definition of Outdoor Recreational Places," in William R. Burch, Jr., et al., eds., *Social Behavior, Natural Resources, and the Environment* (New York: Harper & Row, 1972), pp. 68-84.

with his environment. He understood his environment and his role in it. (In fact, in the beginning, before Adam took his first bite of the apple, he lived in paradise and his sense of place was total.) As science progressed and new technologies were developed, a fundamental disruptive process was initiated and man began to lose his sense of place in the rapidly changing environment. In grossly oversimplified terms, contemporary tensions, ulcers, and mental problems became far more prevalent than these were in "simpler" environments.

Numerous literary hearings have been held on why man, particularly Western man, has so mismanaged his environment. The poles of discussion are many: subject vs. object, mind vs. matter, man vs. nature, contemplative vs. exploitative, spiritual vs. materialistic. Aldo Leopold, for example, suggests that we have as yet no ethic dealing with man's relationship to land save that which is strictly economic, entailing privileges but not obligations.[4] Lynn White, Jr., on the other hand, argues that Christianity, especially in its Western form, is largely at fault, that Christian tradition has taught us to be "superior to nature, contemptuous of it, willing to use it for our slightest whim."[5]

And God blessed them, and God said to them, "Be fruitful and multiply, and fill the earth and subdue it; and have dominion over the fish of the sea and over the birds of the air and over every living thing that moves upon the earth." (Genesis 1:27-28)

I do not wish to be misunderstood. I am not pleading for a return to a position of subserviency to the natural landscape. I merely wish to point out that between now and the end of the century we will probably do as much building as civilized man has done throughout history. We are in the process of creating a world that will be largely man made and man controlled, and for which we are attempting, albeit poorly, to develop a new set of values. We may look back and conclude that our technological world was the best of the alternatives after all. At present, however, it is fit to ask: "What will we be aban-

[4]"An Ethic for Man-Land Relations," in Roderick Nash, ed., *The American Environment: Readings in the History of Conservation* (Reading, Mass.: Addison-Wesley, 1976), pp. 105-109.
[5]"The Historical Roots of Our Ecological Crisis," *Science*, 155 (10 March 1967), 1203-1207.

doning?" Are we, as Leopold suggests, about to remodel our Alhambra with a steam shovel?[6]

One of the problems before us today is to decide which vestiges of the past and conditions of the present we desire to carry with us into the future. Most of us are concerned not so much about whether we should preserve as about what to preserve of those rare, unique, and distinct features of Mississippi that provide a sense of place. Simply because something is rare, unique or distinct does not necessarily imply a need to preserve it. Also to be valued are the characteristics that distinguish it as worthy of preservation.

Preservation is not new in American history. Far-sighted public officials involved themselves in preservation as long ago as 1858 when George Washington's home at Mount Vernon was designated a national shrine. The private sector also became involved in preservation at an early date. In 1895 Andrew H. Green formed a state historical organization in New York, which in 1901 reconstituted itself as the American Scenic and Historical Preservation Society. In brief but eloquent fashion, this group in 1914 put its feelings about preservation on record:

No doubt one great reason [for preservation] is the feeling that it is well-nigh criminal to destroy or to undo great works of art and architecture which embody the labor and the genius of so many men of so many ages. It is like nullifying the lives of so many generations of men—like obliterating them from the scroll of time—as far as their productive labors are concerned. It is like setting back the calendar of years to the time before those works were made, and creating a condition the same as if the works had never been performed. It is depriving the world of what makes for civilization and of what civilization is entitled to have, namely, the accumulation of the best products of human genius of all preceding generations.

But there is another reason of more universal application than the foregoing. The reason which we have just mentioned is based largely on the consideration that the monuments ... are great in themselves; and that they possess intrinsic value, either on account of their magnificence or their artistic refinement. But an historic monument may possess value through an association of ideas irrespective of its intrinsic value, and this is true equally of the palace and the cottage.[7]

[6]Leopold, "An Ethic for Man-Land Relations," p. 109.
[7]"Nineteenth Annual Report of the American Scenic and Historic Preservation Society," in Roderick Nash, ed., *The American Environment: Readings in the History of Conservation* (Reading, Mass.: Addison-Wesley, 1976), pp. 74-78.

Public Policy and the Environment

To this point I have attempted to show that a sense of place is not only allied with environment, but is in fact a quality condition of the environment. This relationship is significant insofar as public policy considerations are concerned because it is highly unlikely that sense of place, however defined, will stand alone as a major public policy objective. Environmental quality, on the other hand, has taken its place as a national objective. Numerous single-purpose programs cover a host of environmental concerns. Among them are air and water pollution control, natural land preservation, scenic landscape preservation and enhancement, highway beautification, urban beautification, urban renewal, and architectural and historic site preservation. Separately, the many programs are concerned with preserving and ordering the natural environment and with manipulating and creating the artificial environment. Although the objectives of these programs are varied, when reduced to the smallest number of common denominators we find three principal objective categories: physical and mental health, sensory and participatory pleasure, and economic value.[8]

Our environmental programs at all levels of government are adequate to get us started toward providing an environment capable of enhancing the quality of life. Why, then, aren't they working? The problem is complex and certainly beyond my ability to answer conclusively, but two partial reasons come to mind. First, we lack a common currency with which to mutually relate program objectives. And second, perhaps because of the common currency obstacle, most environmental programs have come to serve as constraints to income maximization rather than objectives in their own right. That is, environmental programs add to the income objective the proviso, "subject to the constraint that you do not significantly harm the mental or physical health of human beings, aesthetic or participatory pleasure, or property values."

I have been told that what we in Mississippi are struggling with is

[8]Robert Kates, "Comprehensive Environmental Planning," in Maynard M. Hufschmidt, ed., *Regional Planning: Challenge and Prospects* (New York: Frederick A. Praeger, 1969), pp. 67-87.

the dilemma of economic growth and environmental quality. Like many so-called dilemmas this one is based on two alternatives that are made to appear mutually exclusive. They are not. They are objectives which can be compatible and made to blend in such a way that social control in the form of environmental policy (public policy being a form of social control) safeguards the freedom for economic development. The problem is not a matter of having our cake and eating it too. It is, rather, a problem of first arriving at an objective function for environmental planning, then translating the objective into a set of indicators that are equally applicable in measuring characteristics of both the social "system" and the economic system. One should not have to follow the question, "Are you for the freeway, or do you want to see the city lose x-million dollars?" with the statement, "If you build the freeway, the fourth oldest house in Mississippi will be destroyed."

In closing I would like to respond to a rhetorical question, "If we can put men on the moon, why can't we solve our own earthly problems?" The answer is relatively simple. Three essential facts were known about the moon trip. We knew where we were, where we needed to go, and what means were necessary to get there. Developing policy on environmental issues is made difficult not only because it is likely to be politically controversial but also because it is technologically bewildering. Moreover, it is difficult conceptually because we do not all agree on what we see as either environmental quality or the factors that shape a sense of place. Furthermore, we have no scale of measurement, let alone a clear sense of the direction we would take if we did have one. I think we agree, however, that we do have a vested interest not only in identifying what we perceive as being distinctly Mississippian but in examining our environment—our sense of place—in order to describe where we are and where we should be going.

Preserving the Sense of Place:
State Policy

PATTI CARR BLACK

When we speak of "preserving the sense of place," we often speak in terms of sites and structures, but historic preservation cuts a wide swath. It may also mean preserving artifacts, documents, music, folk customs, foodways and speech, to name a few areas. It is this all-encompassing definition that I use, and it is primarily the policies of one state agency, the Mississippi Department of Archives and History, which I cursorily describe.

Preserving the sense of place has been a matter of state policy in Mississippi for over seventy-five years. In 1902, as the second state in the union to do so, Mississippi established a Department of Archives and History. Its primary purpose was to collect and preserve written and published materials bearing upon the history of the state. The objectives set forth in the law were broad enough to encompass all historical resources, and by the second year of its existence the department had begun to collect historical artifacts.

As is true of most government functions, historic preservation grew out of activity in the private sector: there was prolonged concern which we can trace back to the 1850s, when the first Mississippi Historical Society was formed. Organized by B. L. C. Wailes, it was the first effort in the state to systematically collect and preserve historical resources. It had a short life but it laid the foundation for its successor, a revived Mississippi Historical Society, chartered in 1890, which spearheaded the move to establish the Mississippi Department of Archives and History. After giving birth to the department, the Historical Society faded away in 1914, not to be reborn until 1952, when the current Mississippi Historical Society was formed. Today the Society has a membership of over 2,000.

The concept of historic preservation within the Department of Archives and History has evolved through the years, encompassing each year additional aspects of historic preservation. These now include the following areas.

Archives: The archives and library division collects resource material—official archives, private papers, books, broadsides, newspapers, photographs, maps, recordings, videotapes, and all types of historical documents and source material. In 1969 an oral history program was established. We are by no means the only state institution collecting these materials. Several universities have archives and oral history programs.

Archaeology: The earliest archaeological activity in the state began in the 1920s, first with Calvin Brown's work with the State Geological Survey, and in 1925 with the Bureau of American Ethnology investigations of Choctaw lands. The Department of Archives and History assigned a staff member to participate in that study which examined, among other sites, the Choctaw mound, Nanih Waiya. In 1927 the department hired two young men to work during the summers as field archaeologists for the Archaeological Survey of Mississippi, with efforts concentrated in the Big Black River drainage area. By the 1930s and '40s archaeological work was widespread. The Fatherland Site at Natchez was partially excavated by the Department of Archives and History; the WPA surveyed archaeological sites statewide, the National Park Service instigated the Natchez Trace survey; and a significant survey of the lower Mississippi valley was undertaken in 1939 as a joint project of Louisiana State University, the University of Michigan and Harvard's Peabody Museum. Until the 1960s out of state universities and the National Park Service continued to direct archaeological surveys in Mississippi. In the 1960s, at Charlotte Capers's insistence, the Mississippi Department of Archives and History got into the archaeological research business. In 1962 the Department received a grant from the National Science Foundation for an extensive excavation of the site of the Village of the Natchez Indians. In 1968 the Mississippi Archaeological Survey was established by the legislature, and in 1970 the Division of Historic Sites and Archaeology was established within the Mississippi Department of Archives and History. Today the department has seven staff archaeologists, five archaeological sites owned by the department (Jaketown, Liest Site A, Grand Village, Jackson Landing, and Mulatto Bayou), and sixty archaeological sites on the National Register. The larger state universities also have archaeological staffs.

Historic Structures: Federal activities arising from the Depression of the 1930s formed the base of our current surveys of historic structures. The Historic American Building Survey and the WPA historical research project left us valuable material. The private sector again led the way in the actual preservation of historic structures. The Natchez Pilgrimage, established in 1932, insured attention to many historic buildings and was the impetus for later restoration efforts not only in

Natchez but all over the state. Today notable activity is taking place in Vicksburg, Holly Springs, Columbus, Corinth, the Gulf Coast, and in countless other communities. But the first restoration of a historic structure by a state agency was not begun until 1959. The old state capitol had been saved from destruction in 1916 through the efforts of the Department of Archives and History and patriotic societies, and in 1959 the department began a careful adaptive restoration.

In 1965 the State of Mississippi acquired Jefferson College in Adams County, transferred it to the Department of Archives and History in 1971 and began restoration. The first building was opened to the public in 1976.

In 1966 and 1971, piecemeal, the Grand Village of the Natchez Indians was acquired by the Department of Archives and History and opened to the public in 1976. The department has acquired the Van Dorn house in Port Gibson, Windsor Ruins, and the Manship House in Jackson. Restorations are in progress. In 1973 the Governor's Mansion, under the direction of the Department of Archives and History, was completely restored and refurnished.

Outreach activity in the department springs from two important pieces of legislation, one federal, one state. With the passage of the National Historic Preservation Act, 1966 was a pivotal year throughout the nation for the historic preservation movement. This legislation set up the framework which allowed the Department of Archives and History to launch a systematic and far-reaching program of historical preservation. This was done in 1970 through the organization of the Division of Historic Sites and Archaeology (now called the Division of Historic Preservation) within the department.

Another important piece of legislation was the passage of the Antiquities law of Mississippi in 1970. These two laws gave authority needed to administer the historic preservation activities of the department. The Historic Preservation Division has three functions: the review process, survey and planning, grants-in-aid. These programs are handled by a professional staff of historians, architectural historians, and archaeologists.

The review process attempts to enforce the review provisions of both the Antiquities Act and the National Preservation Act. The Antiquities law protects historical, archaeological, educational and scientific sites located on state, county, or municipal property. Theoretically, the Department of Archives and History has the authority to pass on any alterations to such structures, whether it be re-roofing or major restoration work. The problem, of course, is the implementation and enforcement. If federal funds are involved in any project, the department is automatically notified by the federal agency. Unfortunately, tearing down a building or bulldozing an archaeological site does not require federal funds so that it is difficult to police such activities. But we also work with county boards of supervisors and city council planning departments, who are usually aware of the statute. Problems come with small cities and rural areas where demolition and alterations go on unknown and unheralded. Local historical societies and history buffs are helpful in many of these instances in notifying the department. We must depend on the interest, cooperation and knowledge of Mississippi citizens. As of today, only two cities have adopted their own historic district zoning: Natchez and Vicksburg.

The other act, the National Historic Preservation Act, directed all federal agencies to consider the impact of projects on natural and man-made environments. The Department of Archives and History implements the National Historic Preservation Act on the state level, using review procedures adopted in 1974 by the Advisory Council on Historic Preservation. Over 200 projects a month are reviewed.

In addition to the review function, there are survey and planning. Mississippi's initial survey of historic sites and structures began in 1948 with the creation of the State Historical Commission. It had no staff and its duties were absorbed by the Department of Archives and History in 1968, but during its existence, through the Department of Archives and History staff, it identified and erected historical markers at some 375 sites. Survey and planning really got off the ground with the passage of the National Historic Preservation Act, which established the National Register of Historic Places. The register is in effect an inventory of sites and structures worth saving. After the Division of Historic Sites was set up within the department, an attempt at state-wide survey and planning was undertaken. Initially, the emphasis was on individual sites and structures. Today the emphasis has shifted to surveys of entire neighborhoods. For example, Carrollton has recently been surveyed from the data gathered, and 66 buildings will be nominated for the National Register. A survey of Pass Christian has shown 125 buildings worth saving for historical reasons. The great post-World War II boom and the policies of the Great Society activated sweeping urban renewal projects that caused wholesale destruction of neighborhoods. The built environment is becoming homogenized; the sense of place destroyed. The neighborhood preservation program is an effort to keep the uniqueness of a place from being eroded so that people will have a context and a continuity. To date there are only two neighborhoods in Mississippi on the National Register: Smith Park Area in Jackson and Natchez Under the Hill. There are, however, over 200 separate structures and sites in Mississippi on the National Register, with a long waiting list. The Tax Reform Act of 1974 made it attractive for owners of historical properties to get on the National Register.

When the professional staff determines that a property possesses sufficient significance, research is initiated. The choice must then be approved by the Mississippi Historic Preservation Professional Review Board, which is made up of eleven people from the fields of architecture, archaeology, history, law, landscape architecture, and urban planning. Exhaustive research is then completed and the nomination made to the National Register.

Unfortunately, our small staff of four architectural historians makes the task of researching all the worthy buildings in the state an impossible one. The neighborhood concept thus has a pragmatic advantage: an entire district can be spotlighted. The primary objective of the National Register is to make owners aware of the historical worth of their property and aware that they can get help in preserving it.

The final program provides that help: the Grants-in-Aid program. Through monies provided by the National Park Service, the Department of Archives and History can make 50-50 matching grants to restore and preserve individual sites and structures in the state. These grants may be made to individuals or organizations. The award is based on the historical significance of the property, the need of the applicant and the commitment made to preservation standards. The Board of Directors of the Mississippi Department of Archives and History selects the grantees, and their selection is reviewed by the

Historic Review Board. In fiscal year 1978 grants totaling $525,000 were awarded to 20 different structures in the state.

Museum: The museum function preserves a sense of place. For the Mississippi State Historical Museum the traditional museum duties are paramount: the collection, preservation, and interpretation of artifacts bearing on the history of Mississippi. But in addition, since 1973 the museum has led the state in the exploration and preservation of folk culture, not only through the collection of artifacts, but in documentation of folk culture through photographs, interviews, tape recordings of music, and presentation of crafts demonstrations and folk concerts.

I must point out again that I have tried to speak only about historic preservation as it emanates from the Mississippi Department of Archives and History. There are other agencies doing important work. Other state agencies are in the museum business. The Museum of Natural Science collects and preserves specimens of our natural heritage; the Department of Agriculture and Commerce is about to break ground on the new Museum of Agriculture and Forestry. The Mississippi Park Commission administers the Winterville Mound Site; the Nanih Waiya Cave Mound in Neshoba County, and the Nanih Waiya Mound in Winston County. The Grand Gulf Military Park Commission operates the Grand Gulf Site, and of course the National Park Service administers many significant archaeological and historic sites along the Natchez Trace Parkway. These include the Tupelo Battlefield Site, Brice's Crossroads and Vicksburg Military Park. There are, in addition, many excellent projects underway in the state initiated by historical societies, chambers of commerce, county boards of supervisors, and private owners.

The major task all of us face is making the public aware that continued active support of preservation, on the local as well as the state level, is vital if Mississippi is to retain the uniqueness of its man-made environment. Nor should preservation be considered as anti-growth or anti-progress. Retention of old structures can not only be economically beneficial but good for business and the character of the community as well. Historic preservation is tied to growth. It is linked to the educational, cultural, and economic development in the state. Preservation is a progressive concept.

Preserving Cultural Resources

ROBERT THORNE

Mississippians, like people throughout the rest of the nation, are seeking to establish and identify a sense of place and belonging in a land which we have occupied only in the historic period. After the turmoil of the 1960s and the celebration of the Bicentennial, it is once again becoming acceptable and even fashionable to be proud to be an American and to trace and demonstrate our individual past. Obvious indications of our interests include the numerous pilgrimages held each spring throughout the state; the restoration of "older" homes which have no historic "significance" but are of architectural interest; the increased participation in genealogical studies; and steady numbers of people who participate in such organizations as the D.A.R., Colonial Dames and U.D.C. In a lot of ways it is unfortunate that written records do not completely identify activities of the historic period and are totally absent for the New World prior to 1492. Partially as a result of the paucity of written information, there is, and has been for the past ten years, a growing concern for our cultural heritage and cultural resources. Congress and a number of states have passed legislation and promulgated regulations which now allow us to more carefully protect these resources and the data which can be recovered from them.

As Americans we are constantly bombarded with statements of "progress." Frequently we are informed of a massive project, told that it is progress, and then discover at implementation that the project will destroy tangible remains of our prehistoric and historic past. Some of this progress can be very controversial, i.e., the Tennessee-Tombigbee Waterway, levee construction in the Mississippi Delta, urban renewal projects, subdivision development, reservoir impoundment and mechanized agricultural practices. Some projects are funded with governmental monies while others are totally supported by private enterprise. Obviously, the preservation of elements of the past and progressive economic and technical steps come into conflict.

I would like to be able to tell you that there is an easy, clearly defined solution to conflicts which arise between progressive steps and preservations of our cultural resources, but that is simply not the case. To begin with, if archaeological recovery of data is necessary, we will immediately set about destroying the very things we are determined to protect. As a result, as archaeologists we must continually strive to record the maximum amount of data. Many people who call themselves "amateur archaeologists" do not understand why "professionals" try so hard to discourage their activities. The case is that such activities ultimately produce a data loss greater than that which is recovered. Conservation of resources, now billed as *Cultural Resource Management,* is a prime consideration in any formal attempt to mitigate the loss of data which will result from any project.

Conservation of our cultural resources, both historic and prehistoric is a complicated business. In Mississippi we have had an "Antiquities Law" since 1942, when the statute was first entered on the books. It was revised and strengthened in 1970. It can only be enforced, however, on publicly held lands or on privately held lands which have been declared an "Archaeological Landmark." In all cases of privately held lands, tangible remains of the past belong to the landowner and may be treated in whatever manner he chooses. When a man calls and says he intends to "doze" down a large mound because it is in the way of his farming, how do we convince him otherwise?

Conservation of resources on federally held lands or on federally sponsored projects operates on an entirely different legal base which supersedes the existing state statutes. It should be noted here that any work which is carried out on a federally funded project is coordinated through the offices of the State Historic Preservation officer. As a result, an attempt is made to represent the interests of all the citizens of the state.

National concerns for cultural resource management began in 1906 (Act for the Preservation of American Antiquities) and was continued with other legislation in 1935 (Historic Preservation Act); in 1960 (strengthening of 1935 act); in 1966 (Preservation of additional properties and establishment of National Register, advisory council on Historic Preservation) and in 1969 (National Environmental Policy Act). Even with the mandate of these laws, federal agencies did little until recently to preserve resources or recover data—largely because funding was not available and the impetus was not present. In 1971 Richard Nixon signed executive order 11593, which was a specific directive to all federal agencies to carry out the mandates of existing preservation statutes. Probably the major impact on preservation and conservation came in 1974 when Congress passed public Law 93-291. This act empowered federal agencies to expend an amount equal to one percent of construction costs on the preservation of resources or the mitigation of data loss as a result of construction.

Executive Order 11593, the Environmental Protection Act and its revision and Public Law 93-291 have had a tremendous impact on our definition of place. With these three elements as a legal background, archaeologists, historians, and architectural historians have done more in the last ten years to develop an understanding of our past than was done in the preceding half century, although there were some notable points during the earlier period (W.P.A. projects, TVA projects, River Basin Surveys).

Our professional roles as "Stewards of the Past" is more difficult now than it has ever been, even though large sums of money may be available. The preservation of cultural resources is frequently caught between the private citizen's attitudes about construction projects and the federal agency's intent to carry a project out. We are frequently seen as an extension of the agency and on their side when property owner permission must be obtained. (That permission *can* be difficult to obtain.) Essentially the problem is one of education or the lack of it. Many people see no value to a "resource" which generates no income, even though the resource is being lost and cannot be replaced. The responsibility for this lack of education begins at the elementary school level when students are first introduced to historic events, places and people; it extends to the post-college level and to the responsible State agencies and individuals.

If we are to conserve our cultural resources and enhance our sense of place, public education must first come. As professionals, we must grasp every opportunity to explain that the tangible remains of our past are truly a non-renewable resource and that they should be protected.

Zoning:
A Means of Encouraging and Protecting
The Sense of Place

VOLNEY CISSNA

Whether it be a community, substate region, or state, a sense of place is the composite reflection of an area's past accomplishments, aspirations and conflicts blended into the present through public recognition and acceptance. It is more than just a heritage; the term connotes a living, emotional involvement that finds, within the feeling of identification, a constructive sense of purpose.

In this brief presentation I will be considering the preservation and conservation of historic buildings and properties by local governments—in essentially a compatible environment, one that protects a desired character of a neighborhood or district and strengthens a community's aura.

Zoning is regulation of land use by local units of government and a valid exercise of police power in support of the public interest through promotion of the public health, safety, and general welfare. The United States Supreme Court in 1926, with its decision in the case of *Village of Euclid v. Ambler Realty Co.* found that zoning did not deprive landowners of their constitutionally protected rights. In "Zoning Law in Mississippi," *Mississippi Law Journal*, Number 2, April 1974, one finds:

Prior to *Euclid*, and for sometime thereafter, the Mississippi Supreme Court was reluctant to recognize zoning as a proper exercise of the police power. However, in the 1932 case of *City of Jackson v. McPherson*, Justice Griffith eloquently brought Mississippi in line with *Euclid* by recognizing compelling social and economic reasons justifying zoning. Evidencing extraordinary foresight by anticipating that urbanization would be accompanied by increasing conflicts between rights incident to land ownership and the public welfare, Justice Griffith bridged the gap between pre-*Euclid* attitudes and modern socio-legal thought.

Local government, as a creature of the state, derives zoning powers from the Mississippi legislature. For the valid enactment of a comprehensive zoning ordinance there are certain statutory requirements that must be satisfied:

Development of a Comprehensive Plan for the community
Notice of Public Hearing to consider the Zoning Ordinance
Accomplishment of the Public Hearing
Formal Adoption of the Zoning Ordinance

These four major requirements may take extended periods of time for their accomplishment and represent months of diligent work.

Zoning is enacted to promote the public health, safety, and general welfare. Since 1926, these terms have often served as a basis for a gradual broadening of zoning applications in the regulation of land use and community development. There is also a growing use of the term "public interest" to describe actions of public benefit that may include one or all of the previously stated terms. Charles M. Haar, Professor of Law, Harvard University, states on page 310 of his 1959 *Land-Use Planning*:

In the case of the *City of New Bedford v. New Bedford, Woods Hole, Martha's Vineyard & Nantucket Steamship Authority* . . . this court took judicial notice of the general characteristics of the island of Nantucket and of its great interest in the entertainment of summer visitors. We may also take judicial notice that Nantucket is one of the very old towns of the Commonwealth; that for perhaps a century it was a famous seat of the whaling industry and accumulated wealth and culture which made itself manifest in some fine examples of early American architecture; and that the sedate and quaint appearance of the old island town has to a great extent remained unspoiled and in all probability constitutes a substantial part of the appeal which has enabled it to build up its summer vacation business to take the place of its former means of livelihood. . . . There has been substantial recognition by the courts of the public interest in the preservation of historic buildings, places, and districts. (Citations omitted.)

Sensing the importance and public interest in historic preservation, Congress passed the Historic Sites, Buildings and Antiquities Act of 1935, declaring "that it is a national policy to preserve for public use historic sites, buildings and objects of national significance for the inspiration and benefit of the people of the United States." The national position was further strengthened by Public Law 89-665 of October, 1966, which states:

Be it enacted by the Senate and House of Representatives of the United States of America in Congress assembled, That: The Congress finds and declares

(a) that the spirit and direction of the Nation are founded upon and reflected in its historic past;

(b) that the historical and cultural foundations of the Nation should be preserved as a living part of our community life and development in order to give a sense of orientation to the American people.

The Act goes on to say:

(c) That in the face of ever-increasing extensions of urban centers, highways, and residential, commercial and industrial developments, the present governmental and nongovernmental historic preservation programs and activities are inadequate to insure future generations of a genuine opportunity to appreciate and enjoy the rich heritage of our Nation; and

(d) that although the major burdens of historic preservation have been borne and major efforts initiated by private agencies and individuals, and both should continue to play a vital role, it is nevertheless necessary and appropriate for the Federal Government to accelerate its historic preservation programs and activities, to give maximum encouragement to agencies and individuals undertaking preservation by private means, and to assist State and local governments and the National Trust for Historic Preservation in the United States to expand and accelerate their historic preservation programs and activities.

Under provisions of the Tax Reform Act of 1976, historic districts may be eligible for certain tax benefits. State and/or local statutes must be certified by the Secretary of the Interior (acting through the National Park Service) that such statutes, including any by-laws or ordinances pertaining to the historic district or districts, contain criteria that will substantially achieve the purpose for which the district was created—that of preserving and/or rehabilitating buildings of "historic significance."

Recently, enabling legislation has been passed by the State of Mississippi in the form of the Mississippi Local Government Historic Preservation Act of 1978: "An act to provide for the establishment of historic preservation commissions by counties and municipalities; to permit the establishment of local historic preservation districts; and for related purposes."

From the foregoing citations of laws and findings of the courts, I believe, as a professional planner, that the creation of historic districts by local units of government is a valid exercise of the police power in the regulation of land use. It promotes the public interest and is in keeping with the intent of Congress and the Mississippi State Legislature. Such districts are a means of preserving and restoring buildings and properties that are tangible ties with the past and contribute to a community's special character and identity. By use of zoning regulations new construction, as well as rehabilitation, must be compatible with the desired architectural appearance and use. New development is encouraged to complement existing character of an area and to protect the community's sense of place.

A Sense of Place
for Today and Tomorrow

FRANK E. SMITH

The influence of the sense of place felt by Mississippians about their state and their individual communities and neighborhoods has often been exaggerated. At the same time it has been ignored. It has been used for many dubious and devious purposes, as well as for broadening the coalition umbrella for meritorious or at least semi-meritorious causes.

The sense of place in Mississippi has always been stronger than in most other regions of the country. It has influenced public policy in the past and it still influences public policy. We need to know more about how to make that influence more useful in improving the quality of life in the "place" that is Mississippi. This paper will discuss primarily the influence of the sense of place on the continuing industrialization of Mississippi, and of that same sense on public policy decisions as they have been made, and are being made, in that field.

The mystique, or the myth, or a sense of place has been created and called up since the Civil War, as it suited usually sincere people who wanted to make points about public policy. Often, however, the sincerity of those involved is very much open to question, as it too often is on many public issues.

I remember the first aggressive efforts to organize sentiment to bring industry to my home town of Greenwood, thirty years ago in the years immediately after World War II. These efforts were strongly opposed by a group who wanted to "keep Greenwood like it is," or "was," or more accurately, like it was remembered. The remembrance went back a convenient twenty-five years, to the days of dollar cotton, and almost dollar cotton, after World War I. Overlooked was nickel cotton, and the decade before World War II, when WPA and NYA jobs (administrative) became a successful way of life.

The organizers of the effort to block industrial development were afraid of anything that might limit the supply of surplus farm labor, or raise the wage level in existing industrial employment. They could not openly broach this theme in a community so fresh from depression, but they could talk about "losing the look" of the "town we love," and about an ominous and vague threat to "our way of life." This phrase had not yet become "our Southern way of life," but even without the word "Southern" there was no trouble in using it to conjure up vague fears about "uppity nigras" and maids and cooks who had belonged to "Eleanor Clubs," and were already asking wages that were more than anybody could afford to pay.

If the anti-industry effort had coincided with the Civil Rights campaign, it might have been a victim, for a limited time, of racial strife. It did not, however, and most of the Delta planters who had opposed industrial development were within a few years actively espousing it through organizations like the Delta Council.

The opponents of industrial growth who have evoked the sense of place in Mississippi have not been limited to those seeking to hold down the wage scale, however (although they may be indirectly contributing to such a result). The fear of a destroyed place has been high on the list of the images raised by the opponents of the Tennessee-Tombigbee canalization. They regularly call up the vision of the happy agrarian South, with each place and scene to be etched forever in actuality and not just in memory.

The agrarian theme has been part of a concept of southern intellectuals since Thomas Jefferson wrote *Notes On The State of Virginia* not quite two hundred years ago. Jefferson the philosopher, naturalist, and early environmentalist, was willing to "let our workshops remain in Europe." Jefferson, the national politician of a few years later, was not. He did enunciate a political philosophy which glorified the leadership of the farmer, but he was careful to accept the fact that industry and commerce were an integral part of the new nation, including Virginia.

The major effort to enunciate an agrarian philosophy for the South, and to keep the workshops out, was delivered fifty years ago by the Vanderbilt Agrarians, or the Nashville "Fugitives," when they published *I'll Take My Stand*.[1] The Agrarians spoke out at a time when the South was still overwhelmingly agricultural, when theoretically it might have been possible to resist the tide of industrialization. Their regional approach was so strong that they felt it necessary in the introduction to *I'll Take My Stand* to make it clear that they did not favor secession, some sixty years after that failure. They were called the "Fugitives" because they sought at least philosophically to flee from industrialization, but they set a theme for Southern intellectuals which still persists.

The very term "Vanderbilt Agrarians" is highly accurate, for the Southern Agrarian life they described could only have been concocted from the ivory towers of a secure and well established university. Both the pre-Civil War agricultural life and the farm life of the 1920s lacked the charm and the strength which were often attributed to them. In some of the Agrarians' own scholarly research, notably that of the historian Frank Owsley, this fact had been demonstrated, but it is not unusual for polemicists to ignore inharmonious facts.

In the first paragraph of the first of the twelve *I'll Take My Stand* essays, John Crowe Ransom claims for his group priority in appreciation "for a certain terrain" and subsequently claims for the South acceptance of the role of place as a quality which helps distinguish the region above others. From that point there is general reiteration of a theme that the sense of place can only be properly preserved in a South which turns away from industry and commerce.

Obviously the "certain terrain" provided a sense of continuity to the new Southern intellectuals which was heartening in the midst of the vastly changing world of the decade after the first World War. Place could provide a bulwark against a bewildering time, and also become

[1](New York: Harper and Brothers, 1930). Subsequent references appear in the text.

a bulwark against a fearsome change. The vision of an idealized place became so strong that it obscured the conditions that cried for change. There was not enough reflection upon the possibility that "place" might provide the continuity which could coordinate and control change, to provide a stability that enhances the changed new world.

Andrew Nelson Lytle's essay is entitled "The Hind Tit," but it includes the most romanticized version of Southern farm life of any in the compilation. There is considerable confusion between the idealized yeoman farmer and the old plantation—his farm house has to be almost a plantation manor to afford the comparative luxury of the establishment he describes. The implication is that the comforts and leisure of farm life come without the contribution of unrewarded tenant labor. The absence of any comprehension that ease and comfort are achieved only with the help of less-rewarded labor is characteristic of references in *I'll Take My Stand* to Southern agricultural life.

In actuality, of course, Southern agricultural life in 1930 was still largely based on a concept that success came through a limited reward for tenants or hired labor. The idealized yeoman farmer, working his land only with the labor of his family, usually struggled to maintain the same level of life as the tenant and the sharecropper. In 1930 neither planters with hundreds of acres nor yeomen with twenty acres and a mule lived a life which enabled more than the merest handful to justify John Crowe Ransom's description: "He identifies himself with a spot of ground, and this ground carries a good deal of meaning; it defines itself for him as nature. He would till it not too hurriedly and not too mechanically to observe in the contingency and the infinitude of nature; and so his life acquires its philosophical and even its cosmic consciousness" (pp. 19-20).

It is important to look at what the Vanderbilt Agrarians said because for fifty years they have represented the intellectual opposition to most change in Southern life. Too much of their whole thesis was based on a romanticized version of both the past and the present (1930) South. They asked for a stand against "progress" in all the best and worst of that term, at a time when all the inexorable forces of both economics and human nature were seeking change in almost any form to alleviate human suffering.

Of course the fullest explanation of the Fugitive essays shows that the authors did not fully share this view, as a look at their subsequent careers and subsequent writing makes clear.

The best message for today from *I'll Take My Stand* comes from Stark Young, the only Mississippian represented among the essayists. (He was the only one with no close links to Nashville; he was already well known as a critic, but not as the author of *So Red the Rose*.) Young said:

There is no reason now that we should pass through quite the state of mind that went, in the rest of the country, with the mechanization of the past decades. We can begin close to where the better sort of thinking and better conditions have by now arrived. We can, if we only would, see industrialism as it spreads in the South, and study it, from the vantage ground of theory, criticism, and error elsewhere developed from experience and long observation. We can accept the machine, but create our own attitude toward it. . . .

That a change is now in course all over the South is plain; and it is as plain that the South changing must be the South still, remembering that for no thing can there be any completeness that is outside its own nature, and no thing for which there is any advance save in its own kind. If this were not so, all nature by now would have dissolved in chaos and folly, nothing in it, neither its own self nor any other. (pp. 355, 359)

The opportunity that Stark Young suggested still exists, if not in the same great void as when he presented it. We have moved into industry on a large scale, with few reservations, but on the whole it has not been in the same pattern as that of the Northeast, or Great Lakes, or even the textile mill towns of the Carolinas, to cite a closer example. In other words, Mississippi can still continue its utter abandonment of the stand of the Agrarians and retain the value of a "certain terrain." We have accepted the machine, to paraphrase Young, but we can do far more about a more positive attitude against its destructive force.

The great value of the sense of place to Mississippi can be that it identifies for us a physical location of the experiences of our life that will continually evoke a sense of pleasure and satisfaction. For many of us these were the human relationships that we achieved in spite of surface barriers that could otherwise have led into discord or even violence. We identify these experiences with places.

Why is our sense of place different from that in other parts of the country, or other parts of the world? Perhaps it really is not, but seems to be for us, and that seeming becomes reality. Perhaps it is because of our climate—we have not been too far removed from it because it is generally comfortable most of the year, and when it has been too hot or too cold we have not been able to afford any but the most elemental relief from the excesses of nature.

The places we remember with affection are often identified with relief from the heat—porch, tree, pond. (What I remember about the Confederate monument on the lawn of the Leflore County Court-house is that the marble corner niches opposite the sun were cool places to sit and read.)

Because we haven't had large cities, and have had relatively little in the way of organized or commercialized recreation, our places are more likely to be hunting fields and fishing banks and country roads than theaters, coliseums or city streets. Churches and post offices and school houses are more likely to be the buildings. Our small towns have identified themselves around school football teams, however, so that unprepossessing athletic fields are major places for us, by contrast with huge stadia or field houses.

But place involves an identification with names—post offices, churches, schools—that seem to mean more to most of us than to people from other places. Perhaps the identification comes because we lacked other things for prideful identification, because we knew firsthand the actuality instead of the myth of defeat in the Civil War, the unacknowledged repression of the conflict between racial mores and professed Christian ethics, the shameful lack of recognition of human values which every black person knew, and felt, either instinc-tively or in actuality.

All of the above is by way of saying that a sense of place is a very real thing in Mississippi, as difficult as it may be to agree upon identifica-tion. All of it adds to the problem of preserving the existing place and creating a sense of identification with new place. Part of the reason for the strength of our sense of place has been a long-time void in public policy. Will current decision making which establishes public policy work to destroy a sense of place?

I believe it would be inaccurate or unwise to claim a crisis in maintaining our sense of place. It can be lost or destroyed, of course, but if we have developed and retained it by happenstance through two hundred years of existence, it is not likely to disappear overnight. Among other reasons, as long as we are on the bottom of the economic ladder we retain some of the same strong influences which have brought about our sense of place.

The opportunity and the obligation to continue to develop and to maintain the sense of place is greater now because of another factor in our existence. There are very concrete and hopeful signs that Mississippi can be a real national leader in taking our region and our nation out of the travail of racial conflict. The very existence of the widespread appreciation of a sense of place is one reason that we can, and we must retain that sense if we are to fulfill the obligation to develop a racial pattern that is a demonstration of both the American and the Christian ethic.

We are not in the midst of a millennium, or even a defined path toward it. But we have the opportunity because we have had so far to come along the way that we can forego many of the time-wasting preliminaries and shadowboxing that inhibit forward movement. I would not propose here to draw a blueprint for this continued progress in enlightened race relations, other than to say that it must have a firm foundation of rapidly advancing economic opportunity and the continuing advantage of the factors in our environment which helped keep us together even in the midst of the worst racial discord.

Black people from Chicago do not come back to Mississippi to fish in the shade of the bayous and horseshoe lakes of the Delta because they have to have the fish for supper, as they or their parents once did, they come because of the place. The grandfather who stayed in Mississippi never loafed on one of the benches of the courthouse square on Saturday—he used the curb of one of the streets which became Blacktown on Saturday—but the court square was such a place that one of the rewards of voting citizenship is to be able to share its bench and its shade in the midst of the milling crowd.

This is part of what we must preserve to maintain our sense of place. The fish in too many horseshoe lakes have been killed or vastly reduced by the intake of unchecked agricultural chemicals. Too many places have been lost because nobody assumed a responsibility to speak up for them.

Court square property owners now know that maintaining the traditional appearance, and restoring it as much as possible, helps hold business and helps hold property values. Too many, however, overlook the danger to small town values of strip development, unorganized and unplanned. There is little realization that water and sewage facility extension should not be allowed or authorized without provision for the small park equivalent of the court square.

We are creating new places in Mississippi with our improved agricultural practices. The awareness that most of our farm land can best be used for pasture and timber is rapidly increasing our overall income from this resource, even if a good part of the added income goes into a corporate exchequer. The result is more often green hills and green valleys bordering our highways and byroads. The metal trailer houses are sometimes hard to blend into the landscape, but the viewer can be aware that the housing comfort they provide conditions the eye of many other beholders.

Our seasonal changes are not enough to give us the complete spread of autumn color that is the glory of so much of the American countryside and the joy of the windshield nature lover, but we are reaching a period of vast improvement in our landscapes. The ugly gullies and red erosion are all but gone. The dreary mud of fall and winter is yielding to year round grass, and winter cover crops in the Delta change some of the leafless hardwoods from bleak, stark nakedness to picturesque stark outlines against the sky.

We already have a goodly share of winding back roads and gently sloping hills. We can have pastoral beauty combined with intense cultivation, as any of us can attest who have seen the rolling hillsides of England. Improving the quality of rural life can offer an increasing opportunity for a certain terrain that is a part of the heritage and spiritual influence shared by all Mississippians.

There will never be a magic formula for preserving the sense of place for Mississippians. We cannot create a department of state government dedicated to that purpose, or rather it would be futile to do so. Every department should have such a goal as part of it sense of purpose, however, and that will come only when a coherent body of public opinion makes itself known on the public issues—such issues, for instance, as those that deal with visual pollution as well as air and water pollution (even though these pollutants are usually directly related).

The candidates for governor and the legislature who once talked about preserving our traditions and our traditional values have already learned to be cautious about talking about "traditions," but they also must be made aware that one of the greatest values for citizens is their sense of the place and the necessity for all to have full access to the place that is their special terrain.

As far as preserving the quality of place in Mississippi is concerned, our state government has less to do with determination than does local and national government. State government has played a minor role, usually because an active role would cost money which is unavailable in competition with other supplicants. The role of state law has been most often utilized to strengthen traditional property rights about land, the law being interpreted to give the property owner the right to abuse his property to his immediate benefit and the public's long-range loss.

Our constitutional system of weak governors limits the hand of even the most enlightened executive in attempting to guide public policy about use and preservation of our land and water and the combination of these resources which has established our terrain and will control its change or deterioration. Federal grants programs of the past ten years have greatly increased the power and influence of the governor without benefit of any change in state law, and any governor could greatly increase his achievements in this field with only a minimum of intelligent planning and direction, by contrast with virtually no policy in the past.

Federal policies are the major influence on our natural resources. Federal programs are responsible for soil conservation and related land improvement which has completely changed the face of Mississippi agriculture. Federal programs are responsible for flood control and navigation and a continuing reforestation. Most of our new housing development, both rural and urban, is subsidized or otherwise benefited through various federal programs administered by a number of federal agencies.

On the whole, the influence of these federal activities has been vastly to our benefit, both from a short-range and a long-range view-point. The kind of federal control which has resulted has not been the iron grip of big government, but the light touch of a sometimes not very observant big brother, who speaks most often from the viewpoint of what might be called the traditional establishment within the state, as expressed through our congressional representation. The federal programs have not been ironhanded, but on the whole they have been fairly and honestly administered, both because of the responsibility accorded the congressional intermediaries, and because the federal government has been on the whole fair and honest—far more so than a large sampling of state and local government.

The comparative quality of the federal programs does not mean that they have accomplished the maximum potential benefit for Missis-sippi. Aside from the general agricultural programs, the major federal resource activity through the years has been the work of the Corps of Engineers on the Mississippi River. Their work has brought virtual assurance of protection from floods from a valley once subject to regular depredation from the river. Stability of the channel has brought a flourishing barge traffic that exceeds in use of the river the steamboat era which began 150 years ago.

Despite the benefits of both these programs, however, the river has been no source of salvation for thousands of people who live within the valley. One of the highest incidents of poverty in the nation exists among the black citizens of the lower Mississippi Valley, including, of course, those in Mississippi. The resources of the river have never been fully coordinated toward helping all of the people of the valley.

Private citizens, acting individually or through all manner of organ-izations, have a greater voice in federal programs today than ever before. There are already many evidences here in Mississippi of how this influence has been felt—in most cases to help preserve a better place. Perhaps more important than direct influence upon the agen-cies, informed public opinion quickly reaches the congressional emissaries to federal policy.

Preserving places, and providing new ones, however, is most essen-tial in citizens' action at the local level. Our special terrain is most directly controlled by the county board of supervisors and the town board of aldermen. They pass, or fail to pass, the zoning regulations and provide the building permits for planned or unplanned development. They are the most subject to corrupt pressures, direct and indirect, but they are also among those most strongly motivated by the desire for service to fellow citizens. They are also the public officials most influenced by individual requests and by individual votes.

As with every other part of the process of movement in our society, local government can be moved to protect the best of what we have and to increase its availability for the future. The general educational process is the best method of pressure and achievement by an informed local citizenry. What is more important, the benefits of the educational process are not limited to public officials. The process will benefit the business and professional community and motivate the enlightened self-interest that is always the most effective influence on the decision making process.

In our efforts to preserve and improve the sense of place in Mississippi we may never arrive at a definition of the term satisfactory to all of us. Perhaps that is to the good, because the vagueness of the term can attract a broader band of allegiance and make it harder for us true believers to become diverted by disagreements about whether my place is better than yours or by the many other possible distractions.

The relative poverty of our material existence has more than anything else led to our reliance on a sense of place. We are far more subject now to national, non-regional, influence than when we first began to establish place, but we are also likely to retain our relative poverty. That means that a substitute for our traditional sense of place would likely be a cheap imitation. Let us preserve the real thing, that which we gained in the midst of the most severe handicaps. Place was a means, more than anything else, that held us together.

In the great opportunities that lie ahead, let us utilize our sense of place to make their fulfillment and their impact even greater. To each of us our places will always differ because of the difference of our perspective. The perspective is inevitably narrowing, both from the reduction of racial and economic barriers and the overall elimination of communication distances in our national and world society. As the perspective changes, the places we share can bring us even closer together.

Mississippi in the Media

GARY A. STRINGER

Paul Pittman, publisher of the *Tylertown Times* and moderator of the panel, presented the first paper of the session. Having lived through and written about the social revolution of the last twenty years, Pittman stressed the cultural displacement this phenomenon has caused for all Mississippians over thirty years of age, black and white alike. Pittman's speech showed that he himself has not escaped the unsettling effects, his presentation moving between analysis and lament. Though he blamed national TV for instigating the "rising hopes and expectations" in the black citizens of the South, for instance, Pittman viewed racial equality under the law as an idea whose time had come by the early 1960s, a concept that could no more be repelled by the white political establishment than legitimately ascribed to the agitation of outsiders.

Pittman credited the news media of Mississippi with only a second-rate job of reporting the "big story" of the last twenty years, though he extenuated this shortcoming in terms of a natural human resistance to change. In his view, both newspapers and television in Mississippi have evolved toward greater social responsibility in recent years, though this change has been largely voluntary on the part of newspapers while it has been forced on television by the Federal Communications Commission. As evidence of the latter proposition, Pittman cited the FCC's pressure on WLBT-TV during the Ole Miss integration crisis, the final result of which was the reassignment of the franchise and appointment of the first black station manager of a nationally affiliated television station in America.

Pittman reiterated his perception of a cultural displacement felt by Mississippians, a condition he said was responsible for a recent revival of interest in the institution of the family reunion. He concluded that nobody can know with certainty what lies ahead for Mississippi and her citizens' sense of place.

Following Pittman, journalist Sarah McClendon, a native Southerner who has lived for years in the nation's capital, presented an outsider's view of the state, relying necessarily on second-hand material. She attributed some of her impressions to conversations with Mississippians Pat Derian and Hodding Carter, both of the U.S. Department of State, and cited an article by journalist Alice Bonner of the *Washington Post*. Other observations appeared to derive from the national news media. The place McClendon described is characterized by poverty, disease, racism, sexism, corrupt government, and educational and economic backwardness.

McClendon stressed the reluctance of big business and industry to locate operations in a state that fails to provide its citizens with even basic educational and cultural advantages. She delineated an educational picture in which even college graduates and teachers can scarcely read and write, an economic profile shaped by hunger and privation, and a social topography bounded by Ku Klux Klanners, anti-feminists, and brutal police. The salvation of Mississippi, in McClendon's view, lies mainly in doing whatever is necessary to attract business and industry from out of state. Such economic improvement, she implied, would promote the social and cultural advancement needed by Mississippi's (largely disadvantaged) populace. As the question-answer session later showed, McClendon's remarks evoked reactions ranging from polite skepticism to outright hostility.

The third speaker, Rea S. Hederman of the *Clarion-Ledger* in Jackson, Mississippi, focused on the possible influence of a newspaper on the sense of place. Hederman noted the newspaper's responsibility for discovering and reporting the realities of life in a region, observing that these realities may conflict with the typical images presented by a region's artists. He predicted that Mississippi would be drawn more into the mainstream of American life by such factual reporting. Hederman stressed the commitment of both time and resources that a newspaper wishing to play its proper role must make and noted that identification of trends likely to affect an area's citizenry is the first step toward solving critical problems.

As examples of what the *Clarion-Ledger* has done to inform Mississippians of crucial issues, Hederman cited stories on the Frost Belt-Sun Belt confrontation (a matter one of whose results might be the loss of federal anti-poverty programs) and coverage of zoning procedures in Jackson, the latter an issue that directly involves the sense of place in Mississippi in that residents of the city have formerly not been apprised of plans to demolish historic sites until after the administrative fact has been accomplished. Hederman regretted the possible loss of a sense of place that such destruction might entail as the state moves toward "Americanization"—renewal of downtown areas, proliferating of fast-food restaurants, construction of inter-state highways, and removal of all traces of Mississippi's rural past.

Hederman next speculated about the possible effects of the modern Southern newspaper on the "New South" artist. He cited classic precedents—Chaucer and sculptor Peter Parler the Younger, for instance—in which artists had achieved vitality by playing off contemporaneous reality against a received stereotype, and he voiced the hope that journalists might help to provide the factual ingredients for such blending in the present time. He concluded by referring to the importance of journalistic reports in recording and publicizing those events and objects that collectively determine any region's sense of place.

The last formal speech was delivered by Bert Case, news director for WLBT-TV in Jackson, Mississippi. Case began by noting that Mississippi ranks last in per capita income and lamented that nobody, including those in the Research and Development Center in Jackson, seems committed to changing this fact. Case even conjectured that a kind of perverse pride in being last has taken root in some of Mississippi's citizens.

Case commented that Mississippi has moved a long way from the "closed society" described by James Silver in the 1960s, though it still has far to go, and argued that one of the biggest obstacles to progress is the antiquated Mississippi Constitution, which dates from 1890. Partly owing to the deficiencies of this document, especially its establishment of the powerful boards of county supervisors, Mississippi is, in Case's opinion, one of the most inefficiently run and corrupt states in the nation. He suggested that the corruption has generally escaped exposure because of the news media's failures and weaknesses. Another problem Case mentioned was Mississippi's selection of poor leadership at the state level. He suggested that Mississippi's last three governors lacked organized plans for the state's advancement; furthermore, whatever programs they did offer, Case noted, were thwarted by an all-powerful legislature whose dominance is guaranteed by the old constitution.

Case also cited a public toleration of corruption as one cause of Mississippi's problems, referring specifically to violations of a constitutional prohibition against a person's serving in more than one branch of government at a time. A suit pending in the Hinds County courts to force legislators off boards, commissions, and agencies, said Case, has been repeatedly swept under the rug and judicially delayed.

The above analysis of the state's ills behind him, Case turned to a consideration of the news media in Mississippi. He observed that things had changed radically since his arrival in Jackson in 1965, when he became, along with a single photographer, the "news department" of a local television station. Newspapers, particularly the *Clarion-Ledger*, have recently begun to invest the time and resources necessary to expose corruption and inefficiency in state government, an effort in which, Case said, Rea S. Hederman has played a hero's role.

In comparing television and the newspaper, Case noted that his news department at WLBT-TV had broken the story on the scandal involving state senator Bill Burgin, but conceded that the *Clarion-Ledger* had provided the thorough reporting required to inform the public fully. Case urged the audience never to rely on television as the sole source of news (though 66 percent of all Americans presently get most of their news from TV) because this medium does not have the time to do detailed reporting. Despite the intrinsic limitations of television news coverage, however, Case stated that he has witnessed substantial progress in television's coverage of the news, citing in particular an increase in the number of reporters employed by Mississippi stations and mentioning that his own station now has a news department of sixteen people. Another hopeful sign for television news in Jackson, Case noted, is the presence of his boss, Bill Dilday—the first black ever to head up a nationally affiliated television station. Case praised Dilday as a dedicated newsman and efficient manager, who has brought about remarkable progress. But even with the best of management and reporting, Case stated, television news will never be able to equal the newspaper for in-depth reporting. The limitation exists despite the magic power of motion, an attribute that television alone enjoys.

Case concluded by speculating that positive changes lie ahead for television—the likelihood that viewers will soon be able to "talk back" to their sets and the probability that the communications satellite will make possible many instant, on-the-spot transmissions from event to the home. Case's general mood about Mississippi, he said, is optimistic. He prophesied that Mississippi will be brought willy-nilly into the twentieth century, that there will shortly be an enormous influx of people from the North into the Sun Belt, and that Mississippi, if the South can avoid the errors of the North when this migration comes, will one day get off the bottom of the economic ladder.

A question and answer session followed the speeches. As is usual in these situations, more people wanted to testify than ask questions. Several conferees took the microphone to refute the criticisms that McClendon and others had leveled at Mississippi. After this catharsis, a few questions arose.

Asked about competition with William Minor of the *Capital Reporter* in Jackson, Hederman responded that his paper practiced a different kind of journalism from Minor's and disagreed that the two were in competition.

All the newspapermen were asked about the demise of the small paper and the prevalence of large conglomerates. Pittman lamented this development, saying that the small paper could scarcely compete with the large companies. McClendon condemned the syndicates as absentee landlords who homogenize the news and dilute a paper's regional flavor. She praised Hederman for putting money into his paper and making it financially sound. Hederman agreed with

Pittman and McClendon that the buying up of small papers by con-glomerates was generally deplorable, but noted that sometimes the newspaper chains improve the properties they take over.

A question next arose about the effectiveness of radio for local news coverage. Pittman was of the opinion that radio tends to be very good in this area.

The final question concerned the current salary scale for reporters. Pittman said his reporters earn $150 to $165 per week. Hederman refused to divulge figures, saying only that he recruits reporters na-tionally and pays competitive salaries.

Change in Mississippi and the Media

PAUL PITTMAN

For Mississippians over thirty years of age, and especially those involved in the media, the place of one's being in the year 1978, the pace, the mood, the changes all can be an unsettling thing. Events of the past decade or more, particularly, have altered a way of life, a culture, in a manner that has been deep and abiding and, I might add, unsettling.

In the early 1970s, sitting around the bar of LeFleur's Restaurant with several journalists, including Dub Shoemaker of Kosciusko, Hodding Carter III, once of Greenville, now of Washington, D.C., Professor Gayle Denley of Bruce and Oxford, I recall making the comment that there was nothing else to write about. The big story, you see, not just in Mississippi but in the Deep South, had been the social revolution that was going on. The sense of place and time and cultural ties had been disrupted in an outpouring of violence and even bloodshed in Birmingham, in the Mississippi towns of McComb, Grenada, Oxford, Philadelphia, Hattiesburg, Meridian and in Bogalusa, Louisiana.

From all over the country journalists had come to see and hear and ask, and, yes, write about the big story—the evolution of the black and the white (remember that I equate them in this context), the displacement from the sense of place that was so secure and dependable and understood.

Not many days went by for media people in Mississippi, especially the more knowledgeable and thoughtful ones, but that a reporter from up North or East or West was in the office asking how it was and what was going on in Mississippi. We blamed it then—the eruption I mean—on the outside agitators and the federal judges and the Kennedys. We were wrong, as it turned out. For, under the U.S. Constitution, the time had come when blacks in Mississippi could no longer be denied parity under the law. But the cultural displacement left all of us, black and white alike, in a state of shock.

I'll have to say that I blame the medium of television for instigating the rising hopes and expectations among blacks all across the South. Illiterate blacks, living in shotgun shacks and worse throughout the labor-intensive cotton fields of the Mississippi Delta and all across the state—unskilled and untrained—did not read the *Clarion-Ledger*, or the *Washington Post* or the *New York Times* or, for that matter, the Sears and Roebuck catalog. But, invariably, as you travelled over the backroads of the state, you would see those homes with a television antenna sticking out of the roof. The networks brought into their homes the national commitment that was in the works on civil rights. It was a burgeoning thing and simply could no longer be ignored.

The politicians of the intractable Deep South fought on. Because of time, sense of place and circumstances, they had no other choice. Their constituencies demanded it and fed on the spurious hope of state's rights, long since abrogated and abandoned, even interposition and finally civil rebellion in the case of the University of Mississippi and Governor Ross Barnett and a guinea pig black named James Meredith.

I have two parenthetical comments here. One is that the WLBT-TV case stands as a fascinating monument to the change in the media in Mississippi. The other is that the weekly and daily newspapers of the state have adjusted, with considerable credibility, to the revelation that here in this state, sense of place notwithstanding, we have two separate and now presumably equal-under-the-law cultures, co-existing side by side and doing it with grace and good will. That is the amazing thing to me, and I refer back to the idea that the big story, at least for me, is over and done with, and now I write, when I write, about the racial harmony. Generally speaking, good news is no news. It is the man-bites-dog syndrome that tickles the palate of editors and readers.

But let me get back to the WLBT case. During the 1962 desegregation of the University of Mississippi student body—when the issue was at a white heat, federal troops, marshals, federalized national guard and all—the manager of WLBT, one Fred Beard, took a partisan, that is to say, the right of center white man's view, of the whole proceedings. The station was licensed at the time to Lamar Life Insurance Company, a prestigious firm, and no doubt the views Beard expressed on television as Ross Barnett was resisting the effort to register James Meredith reflected the views of most white Mississippians. To make a long, now drawn-out, story short, Lamar Life's right to the license for the lucrative television frequency was challenged on the basis of accountability for Beard's actions and the station's policies during that era.

Robert McRaney, Jr., a bright young television operative, was brought in as station manager by the company, replacing Beard. It seemed to me that he leaned over backward to adjust WLBT's policy and image, but accountability was the key for the Federal Communications Commission, which awarded an interim operating license to Communications Improvement, Inc., an organization that named Bill Dilday as station manager. Dilday is the first and only black man to manage a major network affiliated television station in the United States.

As for the print media, I thought the other night, while the Miss America pageant was underway, about the changes that have occured. Rea Hederman's *Clarion-Ledger* used to figuratively consign nuclear destruction and World War III to the back page or to burial deep inside to report in detail every move that Mississippi's entry in the pageant made. What she ate for breakfast, what she wore to poolside, how she reacted to the judges' stares and questions—all this was reported in detail on page one. At least one or more reporters were dispatched to Atlantic City at great expense to catch the action and report to the readers back home that southern belles and Magnolia blossoms and grits and redeye gravy were not only still alive and well, but would prevail and endure forever and ever. No more. A wire service photo of Miss Mississippi and others frolicking on the beach, cheesecake showing, and a two paragraph, maybe three, story of who won now does the trick.

The *Clarion-Ledger*, as it turned out, was the villain in more than one plot during the transitional days when objective reporting would have been surprising to some and welcomed by many. To say that Mississippi had a monolithic white mind, fueled by most of the press, certainly the politicians and even some of the clergy, would be putting it mildly. Change in their sense of place and time did not come easy for most of us Mississippians.

What is often overlooked, however, is that the trauma of change in this exciting decade or so has not been limited to whites alone. Blacks, unsure of themselves with the chance of breaking out of their historic minority, have suffered their own brand of cultural schizophrenia.

There was a time when a polite white called a black man "colored." Later, it was properly "Negro." Then finally, "black." "Black is beautiful" became the battle cry. Well-meaning whites hardly knew what to do. Neither did well-meaning blacks in their new roles. But there appeared on the walls of the most modest of black homes pictures of the Rev. Martin Luther King and the late President John F. Kennedy.

I have dealt in detail with the social revolution—black on white, white on black—that has come to Mississippi in the past two decades. A little reported story that could have changed history ought to be reported here. In the spring of 1961, after Jack Kennedy became president, Attorney General Robert Kennedy summoned a selected group of Mississippians to Washington to talk to Burke Marshall, the attorney general for civil rights, about the racial situation in Mississippi. The politically oriented Kennedys intended to ride the issue down to the wire. The question was: What will happen if a black student tries to enroll at the University of Mississippi?

It was Hodding Carter III, I recall, who said, "The rednecks in north Mississippi will come out of the hills, and there will be some blood shed." I recall asking about the wisdom of going for school integration as opposed to getting the franchise for every qualified citizen to vote. Marshall's response appeared to be negative to me. Knowing that the heat was on and that President Kennedy was going to pursue the civil rights issue, I thought the idea of giving every citizen the vote was far more viable than the more emotion-ladened concept of putting black and white students in the same school. My idea did not sell, as history records.

But, as it turned out, the franchise, finally achieved for black voters, has worked a profound change in Mississippi political leaders. Imagine, if you can, white candidates for sheriff meeting with black leadership groups and acceding to their requests for black deputies, black office workers and the like.

Today in Mississippi the black voter holds the balance of power in many counties and districts. The myth is that this represents a bloc of votes. It does not. The truth is that the black vote is fragmented, bought off in some cases by artful whites, but no longer stuck with having to vote a certain way to prove a point. The same is true, to some degree, for white voters.

During this transition, how has the Mississippi press reacted? First of all, the television and radio stations have been under some pressure from the Federal Communications Commission to deal fairly with touchy racial issues. Not so the weekly and daily press. They have no federal agency which influences policy in such matters. Thus, it is interesting to note that cultural change in Mississippi has been accompanied by a change in the handling of the news.

In many of the papers, "News of our Colored Friends" has been replaced by run of the paper use of items regarding blacks. Moreover, some papers use social items about blacks on the heretofore Magnolia blossom society pages, and more papers use courtesy titles when referring to black men and women.

My emphasis so far has been on black-white relationships in Mississippi. But there are other changes—these universal—in the way of life. The white aristocracy in the South, now enshrined in the ruins of the Civil War, made a fetish of protectiveness of their women. The woman, tradition dictated, was to be set apart, protected and even exalted in words if not in deeds. Even this position, a romantic hallmark of a changing South, is under challenge. The women's liberation movement, which has caught the attention of key women— maybe even former southern belles—allows little of the fawning, self-effacing woman of yesteryear. Chauvinists contend that women should not have the opportunity of having it both ways—sheltered woman on the one hand, freed woman on the other.

Now, where do these changes leave our sense of place?

Well, I contend that Mississippi has been drawn unwillingly, perhaps kicking and screaming, into the twentieth century, for better or for worse. The media have done a second rate job of reporting the shift, but the fault should not be put on them. The fault is a human one, that of resisting change, of having difficulty in assimilating the unfamiliar—this applies to both black and white—and the media have the added burden of having finally to answer to the business office—the profit line.

I think of some of the very good journalists who have taken the trouble to play their hand out on this scene. Oliver Emmerich of McComb is one. And I put Charlie Gordon in the same category. Emmerich is dead, but Gordon writes on, sardonic, sarcastic, incisive, too lengthy, but very good in essence. Hodding Carter III wrote well and was a helpful gadfly. But, he has gone on to politics, a first love, which clouded his reason while sending him to President Carter's Washington and the State Department. I doubt he's happy, shilling for Carter. But a journalist can hardly ever have it successful both ways.

I have dwelt too long on the ramifications of the social revolution involving black and white in our state. But my distorted and uprooted sense of place demanded that I do just that.

Mississippians have not grasped what all this means. Rural Mississippi still clings to the stability of family reunions. Incidentally, they have proliferated in recent years, and I would argue that they have proliferated in direct proportion to the suspicion that the old sense of place is being destroyed.

Then, there is the shift from rural to urban. It is begging the question, in a sense, but the statisticians tell us now that for the first time Mississippi has more estimated population in "urban" centers than in the rural areas. And there are the pressures of industrialization, unionization, organization, arbitration, mediation and the new patterns of life that all of this brings.

Apace with all that has been said are the basic pressures that come with the attempt to move an agrarian state (maybe the most purely so in the Deep South) to an industrial-commercial one. This change, taking place in a complex world that brings a new dependency on trade relations not only with other states but with other countries, creates its own universe of problems.

If there be a truthful thread running through all of this, it is that a Mississippian's sense of place is a transient thing. The past cannot be dismissed. It will always be with us. But the future imposes itself, day by day, upon us.

Rooted in the past as I am, I am naturally apprehensive about the changes and the future. Past the age of being reflexively optimistic, I know that both our place and sense of place have changed. I don't know, and I don't believe any credible witness knows, just how much or what kind of change still lies ahead for Mississippi.

Mississippi's Image:
A View From Washington

SARAH McCLENDON

The image of Mississippi outside of Mississippi is still that of the greatest poverty, a place where many adult blacks have no education and therefore no future, where schools are integrated but where large numbers of black kids cannot afford to go down the line at the lunch counter at noon because they do not have the cash, where integration is still a token thing.

Industrial tycoons do not want to locate in Mississippi unless they are seeking cheap labor. Governmental agencies get mass protests from their employees if Senator John Stennis of Mississippi proposes locating one of the prime payroll sources in the state. Why? Because people think of Mississippi as a state that is not a good place to live. Industry wants to go where their people can have good schools, churches of all faiths—free of prejudice—no Ku Klux Klan, no adverse social conditions that gnaw at society and cause unrest in cities. They want to be sure the schools rate well educationally as compared to elsewhere in the nation and that there are good teachers from grade school on up. They do not associate these with Mississippi, where graduates of colleges often cannot read yet become the teachers of Mississippi youngsters.

Were you one of those who in recent years carried a bumper sticker on your car saying "Mississippi is the most lied about state in the nation"? A prominent Mississippian told me that was basically a defensive bumper sticker.

There have been great improvements in your number of people registered to vote who were intimidated before and not allowed to vote. There has been improvement in your schools. Some 11,000 adults in your state are now enrolled in a right-to-read program jointly funded by federal and state governments. And others are being taught to read in schools and colleges and communities under this program. It will in time improve the quality of teaching.

I talked to two prominent Mississippians before I came here. Pat Derian, an assistant secretary of state for human rights, is virtually running a good part of the nation's foreign affairs and now heads a working group that decides whether the United States trades with a nation or cuts off trade, depending on their progress in human rights. Hodding Carter is not only the assistant secretary of state for public affairs but is the spokesman for the State Department. This means he is often the spokesman for the nation before the world. In fact, the White House frequently refers reporters' more difficult questions to the State Department for answers.

Both Derian and Carter told me how great were the improvements in Mississippi. Carter said he saw a decided change in the conversations of his close friends on the subject of integration when he last visited. He cited the number of Mississippi blacks now holding public office. But Derian mentioned the unpaved streets in black neighborhoods and the open storm sewers as a source of filth and disease and danger to kids.

Carter mentioned the need for complete reworking of the tax base so that so many big firms do not escape taxation. He mentioned that many residences are under-taxed. This tax escape, of course, cuts down on the amount available to pay higher salaries for better teachers who would in turn raise the state's pitiful education level. Carter talks about the large number of adult blacks who have had no education and so are doomed for the rest of their lives to eke out a living, unable to earn the income from industry that they might have if they had been taught skills. He mentioned that this is part of the vicious cycle that hurts Mississippi so much—her people do not have the skills and educational level to attract more industry which would provide more payrolls to pull them out of their economic imprisonment.

"I do not have the answer," Carter said with downcast eyes from a heart in agony at the situation. "But things are so much better than they were. Of course, this is offset by the fact things ought to be much better."

Alice Bonner, a black woman reporter on the *Washington Post* whom I know and for whose accuracy I have great respect, recently researched and wrote an outstanding article on Mississippi for her paper. She told how the food stamp plan is helping 312,000 people in Mississippi, more than it does in 25 other states. But there still are people in the Mississippi heartland, she writes, "who tell of going to bed regularly on empty stomachs or of lying awake to the sound of neighbors' children scavenging in garbage cans for food. Others say they have nothing but a package of dried beans for supper." There are protests from the poor about the state administration of the food stamp program, accounts of abusive and even illegal treatment of those who must depend on food stamps.

Mississippi is one state where the rich critics of the welfare system can be happy. No one seems to make money from being on welfare rolls, and I am told that whether a mother has ten children or two she gets the same small amount each month, about $50, not enough to keep body and soul together.

There is soon to be another session in the state, I am told, to further assess police brutality as alleged in Jackson. The Southern Regional Office of the U.S. Commission on Civil Rights has asked for outside professional help in setting up a system that would cure this recurring problem. The Commission does not appear to be asking for too much when it asks that records be kept on all complaints made to the police departments of cities and that the outcome of final investigations be made known to complainants. These procedures would be a vast improvement and would take care of many ills, although they might not lend much encouragement to the black folk who are too frightened to report incidents.

Let me say that racial discrimination is not the only form of discrimination that occurs on a daily basis in Mississippi. Women, too, often look unsuccessfully for jobs, get fired if they find them, and find they are paid lower sums than a man receives for the same kind of work. Sexual attack on a young woman goes unprosecuted; the male offender gets off with a shrug or, maybe, congratulations for a conquest. Check your juvenile court records for conditions which are appalling.

When certain church groups went from Mississippi to the International Women's Year convention in Houston, they publicized the state as one violently opposed to full citizenship rights for women and irresponsibly branded women feminists who supported the Equal Rights Amendment as lesbians. Of course, keeping down minority groups such as blacks and women is not wise economically or socially, and such discrimination adds further to the avoidance of Mississippi by attractive payrolls and by citizens who might bring in new brains and energy.

A black taxi driver in Chicago driving me to O'Hare airport told me, "Lady, it's a shame that I can't live in Mississippi with my family. I love that state and it would be such a beautiful place to live if they just had good schools. But I have to bring my children up here."

Mississippi, which needs outside capital so much, according to the economic experts, might secure investments if it could follow the example of a city I know only a few hundred miles west of here. I am talking about Tyler, Texas. The leaders of the town banded together, as I am sure your state people did, to advertise the advantages of the place to Northern industry. They offered land subsidies and other attractions to electric, glass, metal and railroad companies. But they could offer as well good schools, decent housing, workers educated and well fed, ample recreation—as you certainly have—but mainly a place where citizens could live enhanced lives. (They have their problems, too, of course.)

What are the people of Mississippi going to do about these problems it faces? Perhaps remember them when they go to vote.

You may not think so, but what happens to one under-privileged, half-starved, under-educated person in this country helps tear down all of our country. Right now, we need a stronger nation, and it can only become that if our citizens are educated so they can watch their government and make democracy work. Remember: "A mind is a terrible thing to waste."

The Newspaper's Role
and the Sense of Place

REA S. HEDERMAN

Because newspapers have far more news reporters than do any other type of media, they obviously concentrate on the news gathering process. This reporting can be a major cause of destroying the sense-of-place images—often stereotyped—of the South as portrayed by writers such as William Faulkner and artists such as William Hollingsworth.

Written and painted representations of farm tenant hovels and other living symbols of poverty may be attractive to readers and art gallery viewers, but those living in them may have distinctly different views. And the views of those inhabitants are most often those presented by newspapers. Such living conditions represent serious social problems that can never be solved without objective, in-depth looks at the subject.

But straight reporting by the news media of enough subjects could destroy much of the subject-matter, or rather descriptive settings, upon which state authors and artists have drawn. Such reports inevitably draw Mississippi more into the American mainstream—a process that, while raising the standard of living for state inhabitants and hopefully eliminating some of our social problems, also makes Mississippians more like their neighbors in all other states in the nation.

This will perhaps draw the state ineluctably toward what John Egerton termed in his book by the same name "The Americanization of Dixie"—a process by which, as the title indicates, a sense of sameness replaces a sense of place. In describing the South's sense of place, Egerton noted: "The South as a land of grace and violence, as beauty and the beast, had an irresistible fascination about it. It was evil and decadent, but it also bred heroes and dreamers, and it yielded a tenacious sense of hopefulness that kept the world from going home. It still has qualities that could make the world come back for another look."[1]

In the prologue, Egerton said: "The South may die, but there will be survivors, and they will have something to say about whether we will in fact have a country, and a chance to start a new history. If the South's best qualities succumb and its worst characteristics prevail, all Americans will have cause to lament the Americanization of Dixie and the Southernization of America." It is important that newspapers use their resources of reporting to identify "its worst characteristics" so Southern leaders may work to keep them from prevailing, as Egerton feared could happen. This requires a type of newspaper that has not often been published in the South—nor in fact in many other parts of the country.

Reporters must be given time to explore problems; they must be allowed to do more than cover meetings and press conferences, which seldom, if ever, are of substance. Such reporting takes a commitment of both time and resources. It should not be unusual for a news reporter to spend several months or longer on a story and during that period not write a single piece for his newspaper. Before problems can be solved, they must be identified and well-defined. This type reporting by newspapers can, and should be, the first step toward solving critical problems facing the state.

Ideally newspapers, again by virtue of larger staffs and thereby of capabilities for reporting on more issues, should try to identify those trends which will likely affect a state's inhabitants. Once a trend is identified, work can begin on producing solutions to the long-range effects the trend may have.

The *Clarion-Ledger* was among the first of the nation's news media to report in depth the beginning and continuation of the Frost Belt-Sun Belt confrontation. Reports have indicated that, if early trends are continued, the state's poorest inhabitants could suffer severely through loss of federal funds for poverty programs. Hopefully, with enough persons aware of this trend, something can be done to avoid

[1] John Egerton, *The Americanization of Dixie: The Southernization of America* (New York: Harper & Row, 1974), p. 24.

plunging back into poverty those who are slowly and belatedly moving out of the South's hovels.

To help and encourage preservation of historic areas in Jackson, the *Clarion-Ledger* began extensive coverage of zoning procedures in each area of the city. Before this reporting began, residents did not know until the bulldozers arrived that a neighboring turn-of-the-century home would be demolished and replaced with a convenience store. By reading stories that tell in advance of upcoming hearings or rezoning historic areas for commercial purposes, residents may organize to protect local landmarks.

In addition to covering all zoning stories, the newspaper also reported extensively on requirements for establishing historic preservation areas, which are now being set up by the city. This reporting, of course, was an important factor in preserving and strengthening one community's sense of place.

These are examples of a newspaper's reporting the significance of stories and putting them in perspective for the reader. Reporting of this kind is important in helping readers to understand the events changing their lives and can also be important in helping to preserve a community's sense of place.

Another trend that perhaps should be identified more clearly and reported in depth is the one this conference is concerned with—the possible loss of a sense of place. With the rapid economic growth of the South and with the influx of persons having no understanding of the South as a separate region, the trend will be toward Americanization. But if that trend is followed through to its conclusion, Southerners will lose more than a sense of place. They will have failed to learn from, and thereby to avoid, those mistakes made by "more progressive" areas, and this could destroy the entire region's quality of life.

The advantage of being last is that one can be first if the line does an about-face; however, it appears that the South may not take advantage of its position. Many of the physical signs of this trend may be seen in every city and town in the South—fast-food restaurants, downtown renovations that ignore all traces of past history, and elimination of most reminders of the state's rural past.

The final effects of these changes on artists and residents remain to be seen. The loss of physical signs of a "sense of place" may well have little effect, however, on the spiritual "sense of place." Southerners, while living in a desert of fast-food chains, interstate highways and other modern appurtances that seem nationally to destroy every community's sense of place, may retain a strong sense of individuality that gives a whole new meaning to Faulkner's promise that man will prevail.

Threats to artists resulting from such stereotyping—including the loss of a sense of place—is not new. Chaucer followed a period of literature that was based almost solely on stereotypes—the chivalrous knight, courtly love and numerous other conventions depicted in the *Roman de la Rose* by Guillaume de Lorris.

But Chaucer took these totally familiar images and made them real and individualized. The knight was dressed in a worn tunic, the summoner's face was incurably diseased, the Wife of Bath was married five times. Through the use of the tension between stereotype and reality, Chaucer wrote in the fourteenth century one of the masterpieces of the English language. His blending of stereotypes and individualized portraits of persons in *The Canterbury Tales* furthered the beginning of a movement in literature toward realism, while maintaining a distinctiveness for the characters of his tales. Statues sculptured by Peter Parler the Younger at the Cathedral of Prague during the same period, showing a similar success in blending realism with stereotypes, constitute the first real portraits.

Now, New South artists seem to find themselves in a similar position. Not only are they faced with having to depict Southern characters that have been nationally stereotyped, but they must also deal with the increasing encroachment of the nation, or Americanization, on their characters' individuality. By drawing on the tension between type and reality, as did Chaucer, Southern artists can continue to create works of excellence, even though their sense of place may be weakened.

Richard Ford successfully uses stereotyped traits of Southerners along with individual, distinguishing characteristics to create his critically acclaimed "A Piece of My Heart." Several Southern artists, including Roland Golden, are doing the same with their paintings depicting Southern scenes.

Newspapers can play an important part in providing material artists can employ in works using a Southern sense of place and combining stereotypes and realism. Photographs in newspapers can, of course, be pure art forms that help create images and ideas of the Southern sense of place. These may either further stereotyped images or depict, sometimes harshly, realities of everyday life. Taken collectively, photo stories may help create totally new feelings of a sense of place. When combined with word stories, they can through newspapers be a major factor in strengthening or weakening a sense of place.

While newspapers can improve living conditions by reporting on problems that need attention, they can also focus on those things that give the South a distinct "sense of place." Reporters consistently seek out those things that make the South and its people different. News concerns the reporting of those things which are out of the ordinary, unique and distinctive—things that add reality to stereotyped images. News stories and feature stories, particularly, help keep persons aware of what their neighbors are doing. They can help keep alive those activities which are indigenous to the South.

The Historical Geography
of Extinct Towns in Mississippi

HOWARD G. ADKINS

Towns are places of agglomerated settlement interacting with a trade area. Since 1625 small towns in America have provided economic ties and disseminated socio-political information to a rural population. Their number and size depend primarily upon the spatial extent of the trade area and the economic pursuit of the inhabitants.[1] As trade areas and economic activities change, adjustments in the town landscape may produce increases in size, or the demise, of a place.

Table 1 shows that considerable adjustments have occurred in the town landscape. Perhaps all these places are not extinct, but they have experienced a population change and are no longer reported separately. The data imply that dropping places from the census reports because of population demise has been widespread, although possibly more prevalent among predominantly agricultural states. Mississippi appears to be a rather typical case.

Throughout the nineteenth century and well into the twentieth century in Mississippi most towns were supported by cotton production or by lumbering. As the economic base changed, however, 265 towns were unable to control their destiny and are now extinct (Table II).[2] Most of the extinct towns were established from 1830 to 1860 and

[1]Eugene Van Cleef, *Trade Centers and Trade Routes* (New York: Appleton-Century-Crofts, 1937), pp. 4-5; Marion C. Clawson, "Factors and Forces Affecting the Optimum Future Rural Settlement Patterns in the United States," *Economic Geography*, 42 (1966), 283-293.

[2]Fifty-nine towns from Franklin L. Riley, "Extinct Towns and Villages of Mississippi," *Publications of the Mississippi Historical Society*, 5 (1902), 311-383, were included. Others were omitted because they are not extinct or I was unable to confirm their location or functioning as a town.

Table I

The Number of Places Dropped by the United States Census
for Selected States During the Intercensal Decade 1870 to 1960

State	1870 1880	1880 1890	1890 1900	1900 1910	1910 1920	1920 1930	1930 1940	1940 1950	1950 1960	1960 1970	Total
Alabama	10	18	49	14	9	13	25	2	8	3	151
Arkansas	11	8	35	9	11	3	3	7	13	7	107
Indiana	150	25	29	5	6	3	2	2	1	2	225
Kansas	11	3	43	9	4	4	4	1	0	1	80
Minnesota	21	7	14	9	10	5	1	3	2	2	74
Mississippi	13	8	8	10	15	22	23	18	6	6	129
N. Hampshire	4	0	8	0	0	0	3	1	0	1	16
New Mexico	x	x	14	1	2	1	0	1	0	0	19
Oregon	10	0	14	1	7	5	3	3	5	0	48
S. Carolina	8	3	28	17	9	7	20	13	1	3	109
Total	238	72	242	75	73	63	83	51	36	25	958

Source: U. S. Bureau of the Census, *United States Census of Population: Population of Counties by Minor Civil Divisions* (Washington: U. S. Government Printing Office, 1870 to 1970).

Table II

Extinct Towns in Mississippi

Town	County	Popu-lation	Incor-poration	Function	Decade Founded	Decade Extinct
Abbot	Clay	175		Trade	1860	1950
Acona	Holmes	250		Trade	1860	1950
Adair	Carroll	256		Trade	1860	1940
Air Mount	Yalobusha	58	x	Trade	1870	1930
Airey	Harrison	300		Lumber	1830	1940
Alberson	Union*			Trade	1820	1840
Albertson	Jones	328	x	Lumber	1880	1920
Alva	Montgomery	200	x	Trade	1870	1950
Americus	Jackson	50		County	1810	1900
Amsterdam	Hinds*		x	River	1820	1840
Arcadia	Issaquena	305		River	1830	1940
Athens	Monroe*	20	x	County	1830	1930
Atlanta	Chickasaw	105	x	Trade	1870	1950
Augusta	Perry	175		County	1820	1900

Avent	George	200		Lumber	1930	1950
Avera	Greene	340		Lumber	1900	1950
Ballardsville	Itawamba	150		Trade	1840	1950
Bankston	Choctaw*	75	x	Manufacturing	1840	1900
Barlow	Copiah	250	x	Trade	1820	1940
Barton	Lowndes		x	Trade	1850	1880
Basin	George	60		Lumber	1880	1940
Beattie's Bluff	Yazoo*			County	1820	1830
Belmont	Panola*	100		River	1830	1900
Benlomand	Issaquena	182		River	1830	1920
Benela	Calhoun	49	x	Trade	1840	1920
Berryville	Scott			County	1830	
Bethlehem	Marshall	30	x	Trade	1850	1920
Binnsville	Kemper	517		River	1870	1950
Birmingham	Lee	100	x	Trade	1840	1940
Blodgett	Jones	415	x	Lumber	1900	1950
Boneyard	Alcorn*	100		Trade	1830	1860
Bowling Green	Holmes*	77	x	Trade	1840	1940
Brooklyn	Noxubee			County	1830	1850
Brownfield	Tippah	300		Railroad	1880	1950
Brunswick	Warren	130		River	1870	1950
Burnside	Neshoba	105		Lumber	1850	1960
Byrd	Greene	255		Lumber	1910	1930
Camargo	Monroe		x	River	1840	1870
Camden	Neshoba		x	County	1830	
Cardsville	Itawamba	250		Manufacturing	1840	1930
Carmichael	Clarke	300		Trade	1890	1950
Carrollville	Prentiss*			Trade	1830	1860
Cato	Rankin	250	x	Trade	1850	1940
Centre	Attala	101		Trade	1830	1950
Chancy	Quitman	250		Lumber	1900	1940
Cherry Creek	Pontotoc	210		Trade	1830	1950
China Grove	Walthal	73		Manufacturing	1810	1900
Chocchuma	Tallahatchie*			River	1830	1850
Chritton	Coahoma	250		Lumber	1900	1920
Clayton	Leflore			County	1840	
Cloverhille	Coahoma	277		Trade	1880	1950
Clyde	Lamar	250		Lumber	1900	1940
Coar's Spring	Copiah*			County	1810	1930
Cohay	Smith	1092	x	Lumber	1900	1950
Cold Springs	Lincoln		x	Lumber	1870	1910
Coleville	Chickasaw	10	x	Trade	1840	1900

Concordia	Bolivar	164	x		River	1860	1890
Congress	Chickasaw	25	x		Railroad	1890	1920
Cooksville	Noxubee	159	x		Trade	1830	1950
Cornersville	Marshall*	165	x		Trade	1830	1950
Cotton Gin Port	Monroe*	500	x		County	1810	1880
Cotton Plant	Tippah	112			Trade	1850	1950
Cumberland	Webster	200	x		Manufacturing	1850	1950
Cybur	Pearl River	1000			Lumber	1910	1930
Dallas	Lafayette				Trade	1840	1940
Dancy	Webster	147	x		Railroad	1900	1950
Danville	Alcorn*	150	x		Trade	1830	1940
Deasonville	Yazoo	150			Trade	1880	1950
Deemer	Neshoba	750			Lumber	1910	1960
Delay	Lafayette	150	x		Trade	1860	1950
Delta	Coahoma	25	x		County	1840	1950
Dixon	Neshoba	200			Trade	1860	1950
Donavan	George	175			Lumber	1880	1920
Duncansby	Issaquena	275	x		River	1830	1930
Dushaw	Jasper		x		Lumber	1910	1920
Ellzey	Calhoun	50	x		Trade	1890	1920
Emory	Holmes	10	x		Trade	1830	1920
Essex	Quitman	122			Railroad	1900	1950
Eucutta	Wayne	300			Lumber	1880	1950
Eudora	DeSoto	150	x		Trade	1880	1950
Eureka	Sunflower		x		Railroad	1870	1880
Fair River	Lincoln	300			Trade	1870	1940
Farmington	Alcorn*	30	x		Trade	1830	1940
Fearns Springs	Winston	155			Trade	1830	1940
Fenton	Hancock	105			Lumber	1900	1930
Fentress	Choctaw	75	x		Railroad	1880	1950
Ford	Smith	315			Lumber	1900	1930
Fouke	Jasper	500			Lumber	1910	1940
Franklin	Franklin		x		Trade	1800	1910
Furrs	Pontotoc	125			Trade	1850	1950
Gainesville	Hancock*	923	x		County	1810	1960
Gallatin	Copiah*	192	x		County	1820	1900
Gandsi	Covington	105	x		Lumber	1890	1950
Garlandsville	Jasper*	215			Trade	1830	1950
Garner	Greene				Lumber	1910	1920
Gilford	Jasper		x		Lumber	1900	1910
Gluckstadt	Madison	150			Railroad	1870	1950

Goodyear	Pearl River			Lumber	1880	1920
Grange	Lawrence	265		Railroad	1870	1950
Graves Port	Grenada	100	x	River	1820	1940
Greenville	Washington*		x	County	1820	1870
Greenville	Jefferson*	300	x	County	1770	1890
Greensboro	Webster*	323	x	County	1830	1930
Hamburg	Hinds*			River	1820	1830
Hamilton	Monroe*	500		County	1820	1900
Harrisburg	Lee	100		Trade	1840	1860
Hartford	Chickasaw		x	Trade	1830	1890
Hathorn	Marion	150		Trade	1910	1950
Hendersonville	Yalobusha*			Trade	1830	1850
Hillsdale	Pearl River	500		Lumber	1890	1950
Hintonville	Perry	150		Lumber	1900	1940
Houlka	Chickasaw			Trade	1850	1900
Hovey	Harrison	150		Lumber	1910	1930
Huntington	Bolivar	155	x	Railroad	1880	1900
Huntsville	Choctaw	76	x	Trade	1850	1890
Inda	Stone	300		Lumber	1890	1950
Jessie	Leake	165		Lumber	1900	1930
Johnsonville	Sunflower*	150		County	1870	1880
Kendrick	Alcorn	300		Trade	1890	1940
Kingston	Adams*	150		Trade	1770	1930
Kola	Covington	100	x	Lumber	1900	1920
Ladner	Pearl River	75		Lumber	1890	1940
LaGrange	Choctaw*	125	x	County	1870	1920
Lake Carrier	Panola	200		Lumber	1900	1950
Lake Como	Jasper	300		Trade	1840	1950
Landon	Harrison	300		Trade	1830	1950
Langdale	Clarke	200		Trade	1830	1950
Latonia	George	200		Lumber	1900	1940
Leighton	Lee		x	Trade	1890	
Leota Landing	Washington	323	x	River	1850	1940
Leverettsville	Tallahatchie	50	x	Trade	1830	1920
Little Springs	Franklin	200		Trade	1880	1930
Livingston	Madison*	150	x	County	1830	1900
Locopolis	Tallahatchie*			River	1830	1860
Lodi	Montgomery	125	x	Trade	1820	1960
Logtown	Hancock	655		Lumber	1840	1960
Lorena	Smith	215		Trade	1880	1940
Lorraine	Harrison	123		Lumber	1850	1950

Love	DeSoto	150	x	Railroad	1850	1950
Lux	Covington	200		Railroad	1860	1950
Lytal	Prentiss	209		Trade	1870	1940
McDonald	Neshoba	200		Railroad	1900	1950
McHenry	Stone	500	x	Lumber	1880	1920
McLure	Pearl River	200		Lumber	1880	1920
McNutt	Leflore*	103	x	County	1840	1900
McVille	Attala	100	x	Manufacturing	1840	1950
Madisonville	Madison*		x	County	1820	1840
Martin	Claiborn	155	x	Trade	1880	1940
Mashulaville	Noxubee	200		Trade	1830	1950
Mechanicsburg	Yazoo	100		Manufacturing	1850	1950
Melba	Jefferson Davis	100		Lumber	1900	1940
Middleton	Carroll*		x	Trade	1820	1850
Milesville	Holmes		x	Railroad	1880	
Millard	Pearl River	400		Lumber	1890	1950
Mish	Covington	100	x	Lumber	1900	1920
Montgomery	Holmes*		x	Trade	1830	1860
Mountain	Rankin	200		Trade	1880	1920
Muldon	Monroe	300	x	Railroad	1880	1920
Mullet	George	150		Lumber	1890	1920
Myles	Copiah	50	x	Railroad	1870	1920
Nanachehaw	Warren	196		Railroad	1880	1950
Napoleon	Hancock	100		Lumber	1880	1960
Narketa	Kemper	200	x	Railroad	1850	1920
Nashville	Lowndes			River	1830	1850
Neshoba	Neshoba	215	x	Railroad	1900	1960
New Camp	Pearl River	300		Lumber	1930	
New Mexico	Issaquena			County	1820	1830
New Port	Attala	107	x	Trade	1870	1950
New Town	Warren	59	x	River	1870	1890
Nickbyrd	Greene	250		Lumber	1910	1930
Norfield	Lincoln	1399	x	Lumber	1890	1960
Nugent	Harrison	150		Lumber	1890	1950
Oma	Lawrence	200		Railroad	1900	1950
Orisburg	Pearl River	455	x	Lumber	1880	1930
Orizaba	Tippah*	150	x	Trade	1830	1890
Osborn	Oktibbeha	100		Railroad	1880	1960
Overpark	DeSoto	150		Trade	1890	1940
Owens Wells	Holmes	125	x	Railroad	1880	1960
Ozone City	Hancock		x	Lumber	1900	1910

Place	County	Pop.		Type	Begin	End
Palmyra	Warren	60		River	1830	1940
Palo Alto	Clay*	50	x	Trade	1830	1900
Panola	Panola*	192	x	County	1830	1900
Pearl	Hancock		x	Lumber	1830	1850
Pharsalia	Tallahatchie*	200		Trade	1830	1840
Piave	Greene	1000		Lumber	1910	1950
Pine Valley	Yalobusha	102	x	Lumber	1850	1940
Pikeville	Chickasaw*			Trade	1840	1850
Plattsburg	Winston	500		Trade	1840	1950
Plymouth	Lowndes		x	River	1830	1860
Plymouth	Pontotoc	25	x	Trade	1830	1950
Poplar Springs	Union	89	x	Trade	1870	1930
Port Royal	Coahoma*			County	1830	1840
Prairie Mt	Chickasaw*		x	Trade	1830	1870
Preston	Yalobusha	250	x	Trade	1830	1930
Prentiss	Bolivar*	200		County	1840	1860
Princeton	Washington*	600	x	County	1820	1860
Rara Avis	Itawamba	155		Trade	1850	1950
Ratliff	Itawamba	115		Trade	1890	1950
Reba	Greene	250		Lumber	1920	
Recluse	Stone	100		Lumber	1900	1920
Redland	Pontotoc	52	x	Trade	1780	1900
Renova	Bolivar	50	x	Railroad	1890	1920
Richburg	Lamar	200		Railroad	1880	1950
Richey	Sharkey	280		Lumber	1880	1950
Richmond	Lee	52		Trade	1840	1890
Richmond	Rankin	300		River	1820	1830
Rio	Kemper	101		Trade	1850	1950
Rockyford	Pontotoc		x	Trade	1850	1870
Rocky Springs	Claiborne	80		Trade	1790	1940
Ruckerville	Tippah			Trade	1840	1880
Sabougla	Calhoun	150		Trade	1880	1950
Salem	Benton*	200	x	Trade	1830	1920
Saratoga	Simpson	70		Lumber	1900	1940
Sardina	Yalobusha*	150		Trade	1830	1850
Sarepta	Lafayette		x	Trade	1840	1950
Sellers	Hancock	160		Lumber	1910	1950
Selsertown	Jefferson*			Trade	1800	1850
Sevenpines	Carroll		x	Lumber	1870	1880
Sheppardtown	Leflore	78	x	River	1880	1900
Shipman	George	200		Lumber	1880	1940

Shongala	Carroll*		x	Trade	1830	1910
Skipwith	Issaquena		x	River	1870	
Snowsville	Choctaw		x	Trade	1840	1880
Soria	Harrison	15	x	Lumber	1900	1920
Spanish Fort	Sharkey	200		River	1830	1950
Sparta	Chickasaw	150	x	Trade	1840	1950
Springdale	Lafayette		x	Railroad	1850	1890
Stallo	Neshoba	200	x	Railroad	1900	1950
Stratton	Newton	231		Railroad	1900	1950
Strongs	Monroe	118		Railroad	1880	1950
Sunnyside	Leflore	250		River	1880	1950
Tallaloosa	Marshall*		x	Trade	1830	1850
Tallula	Issaquena	50		County	1830	1920
Tatumsville	Tate	100		Trade	1830	1850
Tuscahoma	Tallahatchie*	300	x	Trade	1830	1840
Union Town	Jefferson*			Manufacturing	1790	1830
Van Buren	Itawamba*		x	Trade	1830	1870
Verna	Lawrence	155		Lumber	1900	1950
Vernal	Greene	200		Lumber	1850	1950
Vernon	Madison*	50	x	River	1830	1900
Victoria	Bolivar*	50		River	1830	1900
Victoria	Pontotoc*	300		Trade	1830	
Wahalak	Kemper*	145	x	Trade	1830	1950
Waldo	Neshoba	100		Trade	1870	1930
Walley	Greene	300		Lumber	1920	
Wallhill	Marshall	114	x	Trade	1870	1950
Warrenton	Warren*	600	x	County	1810	1920
Webster	Winston	100	x	Trade	1830	1920
Westonia	Hancock			Lumber	1880	1920
West Port	Lowndes			River	1830	1860
West Station	Holmes	200	x	Railroad	1850	1910
Westville	Simpson	200	x	County	1830	1900
Whitefield	Oktibbeha*	56	x	Trade	1850	1880
Whitesand	Lawrence	323	x	Railroad	1900	1950
Wilkesburg	Covington	150		Trade	1850	1920
Winstonville	Winston	50	x	Trade	1830	1910
Wisner	Smith	800	x	Lumber	1900	1930
Woodruff	Washington	150	x	Trade	1900	1930
Woodson	Monroe	25	x	Trade	1880	1920
Wortham	Harrison	200		Lumber	1850	1950

Wren	Monroe	200		Trade	1880	1950
Wyatt	Lafayette*	100	x	River	1830	1920
Zama	Attala	707		Lumber	1910	1960
Zeiglerville	Holmes	105	x	Trade	1890	1950
Zion Hill	Amite	505		Manufacturing	1810	1950

*Towns included in Franklin L. Riley, "Extinct Towns and Villages of Mississippi," *Publications of the Mississippi Historical Society*, 5 (1902), 311-83.

1870 to 1900, and extinction which has been occurring since the 1830s increased significantly after 1920. The life span of an extinct town in Mississippi averaged 56 years, ranging from fewer than 10 to more than 150 years, and during the golden era the population average of all towns was 206 persons.

In this study an extinct town is defined as an agglomerated settlement which at some time contained business establishments and a population in excess of 100 (fewer if it functioned as a county seat, land office, specialized manufacturing town, or if it was incorporated) residing in a congregation of houses reasonably near each other, and which has either lost its population or experienced such decline that it no longer resembles nor functions as a town.[3] The extinct towns are classed into functional categories to relate their demise to geographical changes (Figure 1).

The Geographic Base of Settlement

Four regions based mainly upon differences in soil fertility, topography, vegetation, drainage, economic activity, and density of towns are recognized in Mississippi. These regions are the Delta, the Piney Woods, the Hills, and the Natchez District (Figure 1 and Table III).[4] The Natchez District is a narrow triangular wedge of easily eroded loess soil extending along the Mississippi River. In the District the growth possibilities of interior towns were limited primarily because Natchez and other river ports were accessible to those residing in even the most remote area, and because the dominant agricultural

[3]Howard G. Adkins, "The Historical Geography of Extinct Towns in Mississippi," Diss. University of Tennessee 1972, p. 20.
[4]Howard G. Adkins, "The Geographic Base of Urban Retardation in Mississippi, 1800-1840," *West Georgia College Studies in the Social Sciences*, 12 (1973), 35-49.

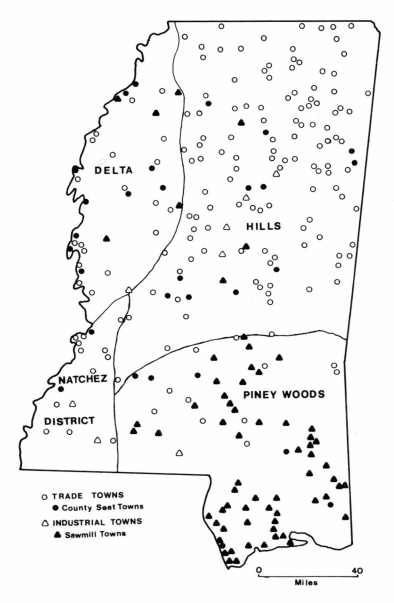

Figure 1: **Regions and Extinct Towns in Mississippi**

system was the plantation, which produced cotton marketed through factors located in the large port cities outside the region.

The Piney Woods region was avoided by the money class of settlers because of difficulty in maintaining soil fertility. One writer asserted that the settlers were "refugees from a growing civilization consequent upon a dense population and its necessities. They were not an agriculturist in a proper sense of the term; true, they cultivated in some degree the soil, but it was not the prime pursuit of these people, nor was the location sought for this purpose."[5]

Table III

Mississippi: Percent of Population by Category and Percent of Employment in Economic Sector by Region in 1840

	Population		Employment sector		
Region	White	Slave	Agriculture	Commerce	Manufacturing
Hills	64.8	53.4	57.5	40.9	54.5
Natchez District	11.7	29.5	23.8	50.9	33.6
Piney Woods	21.0	12.1	13.3	7.0	10.2
Delta	2.3	4.8	5.3	.1	1.5

Source: *United States Census, 1840 Compendium*, pp. 230–237.

Obviously all settlers were not satisfied with the soil features, for Greene, Jones, Perry, and Wayne counties experienced a net population loss to the Hills in the 1830s.[6] Town development in the Piney Woods was adversely affected by the sparse, self-sufficient population and out migration. The first substantial development of towns was realized with the coming of the lumber industry in the 1870s.

The largest region, the Hills, consisting of rolling terrain and variable soils, was opened to settlement in 1832. Large plantations were dominant in an area thirty miles wide that lay east of the Delta in the

[5]William H. Sparks, *The Memories of Fifty Years* (Macon, Georgia, 1872), pp. 331-332.

[6]L. A. Besancon, *Besancon's Annual Register of the State of Mississippi* (Natchez, 1838), p. 190; Jesse M. Wilkins, "Early Times in Wayne County," *Publications of the Mississippi Historical Society*, 6 (1902), 265-272.

Black Belt, a narrow crescent-shaped area west of the Tombigbee River.[7] Otherwise, there was a fairly even mix of large planters, small planters, and yeomen farmers throughout the Hills. The potential markets proved encouraging to merchants, who opened stores in settlements and surveyed town lots around them. As the needs of the settlements for construction timbers, gin, gristmills, blacksmiths, tanners, and artisans increased, towns materialized, and by 1840 the Hills was the most rapidly developing region in the state.[8]

The Delta is an elliptical basin between the Mississippi River and the loess bluffs extending from Vicksburg to Memphis. Its fertile soils, developed from alluvium deposited by the Mississippi and Yazoo rivers, were ideal for the production of cotton. But since only the lands of the natural levees could be safely settled and cultivated without extensive flood protection and drainage, the Delta remained largely unsettled until after 1870.[9]

Agricultural employment was overwhelmingly dominant by 1840. In fact, the ratio of combined employment in commerce and manufacturing to that in agriculture was one to forty. This imbalance would not have been detrimental to urban growth and development had agriculture supported urban related functions, but the per capita investment in manufacturing and commerce was twenty dollars.[10] The wealth of the planters was consumed in purchasing land and slaves and paying tarriffs, freight costs, and commissions, while the annual income of small planters and yeomen farmers amounted to only a few hundred dollars—certainly not enough for investment purposes.

Regional Patterns and Historical Sequence of Extinct Towns
The Formative Years of Settlement, 1770 to 1860
Effective settlement began at Natchez under the English in 1770,

[7]Herbert Weaver, *Mississippi Farmers, 1850-1860* (Nashville: Vanderbilt Univ. Press, 1945), pp. 37-42.

[8]A. J. Brown, *History of Newton County from 1834 to 1894* (Jackson, Mississippi: Clarion-Ledger Co., 1894), pp. 36-44; William A. Love, "Lowndes County, Its Antiquities and Pioneer Settlers," *Publications of the Mississippi Historical Society*, 7 (1903), 362; Mary J. Welsh, "Recollections of Pioneer Life in Mississippi," *Publications of the Mississippi Historical Society*, 4 (1901), 343-356.

[9]Arthell Kelley, "Levee Building and Settlement of the Yazoo Basin," *Southern Quarterly*, 1 (1963), 285-308.

[10]*United States Census, 1840 Compendium*, pp. 230-237.

but was retarded between 1781 when Spain acquired the territory and
1798 when Spain, for all practical purposes, relinquished claim to the
Mississippi Territory. In 1800 settlers were concentrated in the
Natchez District. Land sales were made primarily to settlers more
interested in acquiring plantations to grow cotton than in acquiring
town lots.[11] And although the growth of Natchez was promising, the
towns of Union Town, Greenville, Kingston, and Rocky Springs did
not keep pace with rural settlement because merchants, lawyers, and
doctors frequently used their professions as stepping stones to the
more lucrative and prestigious plantation life.[12] Greenville was noted
in 1807 to contain "one wide straight street nearly half a mile long . . .
intersected by two small cross ones, containing in all forty tolerably
good houses, many of which are now unoccupied. . . . It has a small
church for general use of all christian sects, a small court house, a goal
and a pillory, a post office, two stores, two taverns, and an apothecary's
shop."[13]

Planters conducted business through factors located in the large
port cities, especially New Orleans. This loss of trade retarded the
growth of towns as they were almost totally dependent upon the
seasonal trade of cotton produced by yeomen farmers. In 1842 the
editor of the *Mississippi Free Trader* made the following comparison
between the contribution of the planter class and yeomen farmers to
the economy of Natchez:

[The farmers] would crowd our streets with fresh and healthy supplies of
home productions and the proceeds would be expended here among our
merchants, grocers, and artisans. The large planters . . . do not contribute most
to the prosperity. . . . They sell their cotton in Liverpool; buy their wines in
London or Le Havre; their negro clothing in Boston; their plantation implements and supplies in New Orleans. The farmer has not the credit nor the
business connections to do this; he requires the proceeds of his crop as soon as
it can be sold; and he purchases and pays for, cash in hand, almost every

[11]R. S. Cotterill, "The National Land System in the South: 1803-1812," *Mississippi Valley Historical Review*, 16 (1929-1930), 495-506; Robert V. Haynes, "The Disposal of Lands in the Mississippi Territory," *Journal of Mississippi History*, 24 (1962), 226-227.
[12]*The Louisiana and Mississippi Almanac, 1812* (Natchez, 1812), pp. 28-29; Joseph H. Ingraham, *The Southwest by a Yankee* (New York: Harper, 1835), pp. 165-168.
[13]F. Cuming, "Sketches of a Tour to the Western Country," *Early Western Travels, 1748-1846*, ed. Reuben G. Thwaites (Cleveland, Ohio: Arthur H. Clark Co., 1904), IV, 315-316.

necessary wanted during the year, in the same market where he sells his cotton. [The farmer] hoards no money . . . but he lays it all out for the purchase of supplies, and thus directly contributes his mite to the prosperity of our city.[14]

Mississippi's population increased from 137,000 in 1830 to 792,000 in 1860. This increase was a response to the opening to settlement of 15.7 million acres in 1830 and 1832, and an increase in cotton prices.[15] When cotton averaged fifteen cents a pound, an investment of $21,000 in land, slaves, and equipment on a well supervised plantation would yield a return of between 22 and 35 percent.[16] But cotton was adaptable to cultivation on any scale and, acre for acre, farmers could compete with planters on fairly even terms. Nevertheless, by 1860 regional differences existed among the economic groups. Small farmers accounted for 85 percent of the farm operators in the Hills and 95 percent of the farm operators in the Piney Woods. In contrast, planters accounted for 45 percent of the farm operators in the Delta and loam lands along its margins, and, of course, the ante-bellum plantation system reached its zenith in the Natchez District.[17]

Whenever two or three merchants located at a site accessible within one day's travel to a community of 100 to 150 farmers, a town nucleus was formed. The number of functional units varied, ranging upward to ten or twelve in each center, and often occurred in combination so that the number of establishments did not always reflect the center's importance. At Centre, an extinct town in Attala County, four individuals operated four stores, a cotton gin, gristmill, tannery, shoe factory, saloon, post office, blacksmith shop, and sawmill. In many towns a bank, school and post office were significant adjuncts, but churches were seldom a part of these early centers.[18] Towns on navigable streams contained two or three large warehouses for storages of cotton and goods. Among the inhabitants were "enterprising profes-

[14]*Mississippi Free Trader* [Natchez], 14 April 1842.
[15]*Hunt's Merchants' Magazine*, 13 (1850), 470-472.
[16]Lewis C. Gray, *History of Agriculture in the Southern United States to 1860* (1933; rpt. Gloucester, Massachusetts: Peter Smith, 1958), p. 688; Traugott Bromme, *Mississippi: A Geographic-Statistic-Typography Sketch for Immigrants and Friends of Geography and Ethnology* (1837), reprinted in *Journal of Mississippi History*, 4 (1942), 105.
[17]Weaver, pp. 38-42.
[18]Adkins, "Historical Geography," pp. 42-44, 55, 76-82, 176-177.

sional men and merchants . . . from almost every state in the Union, but they are generally bachelors, and congregate at the hotels, so that for the number of inhabitants in proportion of families and dwellings is very small."[19]

The pattern of extinction shown in Figure 2 suggests that the process was significantly influenced by adjustments following a somewhat hasty settlement. In Table IV towns are categorized according to the major reason for their extinction. Since many county seats were established according to political motivations, without regard to trade area, they often disappeared when boundaries changed and government functions relocated. Small river towns, occupying wetland sites, were susceptible to undercaving and river course changes, and they were almost annually plagued with malaria, yellow fever, and cholera.[20] For these reasons five town sites were abandoned shortly after their founding. Others were able to survive such nature related problems. For example, Amsterdam, "a new and flourishing town of fifty houses . . . on the Big Black River . . . in the heart of a rich cotton growing country," lost about half its population to cholera in the winter of 1832-33. Amsterdam was incorporated the following year and made a port of entry by an act of Congress, but it was unable to withstand the loss of trade to Edwards, a new town two miles north on the Vicksburg to Jackson Railroad.[21]

The War Years and Reconstruction, 1860 to 1880

During the 1860s and 1870s, the town landscape was significantly influenced by a new system of cotton production when the share cropping land tenure system was made possible by crop lien laws enacted in 1867. The creation of large numbers of farm operators and credit advanced on crops stimulated trade at country stores to a degree previously unknown in Mississippi.[22] Many of these country stores

[19]Ingraham, p. 167.
[20]Florence W. Sillers and Wirt A. Williams, eds., *History of Bolivar County, Mississippi* (Jackson, Miss.: Hederman Brothers, 1948), p. 134; "Leota Landing," W.P.A., Federal Writers Project, Department of Archives and History, Jackson, Mississippi; W. A. Evans, "Disease and Doctors," *Journal of Mississippi History*, 5 (1943), 130.
[21]*Niles' Register*, 45 (1833), 189; Riley, pp. 336-337.
[22]Thomas D. Clark, *Pills, Petticoats and Plows, The Southern Country Store* (Norman: Univ. of Oklahoma Press, 1964), pp. vii-ix; Vernon L. Wharton, *The Negro in Mississippi, 1865-1890* (Chapel Hill: Univ. of North Carolina Press, 1947), p. 71.

Figure 2: **Extinct Towns in Mississippi, 1830-1860**

Table IV

Causes of Town Extinction, 1830 to 1860

Change in County Boundary	Trade & Leadership Loss to Nearby Town	Change in Transportation	Unfavorable River Site
Berryville	Alberson	Amsterdam	Hamburg
Beattie's Bluff	Brooklyn	Choccuma	Nashville
Camden	Tallalossa	Hendersonville	Pearl
Clayton	Union Town	Middleton	Port Royal
Madisonville	Victoria	Pharasalia	Richmond
New Mexico		Pikeville	
		Sardina	
		Selsertown	
		Tatumsville	
		Tuscahoma	

were nascent town sites, and with the additions of a post office, church, school, hotels, cotton gins, blacksmith shops, specialty shops, and mule-and-wagon barns, centers of considerable socio-economic importance to the local area emerged.

Under the lien system farmers could pledge anticipated crops for furnishings and supplies. Merchants did not actually charge interest, but the difference between cash and credit prices amounted to an interest charge that in almost every case averaged 25 percent or more. Charges at several stores near Summit, Mississippi, in 1870 ranged between 40 and 100 percent. Fifty years later interest often cost farmers as much as 52 percent.[23] Thus the crop lien held Mississippi farmers captive for three-quarters of a century and deprived towns of profits that perhaps would have stimulated internal growth by passing it on in the form of interest to centers outside the state.

The extinction of towns shown in Figure 3 was due to changes occurring among trade based towns along rivers, to the war, and to political readjustments. The towns of Prentiss, Harrisburg, and Boneyard were destroyed in the War. One soldier described the destruction of Prentiss in 1863 as follows: "We burnt everything:

[23]Robert Somers, *The Southern States Since The War, 1870-1871* (New York: Macmillan, 1871), p. 241; *Yearbook of Agriculture, 1927* (Washington, D.C.: GPO, 1927), pp. 20-22, 240-243.

pianos, guitars, melodeons, superior household furniture of every kind, a store full of goods, the court house with all county papers, the jail, the tavern, and about thirty dwellings, some of which cost $15,000."[24]

Thirteen new counties were created in the 1870s as a result of gerrymanderings of Republicans and Democrats vying for political control. County seat towns had several advantages over other centers, for in addition to the normal function of trade they were centers where county records were maintained, taxes paid, criminals detained, and court battles waged. Also, a county town usually contained a newspaper that imparted to it a degree of community identity and leadership. Nevertheless, with boundary changes government functions relocated, and county towns like Greensboro and La Grange disappeared.[25]

Transition and Change, 1880 to 1920

The disappearance of towns between 1880 and 1920 was more pronounced in the Hills among trade towns by-passed by railroads and among county seat towns (Figure 4). Small towns depending upon the trade of local farming communities continued to dominate the urban scene. Mercantile activities were governed by the seasonal production of cotton, the willingness of merchants to advance credit on anticipated crops and the income of farmers. Farm income in 1900 was about equal to that in 1840, and it did not change appreciably during the next two decades when the average cash income per farm was $605 and that of farm tenants was $106.[26] During the growing season from April to August, there was almost no cash available for retail trade. But after harvest, as David L. Cohn describes, "stores which summer-long have had in stock only the most utilitarian foods such as beans, fat meat, flour, lard, and coffee, now flaunt on their shelves the unaccustomed luxuries of dried figs and raisins, apples and oranges, lemons, and grapes, and tinned California fruit. The drygoods stores now display wondrous suits for men. . . . 'Sunday'

[24]Quoted in John K. Bettersworth, *Mississippi: A History* (Austin, Texas: Steck, 1959), p. 304.

[25]Riley, pp. 328-329.

[26]Charles S. Johnson, Edwin R. Embree, and W. W. Alexander, *The Collapse of Cotton Tenancy* (Chapel Hill: Univ. of North Carolina Press, 1935), p. 1.

Figure 3: **Extinct Towns in Mississippi, 1860-1880**

shoes . . . are now . . . worn everyday. Rayon socks and rayon neckties are bright. . . . Caps will be worn . . . and there are shotgun shells for rabbit-hunting. For the women there are dresses. The stores are crowded."[27]

Settlement in the Delta counties proceeded rapidly with population increasing from 109,000 in 1880 to 332,000 in 1920.[28] Land sales occurred in large units as the fear of flooding, yellow fever, and the cost of draining and clearing the land frightened away small farmers. Delta plantations which were producing almost 50 percent of the state's cotton crop by 1920 were less favorable to town development than had been the Antebellum plantation system. Adjuncts to the plantations that included cotton gins, blacksmith shops, and saw mills had a decentralizing effect on the concentration of these activities in towns. The major deterrent, however, was plantation commissaries through which tenants and wage laborers were advanced merchandise valued at an average of $13.00 per month for approximately seven months. After "settling-up" in the fall the average net income of tenants was $227.00. So effective was this captive enterprise that Delta wholesalers reported in 1920 that from 50 to 90 percent of their business was with plantation commissaries.[29] Credit at the commissaries rather than cash loans and wages gave tenants and wage laborers almost no opportunity to patronize nonplantation businesses.

The volume of freight associated with Delta plantations was such that railroads provided personal freight stops, thereby negating nucleation. For example, along the route of the Yazoo Valley Railroad from Vicksburg north to the state line there were 72 stops in 1900, averaging 3½ miles between stops.[30]

In 1920 blacks comprised 80 percent of the population in the Delta. As Alfred H. Stone writes, "every step taken in the development . . . has been dependent upon and marked by an increased Negro population. The railroad rights of way . . . have been cut out by the Negro, and

[27]*God Shakes Creation* (New York: Harper Brothers, 1935), pp. 44-45.
[28]*United States Census*, "Mississippi," 1860-1920.
[29]T. J. Woofter, *Landlord and Tenant on the Cotton Plantation* (Washington, D.C.: GPO, 1936), p. 203; W. J. Carson, "Financing the Production and Distribution of Cotton," *Federal Reserve Bulletin* (1923), p. 174.
[30]Robert L. Brandfon, *Cotton Kingdom of the New South: A History of the Yazoo Mississippi Delta from Reconstruction to the Twentieth Century* (Cambridge: Harvard Univ. Press, 1967), p. 84.

Figure 4: **Extinct Towns in Mississippi, 1880-1920**

every mile of track laid by his hands. These forest lands have been cultivated by him . . . and their subsequent cultivation has called for his constant service. The levees upon which the Delta depends for protection from floods have been erected mainly by the Negro and the daily labor in field and town, in planting and building, in operating gins and compresses and oil mills, in moving trains, in handling the great staple of the country . . . is but the Negro's daily toil."[31] With limited purchasing power, however, blacks contributed little to the town-forming process. They had no vested interest nor active voice in towns.

New towns between 1880 and 1920 owed their origin to railroads and the lumber industry. During these four decades 3,330 miles of track were laid in the state. Railroads certainly speeded up commercial transactions but perhaps were not so vital to the prosperity of the average Mississippian as have been generally assumed. In the first place, railroads promoted almost no industries other than lumbering. Second, as the farmer viewed it, cotton provided the surest means of buying what the "outside" world had to offer, and the railroad provided transportation.[32] But in the attempt to increase their purchasing power, farmers tended to over produce and thus brought on lower prices, increased tenancy, and a further dependence on cotton. Finally, railroads decentralized trade by facilitating the collecting, storing, and buying of cotton in a myriad of places.[33]

Railroad companies provided freight stops, both to acquire the maximum freight possible and in exchange for a free right-of-way. McDonald, an extinct town in Neshoba County, was located on land donated in 1904 to the Gulf and Chicago Railroad for a right of way. At first little interest was exhibited in the town site, but almost immediately after the first train reached the town, merchants from nearby communities and others purchased lots, built homes, and opened businesses. By 1915 the town contained an estimated one hundred

---

[31]*Studies in the American Race Problem* (New York: Doubleday, 1908), p. 87.
[32]Frank Andrews, "Cost of Hauling Crops from Farms to Shipping Points," *Bulletin No. 49*, U.S.D.A. Bureau of Statistics (1909), pp. 20-21.
[33]Ulrich B. Phillips, "Railway Transportation in the South," *The South in the Building of the Nation*, (Richmond, Virginia: The Southern Historical Society, 1909), VI, 305-316; M. B. Hammond, *The Cotton Industry, An Essay in American Economic History*, Part I (Publication of American Economic Assoc., 1897), p. 117.

houses, thirteen mercantile houses, two wholesale firms, a cabinet wood working shop, a cotton gin, gristmill, sawmills, blacksmith shop, a drugstore, two churches, a school post office, ice house, boarding house and hotel, and had two doctors, a mayor, and a constable.[34]

Cotton, the major item carried on railroads in Mississippi at the turn of the century, was shipped from more than 500 stations. Stations in towns that are now extinct averaged shipping less than 800 bales annually whereas the average for all stations at the turn of the century was almost 4,000 bales.[35] Hence, this myriad of cotton-buying, collecting and shipping points resulted in towns of near equal size without the capital, labor, and markets necessary to attract industry.

The large-scale exploitation of the yellow pine forest which began in the 1870s was the occasion for the second boom period in the state. In the Piney Woods the logging operation was a year-round activity with laborers living in company owned sawmill towns. Mill towns were true towns in the sense that they were supported by a primary activity carried on in the immediate area; however, many were viable only as long as the lumber lasted and disappeared shortly after it was exhausted.

Towns were not usually associated with mills cutting less than 15,000,000 board feet annually, and because of the diseconomics of scale, mills cutting more than 500,000 board feet daily were uneconomical.[36] Mills cutting 30,000,000 board feet "needed about 20,000 acres of virgin timberland to supply a ten-year run."[37] It was possible for such a volume to be available to the mill within a three to four mile straight-line haul of the main line railroad using dummy or spur tracks and steam skidder operations. Under these conditions mills could operate at one location for ten to twenty years.[38]

[34]A. E. Cliburn, "A Town of the Past: McDonald, Mississippi," unpublished manuscript; interviews with J. H. Adkins, C. Clark, A. Robinson, and A. E. Cliburn, July 1969; *Neshoba Democrat* [Philadelphia, Miss.], 22 August 1907 and 9 October 1931.

[35]*Bradstreets*, 11 (1885), 99-100; James L. Watkins, "The Commercial Cotton Crops of 1900-1901, 1901-1902, and 1902-1903," *Bulletin No. 28*, U.S.D.A., Bureau of Statistics (1904), pp. 43-46; *Bulletin No. 34*, p. 34.

[36]Nollie Hickman, *Mississippi Harvest, Lumbering in the Longleaf Pine Belt, 1840-1915* (University, Miss.: Univ. of Mississippi, 1962), pp. 158-160, and 178-183.

[37]Hickman, p. 160.

[38]S. G. Thigpin, *A Boy In Rural Mississippi* (Picayune, Miss.: S. G. Thigpin, 1966), pp. 129, 148. In 1907 the holdings of the Butterfield Company at Norfield was 45,000 acres with an average volume of 12,500 to 15,000 board feet per acre, Hickman, pp. 175-176.

Operating, maintaining, and supplying timber to the mill required a large and dependable labor force. Unskilled laborers were recruited locally and from central and north Mississippi, the Carolinas, Georgia, Alabama, and northern Florida. Skilled operators came primarily from the exhausted timber lands of the Great Lakes.[39] As a result of the migration, population in the Piney Woods increased from 164,475 in 1880 to 415,570 in 1920, and the number of towns containing 500 increased from 19 to 63. Hence, the migration into the Piney Woods and the Delta accounted for 72 percent of the state's population increase between 1880 and 1920.

In most lumber towns the company owned commissary store was the shopping center where only the essential items were carried. Most commissaries were large structures measuring 40 by 100 feet, with roofed porches extending across the front. The interior was divided into a doctor's office, post office, company offices, and the general merchandising section. At first, wages were paid in company script redeemable only at the commissary, thereby prohibiting competitive retail establishments.[40] After the turn of the century, however, companies were unable to maintain complete economic dominance as non-company establishments were opened in many towns. In the extinct towns of Bond, Norfield, Hillsdale, and Zama there were barber shops, hotels, garages, churches, schools, post offices, and leisure time establishments that included skating rinks, theaters and Y.M.C.A.'s. Enterprises either supporting or related to the mill operations varied with the size of the operation, but almost invariably there were machine shops, foundries, brick kilns, turpentine distilleries, and planning mills.[41]

Extinction After 1920

Forces related to those that had encouraged establishment and growth of centers led to increased competition, to differential growth, and ultimately to the extinction of the 181 towns which have disap-

[39]Clayton Rand, *Ink On My Hands* (Gulfport, Miss.: Dixie Press, 1940), p. 166.
[40]Rand, p. 20.
[41]Rand, pp. 8-10; *Star Herald* [Kosciusko, Miss.], 23 March 1967; *Clarion Ledger-Jackson Daily News*, 23 June 1957; "Airey," "Basin," "Paive," "Shipman," and "Verna," W.P.A., Federal Writers Project, Department of Archives and History, Jackson, Mississippi.

peared since 1920 (Figure 5). Sixty-two of the places that disappeared were lumber towns.

After the timber was exhausted, closing a company town was accomplished very rapidly. The company simply dismantled the mill and buildings, placed them on rail cars and transported all to new timberlands. Logging trucks and portable mills replaced the rail skidder system and large stationary mills to complete the harvest of widely scattered and small stands of remaining timber. Company owned houses were dismantled and moved to new locations, sold to workers who remained to work in the portable industry, or were simply abandoned as mill hands and their families migrated with the industry or to the larger towns within the Piney Woods and along the Gulf Coast.[42] Several towns reverted to short lived trade centers as attempts were made to cultivate cotton on cutover land.

Trade centers that had been moribund for several decades began to disappear rapidly as consumer orientations and business patterns were affected by changes in land tenure and farm income. Tenancy declined from 225,617 in 1930 to 3,824 in 1974. Farm ownership which had increased from 77,383 in 1930 to 103,053 in 1950 declined to 38,683 in 1974. Farms increased in acreages from an average of 55 in 1930 to 267 in 1974. The average net income per farm from the sale of agricultural products also exhibited a similar change, from $605 in 1930 to $22,921 in 1974. The results were fewer farm people, but people with more money to spend, whose preferences were changing, and who were willing and able to travel farther to satisfy their desires.

In contrast to railroads, the automobile was the impetus for differential growth as it provided farmers with a wider choice of trade centers. However, interest in securing an adequate highway system had been slow to develop. The constitution of 1890 provided that each county be divided into five districts and that each be headed by an elected official with exclusive control over building and maintaining roads in his district. Thus the state entered the twentieth century with a road system that was purely local and that varied considerably between supervisory districts. In 1922 a system of state highways was

[42]James H. Lemly, *The Gulf, Mobile and Ohio, A Railroad That Had to Expand or Expire* (Homewood, Ill.: Richard D. Irwin, 1953), p. 20.

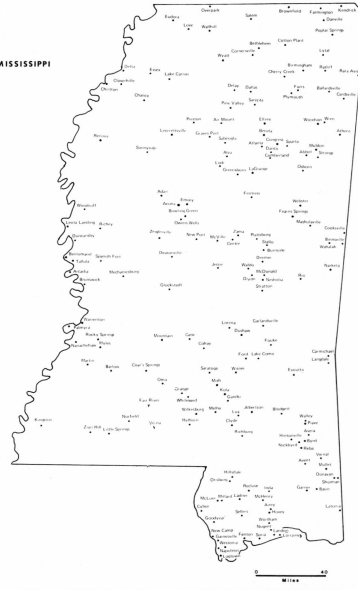

Figure 5: **Extinct Towns in Mississippi, 1920-1970**

authorized to connect the county seats of the state.[43] Eight years later the Stansel Act authorized a 4,000 mile primary road system to connect county seats, principal highways of adjoining states, state institutions, and places with a population of five hundred or more. A secondary road system of 2,000 miles was also established, but major improvements did not begin to occur until after 1946 when the Farm-to-Market road bill provided aid to upgrade the secondary system.[44] For this study, however, it is significant to note that the acts created spatial monopolies by discriminating in favor of county seats and towns containing more than 500 persons. Furthermore, as the network of highways evolved, railroads centralized their operations at county towns to compete more favorably with motor transport.

The centrality of county towns became increasingly important as the state highway system was developed. The population in county towns increased from 364,947 (18 percent) in 1930, to 803,757 (36 percent) in 1970. A significant percentage of this increase could only have come from small towns, since the state experienced out-migration during 1940, 1950, and 1960, and the number of farms declined from 312,266 in 1930 to 53,620 in 1974. One spatial aspect of disappearing towns has been their proximity to county boundaries, with an average distance of 12.8 miles between towns that disappeared and their county seat town.[45] Moreover, almost two-thirds of the places that disappeared were located on unimproved secondary roads.

County towns had several advantages over others. Courthouses were legal centers for the counties and were sites for political rallies and for socializing. Such centers became increasingly important as the number of rural post offices was reduced and as contact between citizens and the government increased. During the 1930s and thereafter, county agents, relief and welfare officials, and county health departments were located in county seat towns. County towns usually contained a newspaper that imparted to them a degree of community leadership and at times campaigned for improvements in appearance, services, and roads.

[43]*Laws of Mississippi, 1924*, pp. 190, 403.
[44]*Today and Tomorrow, An Engineering Analysis of the Highway Transportation System in Mississippi* (Jackson, Miss.: Hederman Brothers, 1949), pp. 18-19.
[45]Distances computed from *U.S.G.S.*, Mississippi Quadrangles, Scale, 1:250,000.

An additional element of centrality was added when the cooperative cotton gin movement, motivated by farmer dissatisfaction with
private gins, was initiated in 1912. County seat towns were selected as
sites for cooperative gins because they were the places most accessible to the greatest number of people. By 1948 the county seat of every
cotton-growing county had at least one cooperative cotton gin.[46]
Farmers sold their cotton to buyers concentrated in county seat towns,
which also had the best communication, transportation, and banking
facilities. And as agriculture was mechanized, implement sales and
services were located in the county towns, thereby contributing to
their spatial monopolies.

The first change in the postal system to have a negative effect on
towns occurred in 1902 when rural free delivery routes were
established along roads passable the year around, and where 100
families could be served along a twenty-five mile route.[47] This elimi-
nated frequent trips to the post office in nearby towns and encouraged
road improvements. The number of post offices declined from 2,048 in
1905, to 1,020 in 1920, 766 in 1940, 540 in 1960, and 494 in 1969.[48]

Retail trade is always influenced by density of population, spatial
extent of the trade area, and social and economic characteristics of the
population. The farming population in Mississippi had promoted a
pattern of ubiquitous small towns similar in size, volume of sales, and
in the level of goods and services offered. As a result, the first *Census
of Retailing*, taken in 1929, noted that 77 percent of the stores, with 68
percent of the retail sales, were located in small towns or in rural areas,
and that 67 percent of all stores sold on credit. But by 1968, 57 percent
of the retail stores, with 73 percent of the retail sales, were located in
towns over 2,500 population.[49] Thus the increase in the range of goods
and services offered in the larger towns has been sufficient to deprive
many small towns of shoppers even for basic convenience goods.

[46]B. K. Doyle and R. W. Shaw, "Mississippi Co-operative Gins," *Bulletin 479*,
Mississippi Agricultural Experiment Station, 1951, pp. 1-35.
    [47]Wayne E. Fuller, "The South and the Rural Free Delivery of Mail," *Journal of
Southern History*, 25 (1959), 511.
    [48]*United States Official Postal Guide*, "Mississippi" (Washington, D.C.: GPO,
1905-1969).
    [49]*United States Census of Business, Retail Trade*, "Mississippi," 1968.

Implications for the Future

The pace of extinction has slowed since 1960. The towns in Table V, however, show declines in population, function, and services since 1930, and they exhibit behavorial patterns similar to those that have disappeared. For the most part they are located in former farming communities on inferior roads and have few centripetal amenities. Perhaps a few will be successful in their bid to attract "footloose" industries. But as long as an open societal system remains many will undoubtedly continue to decline and ultimately cease to function.

If we are to study the past and learn from it, we need to know how towns have responded to change. To understand better which types of towns are able to accept change easily and which cannot, and why, we need to know what they were like during their respective golden eras, for they provide clues to where we have been and where we are going. To achieve this understanding we must study those places that are now coming to grips with change.

Table V

Declining Small Towns in Mississippi

Artesia	Ethel	McLaurin	Satartia
Ashland	Fannin	Mantee	Saucier
Baird	Fernwood	Marietta	Scobey
Baxterville	Fitler	Matherville	Scooba
Beauregard	Gallmann	Mattson	Sebastopol
Beulah	Gatesville	Meadville	Seminary
Bogue Chitto	Gillsburg	Minter City	Sherman
Bond	Golden	Mize	Shubuta
Braxton	Grand Gulf	Montrose	Sidon
Buena Vista	Gunninson	Moss	Silver City
Caledonia	Hamburg	Mt. Pleasant	Slate Springs
Carpenter	Hardy	Myrtle	Soso
Carrollton	Harpersville	Nesbitt	State Line
Carson	Hermanville	Nicholson	Star
Cascilla	Hillsboro	Ora	Stewart
Cedarbluff	Holcomb	Osyaka	Strayhorn
Chester	Homewood	Ovett	Sturgis
Chesterville	Hub	Pachuta	Taylor
Chicora	Ingomar	Paden	Thaxton
Coahoma	Isola	Paulding	Tillatoba
Coila	Johnston Station	Paulette	Tylersville
Crandall	Kiln	Phoeba	Toccopola
Crosby	Knoxo	Philipps	Tomnolen
Dennis	Knoxville	Pinola	Tula
D'Lo	Lake Shore	Pittsboro	Vaughan
Duffee	Learned	Pleasant Hill	Vossburg
Dumas	Leaf	Pope	Wallerville
Duncan	Leflore	Prairie	Walls
Ebenezer	Lena	Prairie Point	Walnut Grove
Ecru	Louin	Pulaski	Waterford
Eden	Louise	Rienzi	Weathersby
Edinburg	Lula	Robinsonville	Weir
Electric Mills	Lyman	Rodney	Williamsburg
Enid	Lyon	Rome	Williamsville
Enterprise	McCool	Sallis	Winchester
	McHenry	Sarepta	Woodland

Source: *United States Census*, 1930 to 1970; *Rand McNally Commercial Atlas*, 1941, 1953, and 1968; and personal visits.

From Prosperity to Poverty:
Economic Growth and Change to 1900

WILLIAM K. SCARBOROUGH

After listening yesterday to the folksy anecdotes and personal rem-
iniscences of returning émigrés from Mississippi, I feel a little out of
place (if you'll pardon the expression) at this symposium. For I have
no recollection of dragging sacks through Delta cotton fields or sitting
on the steps of the old country store or spooning under the magnolia
trees. Instead, I grew up in Annapolis, Maryland, on the banks of the
Severn River just across from the U.S. Naval Academy. I could tell you
about seaplanes rattling the windows in the early morning hours as
they came in for a landing on the river or about crew races on the
Severn or about dress parades on Worden Field. But such accounts
would probably bore you, and they most certainly would not contribute much to defining a sense of place for Mississippians.

Yet, in order to define that sense of place we must have an understanding of the economic forces that shaped the past. That is what I
shall attempt to convey here. And although I am not a native Mississippian, I have resided in the state for the last seventeen years, which
is more than can be said for most historians currently writing about the
South (many of whom are New York-born Marxists). Moreover, I am
here by choice rather than accident of birth—and that ought to count
for something.

The prosperity of antebellum Mississippi rested upon a tripod
consisting of cotton, land, and slaves.[1] That prosperity resulted from a
fortuitous conjunction of circumstances in the late eighteenth and

---

[1] The bulk of the material on the antebellum South is drawn from the author's
chapter, "Heartland of the Cotton Kingdom," in Richard A. McLemore, ed., *A History
of Mississippi* (Hattiesburg: University and College Press of Mississippi, 1973), I,
310-51. In my analysis of the general characteristics of the Southern cotton economy, I

early nineteenth centuries which served to promote the rapid settlement and economic growth of the American South. First, the Industrial Revolution spawned the British textile industry, thereby generating an almost insatiable demand for cotton. At about the same time, Eli Whitney's invention of the cotton gin allowed the hardy, short-staple, green-seed variety of cotton to spread into the southern hinterland, a region uniquely suited by climate and soil characteristics to produce the types of cotton most in demand on the international market. Then, military successes against the Spanish and Indians during the War of 1812 facilitated settlement and cultivation of the virgin lands in the Southwest. Consequently, by the mid-1820s the Cotton South, of which Mississippi would soon be the heartland, had become the world's chief supplier of raw cotton.

Although the Whitney saw gin had been introduced into Mississippi as early as 1795, there was little increase in the territory's cotton production for almost two decades. Early varieties of the white staple proved unsatisfactory in a number of respects, but about 1820 Mississippi growers finally discovered a cotton strain which seemed to meet all their requirements. Characterized by large, wide-open bolls, which made it much easier to pick than its predecessors, Mexican cotton revolutionized the upland cotton industry and, more than any other factor except the cotton gin, served to elevate cotton to its predominant position in the economy of the Gulf South. Further refinements were effected during the next decade, culminating about 1833 with the development of a variety known as Petit Gulf Cotton, which became the ancestor of all later American breeds.

Cotton culture carried with it a high demand for labor. Consequently, as Mississippi's forests gave way to cotton fields, a heavy tide of black Africans poured in from the older slave states to till the newly cleared lands and harvest the white gold. Mississippi's slave population doubled during each of the first two decades of the nineteenth century. But the cotton-slavery boom did not reach a climax until the 1830s when cotton production quadrupled and the slave

have relied heavily on Gavin Wright, *The Political Economy of the Cotton South: Households, Markets, and Wealth in the Nineteenth Century* (New York: W. W. Norton, 1978).

population increased by 197 percent to constitute, for the first time, a majority of the state's total population.

It was in this third decade of the century that Mississippi became the leading cotton-producing state in the nation. Spurred by an abundance of cheap land, easy credit from state banks, high cotton prices, and development of the superior Petit Gulf strain of cotton, Mississippi agriculturists concentrated almost all their resources on that staple. Tens of thousands of immigrants—some prospective farmers and planters, but others simply speculators—poured into the state to take advantage of bonanza conditions. The newcomers, their numbers swelled by an average annual importation of 10,000 slaves, cleared vast areas in the Black Prairie region of northeastern Mississippi and in the bottom lands adjacent to the Yazoo and Big Black rivers in the west-central part of the state. Cotton production rose from 100,000 bales in 1830 to more than 386,000 bales by the end of the decade. More than a million acres of cotton were planted in the state in 1836, when the price reached twenty cents per pound on the New Orleans market.

The cotton boom of the thirties stimulated other forms of economic activity within the state. Land sales skyrocketed, reaching a peak in 1835 when nearly three million acres were sold. In an effort to meet the transportation needs of the state, more than a score of railroads were chartered during the decade. However, most projects foundered in the Panic of 1837, and by 1840 only eighty-three miles of track had actually been laid. Banking activity also increased dramatically. Before 1833 Mississippi had only two state banks in addition to the Planter's Bank, a branch of the United States Bank. But on the eve of the depression the number of banks in the state had increased to twenty-five with total capital assets in excess of $62,000,000. All would succumb shortly, however, to the Panic and to the resulting political opposition of state Democrats in the early 1840s.[2]

Unfortunately for those caught up in the speculative mania of the "Flush Times," the bubble was bound to burst sooner or later. It did so with devastating suddenness in 1837, triggering a depression which

[2] John Edmond Gonzales, "Flush Times, Depression, War, and Compromise," in McLemore, ed., A History of Mississippi, I, 289-94.

would last a dozen years. The financial Panic of 1837, which broke the land boom and drove many banks to the wall, was precipitated by Andrew Jackson's promulgation of the Specie Circular, requiring payment in gold for federal lands. Not only were the speculators ruined, but bona fide cotton planters who had purchased land directly from the government found themselves unable to meet specie payments and thus were threatened with the loss of their property. Notwithstanding these developments, cotton prices remained relatively stable until 1840. Then, as a consequence of a glut in the market engendered by over-expansion of the English textile industry, prices skidded sharply. By the spring of 1840 distress had become acute throughout the state. Not until the mid-1840s did cotton prices begin to rally from their low of five cents per pound, and complete recovery was not achieved until the next decade.

In the long run the Panic of 1837 proved to be a boon to Mississippi, for it generated a reform movement which was to bring far-reaching changes to the agricultural economy of the state during the next generation. Impelled by necessity to reduce their operating expenses, Mississippi planters strove to attain greater self-sufficiency through diversification. They placed more emphasis upon the production of a variety of foodstuffs—corn, sweet potatoes, small grains, fruits and vegetables of all kinds; marked progress was made in the selective breeding of quality livestock; and, finally, by utilizing more intensive methods of husbandry together with such labor-saving devices as seed planters, wheeled cultivators, and scrapers, Mississippians increased their production of cotton.

The results of the agricultural renaissance were impressive. Cotton production mushroomed, not only because more intensive farming methods increased per-acre yield, but also as a result of the expansion of cotton culture in central and northern Mississippi. After 1840 planters began to capitalize, for the first time, on the fertile soil of the Yazoo Delta, previously neglected because of an inadequate levee system. With the rich alluvial delta lands yielding as much as 3,000 pounds of seed cotton per acre, compared to the Southwide average of 530 pounds, Mississippi's cotton growers enjoyed a decided competitive cost advantage by the time of the Civil War.

As cotton production increased, bringing rich dividends to Mississippi planters, so too did the production of food crops and livestock. Corn production more than doubled during the post-depression era, reaching a level of 29 million bushels in 1859. Wheat, rarely planted before 1840, became a crop of considerable importance in north and central Mississippi during the two succeeding decades. Mississippi led all other cotton states in the value of orchard produce and trailed only Texas, Alabama, and Georgia in livestock production at the end of the antebellum period.

Thus, Mississippi's agricultural economy emerged from the depression in a healthy, prosperous condition. Nearly a century would pass before it again approached the degree of diversity and self-sufficiency achieved during the 1840s and 1850s. Perhaps no index affords more dramatic proof of the prosperity of the fifties than land values. During that decade the value of farm lands in Mississippi increased by a whopping 176 percent. At the same time farm acreage in the state increased by 50 percent. By 1860 the cash value of all farm land, implements, and livestock in Mississippi was rapidly approaching $250 million, and the state's population appeared to stand on the threshold of an era which promised even greater prosperity.

The spectacular expansion of Mississippi's agricultural economy during the antebellum years was based on the exploitation of slave labor. As the profitability of cotton production increased, so too did the volume of slave imports. Thus, by 1860 slaves constituted 55.2 percent of the state's total population—a figure exceeded only by South Carolina among all the slave states. As one would expect, blacks became most heavily concentrated in those areas best suited to large-scale cotton culture—the Natchez region initially, and, after 1840, west-central Mississippi and the Yazoo Delta. The greatest density of slave population occurred in the Delta counties of Issaquena and Washington, where, in both 1850 and 1860, blacks outnumbered whites by more than nine to one.

The slaves thus introduced into Mississippi brought wealth and prosperity to many individual proprietors. Indeed, it is fair to say that slaves constituted the predominant form of wealth in the South. And those who owned them prospered during the extended antebellum cotton boom which boosted slave values. At the same time, however, slavery exerted a generally deleterious effect upon regional growth and development by inhibiting the development of a home market, reducing the incentive for entrepreneurial activity in the manufacturing sector, retarding the development of an industrial labor force—either native or immigrant—and discouraging urbanization and internal improvement projects. These deficiencies would later prove to be serious deterrents to the economic recovery of the postbellum South.

Slave labor was employed most profitably on plantations. Farm labor was scarce in antebellum America because most agriculturists preferred farm ownership, and, as land was plentiful and cheap, that goal was readily within their grasp. The resulting labor shortage, however, imposed a serious constraint upon the expansion of family farms in both North and South. Only on Southern plantations, where slavery provided an elastic labor supply, could individual units be expanded sufficiently to produce staple crops for the world market. On the other hand, inhibited by the paucity of labor from growing both staple and provision crops, slaveless farmers chose self-sufficiency as the safer alternative. Thus, according to economist Gavin Wright in his recent book, *The Political Economy of the Cotton South*, the fundamental economic difference between plantation and farm was not productive efficiency or even size per se, but choice of crops.[3]

Whatever may be the merits of Wright's argument, perhaps the best statistical index for differentiating a farm from a plantation is that devised by historian Herbert Weaver, who takes into account the size of both land and slave holdings. Thus, Weaver designates as planters those agriculturists who owned at least two hundred acres of improved land and twenty or more slaves. Using these figures, he concludes that about 20 percent of the agricultural operators in Mississippi on the eve of the Civil War could be classified as planters. Geographically, the plantations were concentrated in the Delta-Loess section of west Mississippi, where planters constituted 45 percent of the heads of agricultural families, and in such northeastern counties as Noxubee and Lowndes in the Black Prairie region.

Attesting to the vitality of the slave-plantation as an economic unit,

---

[3] Wright, *Political Economy of the Cotton South*, p. 73.

there was a pronounced trend toward consolidation into larger individual slave parcels during the late antebellum period. Among the cotton states, Mississippi trailed only Alabama in the number of planters owning a hundred or more slaves each. In 1850 some 206 Mississippi proprietors were listed in that category, but ten years later that figure had risen to 316. Similarly, the number of planters owning 300 or more slaves in Mississippi doubled during the 1850s. Thus, on the eve of the Civil War Mississippi was clearly one of the leading plantation states in the South.

To recapitulate, by the close of the antebellum era, Mississippi's economy, grounded primarily on cotton and slaves, was healthy and prosperous. During the 1850s there was a substantial increase in the average size of agricultural units throughout the state. Simultaneously, land values soared to new heights, reaching $18 per acre for improved land by the end of the decade. Slave prices also rose sharply during this period. By 1860 the average price of an adult field hand on the New Orleans market had risen to $1,800, and the total value of Mississippi's slave property was estimated at $350 million. Alarmed by increasing Northern hostility toward slavery—the foundation-stone of their socio-economic system—and emboldened by the prosperity of the 1850s, Mississippians opted for secession in order to safeguard their economic well-being. It was a fateful decision, destined to leave the state's agricultural economy in a shambles from which there would be no recovery during the remainder of the century.

The Civil War brought devastation to the material and human resources of Mississippi. Twenty-seven thousand Mississippians, more than a third of those who had taken up arms, perished in the bitter, fractricidal conflict—a toll in human lives exceeded only by North Carolina among the states of the late Confederacy. Agriculture, the economic lifeblood of the state, was almost hopelessly crippled by the war. Plantations and farms alike suffered from neglect or abandonment; 60 percent of the state's livestock was destroyed; the Negro labor force became totally disorganized in the wake of emancipation. The once-dominant planter class was ruined, as land values declined precipitately and the huge investment in slaves was lost overnight. Other capital assets suffered a like fate. Investments in Confederate notes and bonds were wiped out, insurance companies became insolvent, towns were decimated, transportation facilities were reduced to ruin, and millions of dollars worth of cotton were confiscated by federal authorities. With the freedmen now classified as population rather than property, Mississippi dropped from fifth among 33 states in per capita wealth to last—a dubious distinction which the state has yet to relinquish.

In the wake of the economic devastation wrought by the war, Mississippi became more firmly attached to a one-crop economy than she had ever been during the golden years of the antebellum period. This was a logical economic development resulting from the unique historical juxtaposition of wartime destruction, favorable cotton prices immediately after the war, and the emergence of the tenancy system. Although the British textile industry peaked about 1860, the reduced southern cotton output—production did not recover to the 1859–60 level until 1878–79—kept prices above normal until well into the 1870s. Encouraged by these high prices, farmers turned increasingly to cotton, a crop on which they could draw cash advances and which could be produced with the unstable labor force then available. The trend toward cotton-specialization was accelerated during the same period by the crop-lien system, which developed in response to the needs of both impecunious farmers and labor-hungry landlords.

Postbellum poverty, however, cannot be attributed solely or even primarily to the tenancy system. Rather, the fundamental cause of economic distress in the Cotton South was a stagnation in the world demand for cotton. Unfortunately, this fall in demand coincided with the increased output resulting from the factors noted above. Moreover, the renewed emphasis on cotton forced the South to abandon the self-sufficiency in basic foodstuffs which it had maintained prior to 1860. In contrast to the antebellum period when family farms concentrated on provision crops, postbellum tenants, who operated more than half of the small farms in Mississippi by 1890, focused their efforts on cotton because they had cash obligations but insufficient land to raise both cotton and enough foodstuffs to achieve self-sufficiency. In sum, then, the demand for cotton on the world market after 1860 was simply too weak to restore economic prosperity based on that staple alone.

The impediments erected by slavery to the development of a diversified nonagricultural economy now came home to haunt Mississippians in the postwar era. Although the Bourbons tried valiantly to stimulate industrial growth, Mississippi remained basically an agricultural state until well into the twentieth century. To be sure, there were a few encouraging developments. With state assistance, railroad mileage doubled during the 1880s. By 1890 Mississippi had 16 cotton mills representing an investment of $3.5 million and 338 lumber mills valued at $4.5 million. Nevertheless, by the end of the century the value of the state's manufactured goods was only one-fourth the value of products in the agricultural sector.[4] Not until the mid-1960s would Mississippi finally achieve the elusive goal of balancing agriculture with industry.

In retrospect, the economic woes which plagued Mississippi during the late nineteenth century appear to have been insoluble. The state's emphasis upon agriculture was not only a legacy of the antebellum period but a logical response to the economic principle of comparative advantage. But the postbellum institutions and circumstances which forced Mississippi agriculturists to concentrate their resources on cotton production undermined the self-sufficiency they had previously enjoyed and exposed them increasingly to such vicissitudes of the market as falling prices and exorbitant transportation and interest rates—evils which plagued all American farmers in that period. The truth is that the problems of Mississippi agriculture were never really solved. Only with the massive out-migration of farm laborers and the gradual development of a diversified nonagricultural sector in the twentieth century did the state begin to register genuine economic progress. Only then did she begin to reverse the trend from prosperity to poverty which had been inaugurated by the demise of slavery and the end of the textile boom.

---

[4] James G. Revels, "Redeemers, Rednecks and Racial Integrity," in McLemore, ed., A History of Mississippi, I, 601-605.

Designing for a Sense of Place
in Mississippi Small Towns*

JAMES F. BARKER

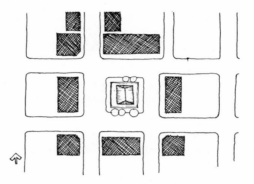

Plan of Ripley Square

America loves small towns. We see small towns as baseball, hot dogs, and apple pie. We believe strongly in the "American village" image. We are inspired by the American symbol of a small town boy, girl, athlete, or politician who makes good. We are dedicated to the idea that the American small town is the proving ground for our national idols and our national leaders.

America hates small towns. Small towns are seen as places where there is a narrowness of thought; where there is a lack of creative stimulus; where morality is more important than knowledge; and where rigid standards stifle intellectual growth.

This love/hate relationship between Americans and small towns is

*All sketches and scores in this paper are taken from James F. Barker, Michael W. Fazio, and Hank Hildebrandt, *The Small Town as an Art Object* (New York: Wittenborn, 1975).

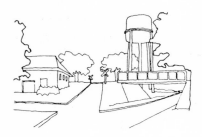

Focal Point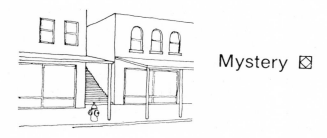

very much a part of today's attitudes. We both idolize small town America for its idyllic qualities and yet scorn it for its provincialism.

Admitting the vices as well as the virtues of small town living, many Americans still feel that the ideal place to live is Small Town USA. In fact, a Gallup Poll conducted in 1968 indicated that we have a high regard for small town living. Americans responded that small towns were more preferable places to live than central cities, suburbs, and rural settings.

Given the problems, it seems important to understand why we have this fascination with life in small towns. When small town residents are asked why they chose to live in small towns, they respond: "It is a good place to raise children;" "There is less crime, less pollution, less traffic congestion;" "I seem to know everyone in town;" "I can count on my neighbors for help;" "I feel secure and safe;" "Individual people seem to have more value as people."

All of these expressions reflect one idea. Small towns are the epitome of community, and even more specifically, small towns are the epitome of a sense of place.

The Sense of Place in Small Towns

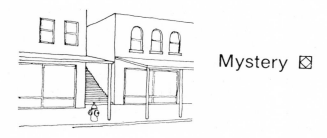

Mystery ◈

Obviously, sense of place is one of the most abstract and illusive concepts that Americans pursue. Understanding what creates a true sense of place in small towns is a complex task because the factors of influence and the forces involved in creating a sense of place are constantly changing, paralleled by changes in the community. We are able to "feel" when these factors fit together to create a sense of place, but an understanding of how and why this fit happens is very difficult to grasp.

A sense of place implies that a community has an accurate reading of its past and present and some idea regarding its future. It is an indication that a small town understands its uniqueness. However, if a small town has its roots too deeply embedded in the past, with little relationship to the present and less to the future, this condition can slowly destroy a sense of place and a sense of identity. Therefore, a sense of place must be part of the past, present and future.

Surprise ★

A small town's sense of place must be kinetic, energy-filled "stuff." If the sense of place cannot change and adapt, it will probably be destroyed by its inflexibility. However, in order to be successful, the sense of place must be anchored by some "truth" that the town holds dear. This "truth" should be fixed and provide a sense of stability and security to the residents of the town. The sense of place should have a base that is static and a surface that is dynamic. Therefore, a sense of place must be rigid yet flexible.

The sense of place in small towns should be simple enough to create an ambiance that is easily comprehended by a visitor to the town. It should establish a spirit that the newcomer can take with him as a memory of what that community holds dear. However, a sense of

Moods

place should be complex enough to allow a life-long resident of the town to discover something new everyday about this ambiance. The sense of place should be comprehensible at every level. It should unfold like a well written novel, with many layers of meaning for all its readers, depending on what its readers need. Therefore, a sense of place must be simple, yet complex.

A sense of place must be part of the town at the largest social and physical scale. It must "hover over" the town at the general scale and establish a comprehensive climate for its residents. However, a sense of place must also penetrate to the details of a way of life in the town. It must be obvious in the tiniest architectural and social detail; from the window frame in a downtown store to the relationship of a pastor and a parishioner. Therefore, a sense of place must be general yet specific.

Significant Details

A small town also needs to have a sense of place that is unified. It should establish a character which translated into physical form should successfully knit the town into a unified whole. It must create a unity of image that makes the various parts of the town work in visual unison. For, truly, this unity of image is a unique characteristic of a small town and it can help to give its citizens a feeling of security. Because of their scale and density, urban areas seem unable to provide this unity of image. A small town has a responsibility to its citizens to provide this unity of image, and it should accept this responsibility seriously. However, it is important that a sense of place also provide diversity. Individual expression must be accommodated in small town living. People's ideas must be allowed to take some physical form. Too much unity produces sameness, boredom, and sterility. Too much diversity produces confusion, tension, and visual chaos. Therefore, a sense of place must provide unity yet diversity.

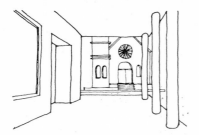 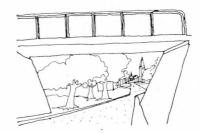

Here and There ◉

A sense of place in small towns must be part of the past, present, and future; it must be rigid yet flexible; it must be simple yet complex; it must be general yet specific; and it must provide unity yet diversity. As is obvious from these characteristics, a sense of place must be all things for all people, and yet it must be a unique quantity of "stuff" that only exists in one spot—in the small town in which it takes its shape. It must be special; it must be impossible to duplicate in any other location. Small towns have the capacity to be the physical manifestation of a true sense of place.

Mississippi Small Towns

Mississippi is a state whose cultural, economic, and social heritage is completely "bound up" with small towns. This state is blessed with a wealth of small towns, and yet we seem to know very little about what makes our towns fail or succeed as places for people.

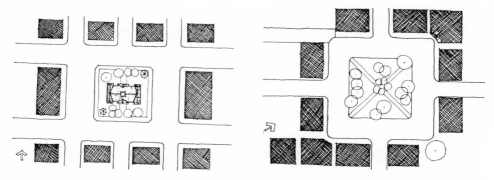

Plan of Holly Springs Square   Plan of Calhoun City Square

Mississippi has suddenly been rediscovered. We are "in." The Southern image is one that more and more people are finding attractive. The combination of America's traditional longing for the small town lifestyle coupled with Mississippi's rediscovery will soon result in a number of new pressures on Mississippi small towns.

These pressures of growth and prosperity can have a very positive effect on a community or they can destroy its sense of place. This growth and prosperity will automatically increase the income of Mississippi citizens, which will in turn increase the tax base for small towns. This will eventually result in better sewage systems, more street lights, new school additions, and street improvement.

But will an increase in personal income result in an increase in the quality of a sense of place? Will this growth and prosperity automatically create a better sense of place?

Probably not. The early effects of this prosperity on small towns can best be symbolized by The Strip.

Tension ⊖

The Strip and How to Live With It

The Strip is a phenomenon of twentieth century America. It is called by other names, including the bypass, the superhighway, Highway 12, 82, 16, or the four lane. It is, as it exists, the enemy of a sense of place, a sense of identity, and a sense of self.

Confusion ?

If a sense of place reflects a small town's uniqueness, the physical form of this uniqueness is certainly not The Strip. The Strip is the epitome of sameness. It is the same in the South, in the West, in the Northeast, in urban areas, in the suburbs, and in small towns. The Strip, full of branch banks, franchised food places, Big Macs, Whoppers, and used car lots symbolizes sameness of identity, not uniqueness. In this regard it is truly the enemy of a sense of place.

Yet, The Strip will not go away, and it should not. It is now an integral part of the economic, social, and political fabric of small town Mississippi. The need to find an appropriate role for The Strip is unquestionably the most pressing need for small towns if we are to gain—or keep—a true sense of place.

It is too easy to criticize The Strip and then say nothing more. It is obviously ugly, confusing, and unpleasant. Yet it serves a need for activity and convenience, and it fits the way we live today.

So, what should the role of The Strip be in small towns? And, more important, what should the role of public policy be regarding The Strip? The Strip is almost all right. It can be a part of the sense of place in small towns if some minor public policy decisions can be made.

First, the visual order of The Strip should strive to reflect some kind of uniqueness about the small town. Sameness of architecture and signage should be discouraged and uniqueness should be encour-

Enframement □

aged. This could be enforced by a "building review committee" which would judge the requests for building permits on The Strip. This committee should fight the franchised food image that produces the sameness of image found on The Strip. The new fast foods restaurants should be encouraged to find something special about the small town and reflect this uniqueness in their architecture and signage. These places should fit where they are.

There is an encouraging trend in this direction by some fast food chains. A few Hardee's and McDonald's restaurants are beginning to sacrifice their standard corporate images in order to fit more comfortably in their specific environments. These small town building review committees should encourage such fast food chains to adapt this idea to The Strip in small town America.

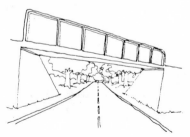

This action leads to the second public policy decision. Using the power of zoning and building permits, the small town should insure that The Strip not become social competition for downtown. A small town can have only one social center and the downtown must remain this center because it provides the best physical framework for social interaction. The Strip can provide healthy economic competition, but it should not be allowed to replace the downtown as the focus for social activity in the small town.

Specifically, public officials should set up a more specialized zoning format that would designate what commercial activities would be allowed on The Strip, in other words, a subset of the commercial zoning category. This would allow only certain types of commercial zoning along The Strip. Only those types of commercial ventures which cater to the automobile for success should be zoned "strip commercial." Included in this category are fast foods, gas stations, drive-in banks, etc. The pedestrian-oriented commercial activities should be located downtown, thus allowing social interaction downtown, and still insuring commercial success of business on The Strip.

These types of public policy decisions are "unAmerican" because they work against free enterprise as we have known it. But they can help to insure the sense of place against destruction for profit.

The Sense of Place or the Place and Its Sense

There is one part of small towns, particularly in Mississippi, that reflects the sense of place more than any other. A few years ago Michael Fazio, Hank Hildebrandt, and I wrote a book entitled *The Small Town as an Art Object*, and we named this part The Place, and its subset The Place Within The Place. This designation came from our concern for the illusive quality of a sense of place. The Place is known by several other terms: the central business district (CBD), the town center, the spot where the action is, and the downtown. Regardless of its name, it is the spot where the sense of place is mirrored or given form.

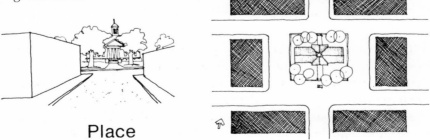

Place

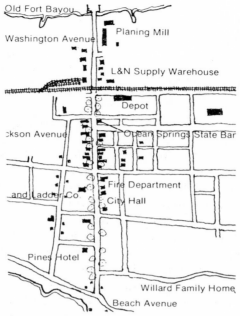

Old Fort Bayou

Washington Avenue

Planing Mill

L&N Supply Warehouse

Depot

Jckson Avenue

Ocean Springs State Bar

Fire Department
City Hall

and Ladder Co.

Pines Hotel

Willard Family Home

Beach Avenue

Plan of Ocean Springs: c. 1920.

Through our research at the Center for Small Town Research and Design at the School of Architecture, Mississippi State University, we have analyzed two basic forms which The Place takes in Mississippi small towns. There are several variations and combinations of these two forms, but their basic configurations are almost always obvious to the small town observer. The linear or link and the square or node are these two forms.

The linear or link Place is the most common in Mississippi. It can be a very strong form. It has the positive aspect of a strong axis. This strong axis can produce powerful image qualities such as closure, terminated vista, focal point, enframement, and anticipation. These image qualities can combine in the appropriate proportions to create a form that symbolizes a sense of place.

In order to create a form that is conducive to a sense of place, the linear Place form generally needs to link two important social/physical landmarks. Examples of these landmarks include the court-

Closure

Terminated Vista ●

house, the water tower, the First Baptist church, the community center, or the city hall. If the linear Place is not visually anchored on at least one of its ends, The Place will generally have the problem of a lack of focus or a lack of termination. This physical problem will have a major impact on the sense of place in the small town. The linear form is potentially strong and can be designed to work significantly in favor of a Place with a sense of place and a Place that makes sense.

The square or node form which The Place takes can be found in a few Mississippi towns. This form is usually referred to as the courthouse square. The Place which takes this square form is potentially very powerful. Its form produces image qualities such as visual venturi, pause, closure, enframement, focal point, and terminated vista. The Place which takes this form has more potential than the linear or link form for creating a strong visual order for the entire town, because small towns with a courthouse square have a grid street pattern that radiates from the square. This establishes the square as the physical, social, and economic focus for the town. This can help to create a strong sense of continuity for the visitor as well as the lifelong resident.

Visual Venturi   ▲

Pause ◇

However, the square Place form must symbolize a comfortable fit between the social and physical aspects of the town. If the courthouse square is the physical focus of town and Jitney Jungle Shopping Center is the social focus of town, then there will be no true sense of place. This battle is being waged in many small towns now, and the courthouse square is losing.

When a small town's Place declines, in favor of the shopping center on The Strip, it affects more than the downtown merchants' association. It directly affects the sense of place and that affects everyone.

Place Within Place

Place Within the Place

Every town center has a center. It is the heart of the physical and social interaction within the small town. It can be a bank, courthouse grounds, or a gas station. It should contain many image qualities, including pause, enframement, focal point, and significant details. Regardless of the form that The Place takes, The Place Within The Place is a nodal point. It must be a spot where people can comfortably meet, write, rush, think, relax, observe, depart, arrive, and know that they are someplace special. If you were asked to take one photograph to illustrate the sense of place in a small town, you should photograph The Place Within The Place.

In the linear Place form, if The Place Within The Place is just another spot along the linear form, it will not create a strong sense of place. However, if the linear form creates a strong axis that is terminated by The Place Within The Place, the result will always improve the quality of the sense of place. Regardless of the form which The

Anticipation 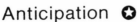   Level Change ⊞

Place takes, the focal point of The Place should be The Place Within The Place.

The square or nodal Place form has the automatic advantage of a predetermined location for its Place Within The Place. This is obviously the center of the square. This location produces a focal point for The Place and for the entire town.

Designing the Sense of Place by Analyzing the Fit

The most appropriate analytical methodology to use in designing for a sense of place in small towns is The Fit. In research at the Center for Small Town Research and Design, we have concluded that an analysis of the architectural or visual images of a small town gives only one view of a sense of place. A community can indeed be well-designed visually, with powerful images at appropriate places, and yet the sense of place feel uncomfortable to the residents because the physical order does not fit with the established social order of the small town. We have also researched towns whose social or mental impressions seemed to be honest and well-balanced, and yet the town's sense of place seemed to physically lack something important. Again in this example, there is not a good fit between the social order and the physical order of the town.

Deflected Vista ○

The Fit is simply a methodology for studying the relationship between the architectural or visual conception and the social or mental conception of the small town. Our conclusion is that the town whose social and architectural conceptions are congruent has a successful sense of place, while the town whose social conception and architectural conception are disparate has an unsuccessful sense of place.

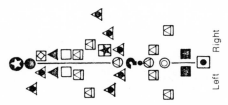

The small town designer involved in an analysis of The Fit in a small town goes through the following steps. The visual or architectural conception of the town is analyzed using the technique of scores.[1] These scores are much like musical scores which record experiences through the movement of time and space. Image elements and qualities are coded and recorded for analysis. Then information concerning the social or mental conception of the town is gathered using questionnaires, personal interviews, and town meetings. These are coded and recorded also using the scoring technique.

Then the architectural and social scores are analyzed to determine The Fit. The scores reveal places where The Fit is socially and architecturally congruent (example: around the courthouse square) and the places where The Fit is disparate (example: along The Strip). The small town designer can then attack those spots where The Fit can be adjusted, either architecturally or socially, to be more successful.

[1]For a more detailed discussion of the technique of scores, see *The Small Town as an Art Object*, p. 3.

The sense of place in a small town can be designed. It is certainly the most complex concept that any designer must deal with. However, the quality of a sense of place can be positively affected by appropriate design decisions at strategic places. The Fit is a method which can aid in making design decisions.

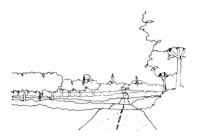

Thereness ◎

Small Town Designers

One factor which contributes to the complexity of a sense of place in small towns is the number and variety of people who are involved in designing for a sense of place. Rarely are the designers architecturally trained. In reality, small town designers are developers, aldermen, store owners, barbers, and garden club members. These people never make decisions that they think will damage the sense of place in their town. They are genuinely trying to improve their community. The decisions that they make, however, often improve one condition and yet harm the sense of place of the community.

Undulation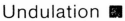

Two examples of this kind of decision-making should illustrate. The traffic in downtown is heavy and there is concern over the congestion. The board of mayor and aldermen decide that a bypass should be built to relieve the congestion in the downtown. (This is a decision designed to improve the quality of The Place). After completion, the bypass begins to sprout a number of gas stations and fast food restaurants. Shopping on the new Strip increases because it is convenient to the new suburbs growing along the edge of town. As the shopping increases, the major downtown store decides that since its lease has expired on its downtown location, it will relocate in a shopping center along The Strip. This significantly decreases the shopping downtown and a number of small shops close or move out of the downtown. This decreases pedestrian traffic downtown and the quality of the environment is allowed to deteriorate. So, a decision made to improve the quality of the downtown actually destroys it.

Here is another example to illustrate the complexity of designing for a sense of place. As downtown begins to decline as The Place for social and physical activity, the downtown merchants' association initiates a campaign to "modernize" the stores in the downtown. (This again is a design decision made to improve the quality of The Place.) A number of store owners respond to this idea and put brightly colored aluminum panels and screens over their building facades to "modernize" their stores. The result is that the unique qualities of their historical architecture are covered by a layer of aluminum. This destroys the uniqueness of The Place. The quality of the sense of place is harmed as a result of giving The Place the sameness of appearance found along The Strip.

Truncation ◉   Infinity ◉

These are two illustrations of a series of design decisions made for the "good of the town," which actually harm the quality of the sense of place.

The citizens of small town Mississippi must realize that they are indeed the designers of their towns. This realization is the first step to improving the quality of life and sense of place in small towns.

Small towns are the epitome of a sense of place. Although the sense of place in small towns is extremely complex, it is being manipulated or "designed" everyday by small town residents. If a community's sense of place works, it will go unnoticed. It is only when a sense of place doesn't work that we become aware of it. This very fragile condition means that the town whose sense of place is working is the town whose sense of place is the most susceptible to damage.

Small towns are places where the best of two worlds, man/nature and urban/rural, can create one community. They are places where sometimes the ideal is equal to the real. America must truly begin to design the sense of place in small towns. Our small towns are worth the effort.

The Development of Mississippi's Economy Since 1950

F. JOHN WADE

A theme in this conference has been change and its effect on our sense of place. My topic is the economic change which has occurred in Mississippi's economy since World War II, or more specifically since 1950. To those of us in middle age, 1950 has a real but "long ago and far away" quality. We remember the events of that time personally, and some of the things that happened to us during the early 50s are still vivid, detailed, and sharp in our memories. To the younger people in the audience 1950 probably seems more like "history." Truman was president, the Korean War started, and the United States was the supreme military and economic power in the world.

In 1950 Mississippi had a population of 2.2 million people—nearly the same as it has now. It was the poorest state in the Union, just as it is now. Cotton was the major agricultural product, just as today. But revolutionary changes in the state's economic base have occurred in the last 28 years. Mississippi is part of an American economy and social framework where one must run fast merely to keep up. It has not only matched the national changes but has evolved more swiftly than many other parts of the country.

The big change in the Mississippi economy since 1950 has been the shift from farms to factories. The most visible indicator of this change is employment. In 1950, 43 percent of the work force was employed in agriculture. Now the percentage is under seven. This employment decrease was associated with improved efficiency. In the immediate post-war period, it required 146 man-hours to produce a bale of cotton. By the early 1970s only 23 man-hours were required, a six-fold improvement. Output of soybeans per man-hour of labor has more than

179

doubled since 1950, and there has been an eight-fold decrease in manpower utilization for poultry production. Mississippi is now producing almost exactly the same total quantity of agricultural products as it did 28 years ago, but with less than 15 percent of the labor. Tractors have replaced mules, herbicides delivered by airplane have replaced hoes wielded by hand, and defoliants and mechanical pickers have replaced long lines of people. One theory of economic history is that all economic growth is ultimately derived from improved agricultural efficiency. When the entire population of a society is required to produce the food and clothing for that society, not many people remain to produce the artifacts and luxuries of an advanced civilization. But when only a small fraction of the work force is required for food production, the remainder is set free to build steel mills, produce automobiles, invent TV sets, launch rockets, and attend symposiums. The theory cannot be applied too rigorously to Mississippi since most of our agriculture is for cash crops, but the release of the labor force from agricultural pursuits has undoubtedly been a major economic force.

Most of the slack in the Mississippi labor force that resulted from the decline in agricultural employment was offset by growth in manufacturing and government. Manufacturing employment increased from 12 percent of the labor force in 1950 to a current level of approximately 26 percent. As we are all aware, government employment has also increased drastically since 1950. The number of government employees more than doubled from about 8 percent to nearly 20 percent. Part of the increase in government employees comes from the increased involvement by government in regulating all areas of life and in providing welfare to larger groups of people. However, the government category also includes teachers. More Mississippians are in school now, and the number of teachers in the state has risen from about 16,000 in 1950 to over 30,000 today.

From 1950 until the early 1960s the loss of farm jobs in Mississippi exceeded the gain in nonagricultural jobs. This net loss in employment was the main factor in the state's lack of total population growth. Hundreds of thousands of Mississippians have left the state since 1950. Actually more native-born Mississippians are living outside the borders of the state than within Mississippi itself.

As we will see later, blacks, who had held most of the disappearing agricultural jobs, constituted the largest group of migrants from the state.

Manufacturing Employment

Manufacturing is the single largest employment category in Mississippi and has been since about 1960 when, for the first time, Mississippi "balanced agriculture with industry." Growth in manufacturing output is the major stimulus to growth in other jobs and in the population: manufactured products are mostly sold outside the borders of Mississippi and, therefore, bring money into the state. Our agricultural products, tourism, and, of course, many federal government programs also bring money into Mississippi. But manufacturing is the largest of these "economic prime movers" and has the most potential for expansion.

In 1950 only about 12 percent of the labor force—about 59,000 people—were engaged in manufacturing, and about half of these were producing lumber, millwork, or other simple wooden products. Food processing and garment plants accounted for another one-fourth of these manufacturing workers, with the remainder scattered among a wide variety of classifications. The lumber yards were there because of Mississippi's forest resources, and the garment plants had moved in because of the availability of cheap labor. Neither kind of establishment requires much capital investment, industrial support services, or skilled labor; and neither kind offers attractive career possibilities for many of its employees. In short, the manufacturing base was small, primitive, and limited in the careers it could offer its employees. By 1976 the employment mix in manufacturing had changed substantially. Lumber and wood products had declined to less than 10 percent of the total, and many durable goods industries with higher capital and technical requirements had grown to significant levels. Among these are transportation equipment, which includes the Ingalls shipyard, furniture, electrical machinery, fabricated metals, and nonelectrical machinery. The manufacturing product mix is still lopsided when compared to that of the United States, however. As a general statement, Mississippi's largest manufacturing employment categories are those which pay the lowest wages. Mississippi still has the second lowest average manufacturing wage in the United States, with North Carolina being the only state with a lower average.

Throughout virtually the entire 28-year period being considered, Mississippi has not had enough jobs to accommodate its working age population. As a result, the labor force participation rate has been low—that is, the ratio of workers to total population. In 1950 this ratio was 35 percent; it has since risen to 40 percent, nearly equal to that of the U.S. The low participation rate, lack of jobs, and the steady decline in agricultural employment all have contributed to the low wage rate in the state.

Income

In 1950 Mississippi had the lowest per capita income of all the states. It still does. Per capita income is the number derived by taking the total annual income of all families and individuals in an area and dividing this total by the population. For instance, if a family of four had a total annual income of $20,000, the per capita income of that family would be $5,000. In 1950 the per capita income in Mississippi was $755, just about half of the U.S. average. In 1977 the figure had increased to $5,030, nearly three-fourths of the U.S. average. Of course a dollar now is worth only about 40 percent of what it was in 1950; but even taking that into account, the average Mississippian has nearly 2.7 times the purchasing power today that he had in 1950. We are still the poorest state in the nation, but we are nearly three times as well off as we were 28 years ago.

For most people, it is easier to relate to median family income than to per capita income. (Median family income has been growing faster than per capita income in Mississippi because incomes are now more evenly distributed between rich and poor families.) In 1950 the median family income for families in Mississippi was $1,198. Half of the households in the state had incomes of less than $100 per month. And three-fourths of the households had incomes under $200 per month. A dollar in 1950 had two and a half times its present value, so the equivalent today would be for half of our families to have annual incomes of under $3,000 and three-fourths to have incomes under

$6,000. By comparison, the actual median family income today in Mississippi is about $13,000. This is really a startling gain. Think of how a family can live today on $13,000 and how it can live on $3,000. If the figures are broken down by race, we find that the average white family in 1950 had an income equivalent, in *today's purchasing power*, of about $400 per month, the average black family about $200 per month. There were no food stamps then either, although many rural families raised much of their own food.

We can identify a number of reasons for Mississippi's being the poorest state in the nation, statistically. Of course the state's economy was completely disrupted and temporarily destroyed during the Civil War, but this was also true of other Southern states. There are other reasons. One is the geographical location of the large cities that serve as financial and distribution centers for much of Mississippi. Three of these cities are outside our borders. If the state boundaries were changed to include Memphis, New Orleans, and Mobile, Mississippi would no longer be the poorest state. Memphis is sited on the first high ground on the east bank of the Mississippi River north of Vicksburg. The site of New Orleans is the nearest practical location to the mouth of the Mississippi, and Mobile developed because of its natural advantages as a port. So for many years Mississippi had no large city to provide a focus for capital formation, finance, and trade. This is still partially true.

Another reason for Mississippi's low per capita income is its former dependence upon an agricultural economic base. For most of its history the state has been almost totally dependent upon agriculture and forestry. In the Delta where the plantation system of cotton culture reached its fullest expression, the economy also depended on large quantities of black labor. This dependence of wealth upon land ownership and upon black labor encouraged a social and economic structure which placed a high value on stability and which resisted change as something unwelcome. Farmers had to cope with unpredictable weather and unpredictable cotton prices. But they could at least try to keep everything else stable. In other more urbanized sections of the country, change has traditionally been viewed as the very life blood of progress, but not in Mississippi during the first half of the twentieth century. This rigidity is the dark side of the Mississippian's reverence for tradition and human values, which is part of the meaning of the phrase "sense of place." It is also true that education often is perceived to have relatively little economic value in an agricultural society. As a book of the 1940s put it, Mississippi farmers put their faith in God, next year's crop, and the Democratic party.

In the last 20 years the pattern of economic and social rigidity has been breaking up, both under new economic forces and through the intervention of the federal government. Whatever else the effect of these changes, they have certainly created economic benefits.

Population Change in Mississippi

Between 1950 and 1970 Mississippi's population remained virtually constant at about 2.2 million people. Since 1970 the population has apparently grown by four or five percent. According to the best estimates the state now contains 2.4 million people. The recent population growth may be due to the fact that, finally, new nonagricultural job opportunities are being created at a much faster rate than agricultural jobs are being lost. But the stable total population figures mask the fact that over the last 28 years an estimated 1.5 million Mississippians have left the state. By race these emigrants were nearly equally divided between blacks and whites. Although blacks and whites left Mississippi in nearly equal numbers, the patterns of this movement differed. Blacks tended to move north to Chicago, Detroit, St. Louis, and other large cities while whites generally moved to nearby southern states. Offsetting this exodus was a counterbalancing inflow of whites, mostly from other southern states. At least through 1970, however, migration of blacks into Mississippi was insignificant. Many people believe that since 1970 blacks have returned to the South in much larger numbers. But the blacks who do return are often professionals or in leadership roles and therefore are more visible in their communities.

The heavy out migration of Mississippians combined with a high birth rate has created a peculiar age distribution within the state, especially among blacks. Most people who move to a new place to live do so shortly after they complete school in their late teens or early twenties. So the population distribution in Mississippi has been characterized by a large number of children, relatively few young adults, and relatively large numbers of older people. This distribution has been particularly true of the black population in Mississippi. In 1970 there were twice as many ten-year-olds in Mississippi as thirty-year-olds. For blacks this ratio was over 3 to 1. This high ratio of dependents to wage earners accentuates the economic problems of many families.

The Effects of Change

We have an army of statistics showing how the Mississippi economy has changed since 1950. The state has shifted from an agricultural society to one based on manufacturing. The purchasing power of the average family has quadrupled. A group of people nearly as large as our total population has left the state, and hundreds of thousands of new people have come in. What has this done to our quality of life and to our sense of place? If today you take a leisurely trip the length of Mississippi, you can stop at Corinth to see telephones manufactured and *National Geographic* magazine printed. You can see pool tables manufactured in Booneville, power tools in Tupelo, chemicals in Aberdeen, and electric motors in Columbus. If you stop in Meridian, you can see a locally-owned business employing 300 people making audio systems for rock bands and other commercial entertainers. In Quitman, you can visit a large plant making knit underwear and pajamas; in Laurel, transformers; in Hattiesburg, a manufacturer of trailers for LP gas; and in Bay St. Louis, a plant making titanium dioxide from imported Australian ore. Towns like Shubuta, Sherman, Preston, Prairie, McCool, Mantachee, and Maben all have manufacturing plants. A friend of mine from New Orleans once remarked, "Mississippi is the most amazing place. You drive along through the woods on some back country road and all of a sudden you come to a plant where they are making electric can openers for Sears Roebuck or something." Most of the people in all these cities and towns have TV sets. You don't go far without finding a Pizza Hut, McDonald's, or Holiday Inn. You can place a telephone call from Sylvareno, Mississippi, to Singapore for $9.

The winds of change are bringing economic growth with all of its problems and opportunities. Although we are partly at the mercy of this change, to some extent we can manage it and channel its direction, if only we can agree on our goals and work toward them. We can reap the rewards of economic growth while maintaining the values embodied in the phrase "a sense of place." Now that the South has been rechristened by the media as the Sun Belt and is credited for virtues which the North has lost or never had, change will come even faster during the next generation than it did in the last 28 years. It is important that Mississippians work together to make this change as benign as possible. This is not an easy task. Frequently, we do not agree on what we are trying to accomplish. When our goals are clear we often lack a strategy for bringing them into reality. Sometimes we know what to do but lack the resources to carry out our plan. But let me at least suggest a few goals.

First, we need to preserve the vitality of the smaller cities and towns in the state. There are more people in Mississippi and in the country as a whole who prefer small town living than there are job opportunities in small towns. This is one reason why wage rates are lower in nonmetropolitan areas. Mississippi's industrial development programs and incentives need to be focused on medium sized and small communities throughout the entire state, not just in Jackson, along the coast, and in a few other large cities.

Second, we need to emphasize the development of Mississippi owned and managed businesses. While plant branches of large companies provide "instant jobs," in the long run we have not gained much if we have merely moved people from monotonous, routine agricultural work to monotonous, routine assembly line jobs. We need career opportunities for people to grow into managerial, sales, technical, and scientific positions. This means that we must have Mississippi-based companies, not merely branch plants. So we need to encourage the formation of small business and industry so that some of these companies, someday, will be big business.

Third, we need to improve the education and skill of young people. We are making good progress here, but our children still score below national norms on standardized tests, and there is still a need for more diversified and extensive academic and vocational training.

Fourth, we place emphasis on maintaining the good environmental quality of our state. For years we have heard it said that, because

Mississippi is later in its development than the rest of the country, we have the opportunity to avoid the mistakes of others. And yet, we seem to go right on repeating the mistakes of others. Urban growth creates junkiness and traffic problems, we bulldoze away trees to save a little money on construction costs, and we do all the other things which create urban problems. We can avoid some of these problems of growth, however, if we pay attention to allocating land for recreational use, if we require esthetically pleasing architectural standards for commercial and industrial development, if we plan our transportation systems to handle future growth, and if our citizens and government officials place value on beauty, order, and tranquility as well as on immediate business opportunities.

A fifth and final point is that we must move in directions which will allow blacks to improve their economic status. The average black family in Mississippi has only about half the income of the average white family. The disparity between blacks and whites is greater here than in any other state. This economic problem is intertwined with a number of social problems having to do with education, health, and aspirations. These are problems not merely for blacks but for blacks and whites alike, and the answers are not easy.

These five goals are difficult ones, and within a free enterprise system, public policy can do only so much. Still, if we work and make progress in these directions for the next two decades, we should be able to look back from the end of the twentieth century and say, "Mississippi is a great place to live, just like always." Of course there never has been a time when it was "just like always." Our state has been changing and will keep changing. Our task is to make it change in the right way.

MISSISSIPPI EMPLOYMENT TRENDS AND GOALS, 1950–2000

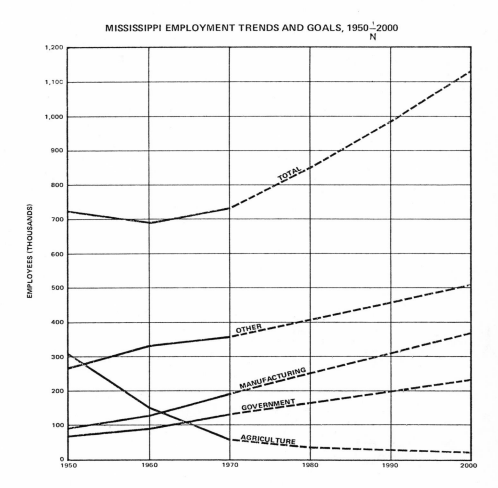

SOURCE: U. S. Bureau of the Census, Census of Population, 1960 and 1970, *General Social and Economic Characteristics: Mississippi.*
Mississippi Research and Development Center estimates.

Myths of Mississippi's Rural Landscape:
Change and Challenge

W. THEODORE MEALOR, JR.

We are all essentially terrestrial creatures identified with a particular town or area. No matter where we travel or what we do, there is in the back of our minds a place we call home. We may have several "homes," each identified in time and space with other human beings and with important events. Unlike our forefathers, our spatial identity can change more easily as a result of education, travel, and occupation. Even though the mobility that is ours in the last one-third of the twentieth century enables us to develop identity with new places, we can and do identify through memories with those previous places that were "home." Our mind usually reflects upon those places through eyes that recall landscapes and people as they were, not as they are today. We are usually shocked at changes that have occurred to a place from which we have been absent for any length of time. Even if we do have an intimate, daily relationship with a place, we may be appalled at the changes that are taking place.

As important as our identification with a place, or our memories of it, is our perception of places where we have never been—a lack of sense of place. Maybe those of us who are not native to Mississippi but who moved here with an erroneous perception of the state would call this nonsense of place. The fact is that we often do not understand the character of a place nor recognize the forces operative there that cause change. Particularly poignant are the cases in which our perception of a given location is so out of date or so erroneous as to be, in fact, nonsense. It is not necessary for us to "like" a place in order to have an understanding of it. It is necessary, however, for us to know the character traits of a place in order to appreciate it and to comprehend its role as a spatial entity.

189

In many ways Mississippi has been one of those places whose "sense of place" has been misunderstood. Not only are outsiders guilty of erroneous perception of Mississippi, but many of her native children are antagonistic toward the state. Their posture is one of defensiveness, not one of pride. In the case of the outsider, the perception may be based on out of date data. In the case of the native, there may be a perception of what is occurring elsewhere without an understanding of the change that is occurring at home. As a colleague of mine pointed out to a group of University of Southern Mississippi students, Mississippi is a state with many good things going for it, a place of growth, a place to dignify, not a place to deride.

Mississippi, of course, shares the heritage of other Southern states. It is perceived by outsiders in much the same way as other Southern states were perceived until recently. The image of states such as Tennessee and Georgia have changed during the last two decades principally because of the growth of such metropolitan areas as Memphis and Atlanta. Certainly Florida is not considered in the same light as other Southern states are. In essence, the nation is realizing that the South and Mississippi aren't really what they were thought to be. David H. Donald, the Harvard historian, made the following statement shortly after Jimmy Carter was inaugurated:

My Northern-born friends have been celebrating the Democrats' nomination of Jimmy Carter as a signal that at last the South is ready to return to the Union. Putting aside the bitterness of the Civil War and the burden of race, Southerners of Carter's generation are, supposedly, representatives of a New South, a South that accepts and emulates the values of the North.

No view of the Carter phenomenon could be more incorrect. It is more accurate to see Carter's nomination as further evidence that, a century after the Civil War and Reconstruction, the United States has finally decided to rejoin the South.[1]

Donald continues by detailing the influence of Southern writers on American literature during the last few decades. He comments on the role that Southerners have played in the political arena of this nation since World War II and notes especially that all national politicians actively court the Southern vote. Attitudes and values long ascribed to Southerners and scorned or even condemned by Northerners are now

[1]David H. Donald, "From Dixie, With Love and Grits," *The Commercial Appeal* [Memphis], 3 Sept. 1976, p. 5.

part of the national value system. Among these values are individualism, a sense of place, and evangelical Protestantism—all of which are projected by Jimmy Carter of Plains, Georgia.[2] Possibly, then, many of the values we have felt called upon to defend from "yankee aggression" are actually points of pride. To this idea Donald added, "Somewhere the ghost of John C. Calhoun must be grimly smiling at this belated national acceptance of his view of Southern superiority."[3]

As part of the "Sun Belt" Mississippi has felt, to some extent, the change in the national perception of the South. Yet Mississippi has not experienced the influx of outsiders, such as has Florida, nor can any of its cities be classified as regional or industrial centers such as Atlanta or Birmingham. Still, changes have occurred, not only in the attitude and values of Mississippians, but also in the rural landscape. Changes made in the Mississippi landscape are a continuing process resulting from man's adjustment to a variety of economic and environmental forces. Still, with sequential changes in landscape patterns, Mississippians have maintained identity with and respect for land and place. For this attribute all Mississippians can be proud.

The patterns that are visible on the Mississippi landscape in 1978 are a result of a dynamic set of forces initiated from both within and without the state's boundaries. From the perspective of the last quarter of the twentieth century, the changes that have taken place since Europeans first entered the area have increased exponentially, with the most profound changes occurring in this century. Changes in landscape patterns have been predicated on a mixture of economic, technical, and political forces generated from outside the state and working concomitantly with the cultural values within the state. These are numerous, complex and interactive, but three forces are easily identifiable: (1) the development of hard-surfaced roads, (2) changes in national agricultural policies, and (3) urbanization.

Transportation

If economic and social changes were to occur in Mississippi during

[2]Merle C. Prunty, "Two American Souths: The Past and the Future," *Southeastern Geographer*, XVII (May 1977), 1-24.
[3]Donald, p. 5.

the twentieth century, they had to be preceded by the development of a viable transportation system. Out of some 38,700 miles of public roads in Mississippi in 1909, only 185 miles were considered improved and these primarily were constructed of gravel or a sand-clay mixture.[4] Although highway improvement continued, encouraged by the Federal Aid Road Act of 1916, it was not until the decade after World War II that the present network was developed. Figure 1 shows the sparsity of all-weather highways that existed in 1939 when a significantly large portion of the state lay more than three miles from a paved road. Today only a few isolated areas are more than three miles from an all-weather road (Fig. 2).

Paralleling the increase in all-weather public roads, now totaling some 66,000 miles, has been the increase in both volume of traffic and weight of traffic. More than 1.2 million vehicles are registered in the state, and the average Mississippian travels more than 5,200 miles annually.[5] The legal weight limit for motor carriers on all federal aid roads is equal to or greater than 57,650 pounds with a maximum of 73,280 pounds. Until 1970, the legal weight limit was only 30,000 pounds.[6]

The construction of black top roads signaled the beginning of pervasive changes in the rural landscape of Mississippi. Prior to the introduction of automobiles and all-weather roads, travel was limited to the immediate vicinity of one's residence. Traveling by horse or on foot meant that only three to five miles could be covered in one hour's time. Because of lack of mobility, people in rural areas tended to be self sufficient for most of their necessities. Also, because of limited travel time, retail outlets, such as the crossroads general store and the plantation commissary, tended to be rather evenly distributed across agricultural areas at three to five mile intervals.

The advent of the black top road changed this pattern. Now one could travel 15 to 30 miles in an hour, bypassing the crossroads

[4]Thomas D. Clark, "Changes in Transportation," in *A History of Mississippi*, ed. Richard A. McLemore (Hattiesburg, Miss: Univ. and College Press of Miss., 1973), II, 285.

[5]W. T. Mealor, "Transportation and Communication," in *Atlas of Mississippi*, ed. Ralph D. Cross and Robert W. Wales (Jackson, Miss.: Univ. Press of Miss., 1974), pp. 137-148.

[6]Clark, p. 285.

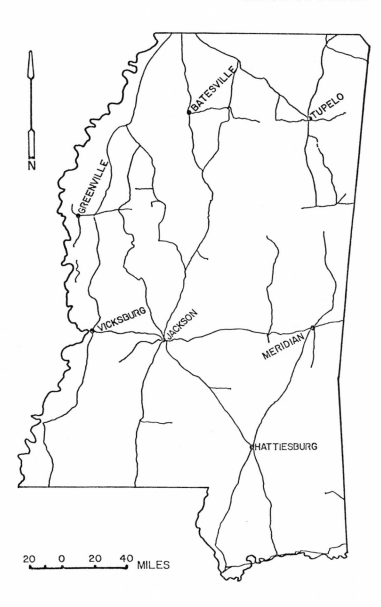

Figure 1: **Mississippi Road Map, Paved Roads 1939**

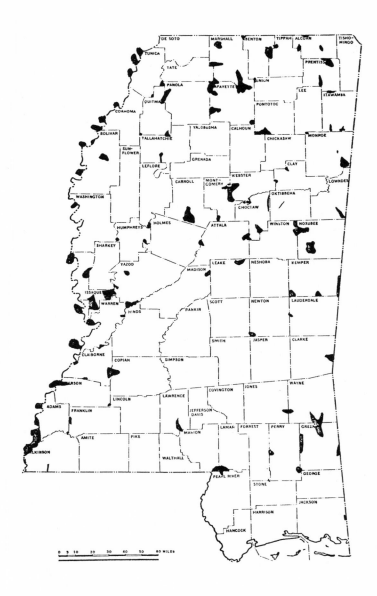

Figure 2: **Areas in Mississippi Three Miles or more from a Paved Road**

general store while going to a larger trade center. The black top road and the shift in travel patterns by rural residents not only caused the economic demise of many of these small trading places; they laid the foundation for population out migration from rural areas. On the other hand, those small communities that were advantageously served by black top roads and that had developed a wider array of retail and social services became increasingly more important. Now they served larger hinterlands. A Saturday afternoon would find these towns crowded with farmers and their families, Model A's and Chevrolets, who had come from 10 to 15 miles away.

Intensification of the transportation network and advancement in automotive technology, coupled with new recreational and leisure opportunities, have created present travel behavioral patterns as different from those of the 1930s as from those of the 1890s. With four lane highways and shorter routes, routes that bypass medium size and even large cities, one is able to travel 50 to 70 miles in an hour. The following series of maps depicts trade area hierarchies for central places in Mississippi with populations greater than 1,000. Figure 3 indicates the 16 largest trade areas in the state. The average range from the central place at this level is 27 miles. The second level within this hierarchy consists of 25 cities, all but one having 10,000 or more residents. The range for these cities is 21 miles (Fig. 4). The next level, containing 72 cities, has an average trade area radius of 13 miles while the last level, having 130 places, has a range of nine miles (Figs. 5 and 6). Note, however, in Figure 6 (which includes all places of 1,000 or more population) that trade centers are spatially more dense in the major agricultural areas of the Yazoo Basin and south central Mississippi than in other areas of the state. In these areas the range for service is about six miles while in other areas of the state, particularly the southwestern and north central portions, the spatial range of trade area services is approximately 11 miles.[7]

Although railroads played a role in the intercity movement of people, they have been more important in moving freight. With the truck, railroads have given Mississippians access to new markets and, of

[7]University Consortium of Mississippi, *Analysis of A Statewide Integrated Transportation System*, Task IV: "Theoretical Analysis of Transportation Network and Population" (Jackson, Miss.: Mississippi Research and Development Center, 1976).

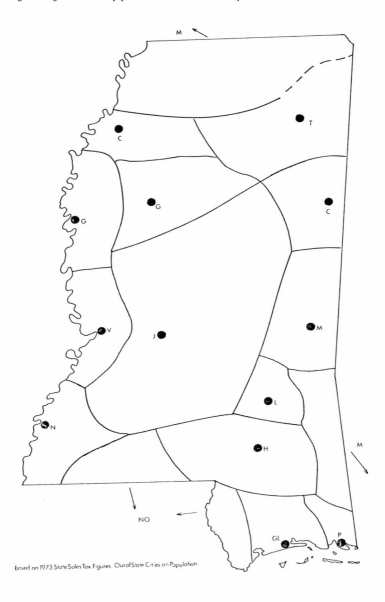

Based on 1973 State Sales Tax Figures Out of State Cities on Population

Figure 3: **Mississippi Trade Areas 16 Cities**

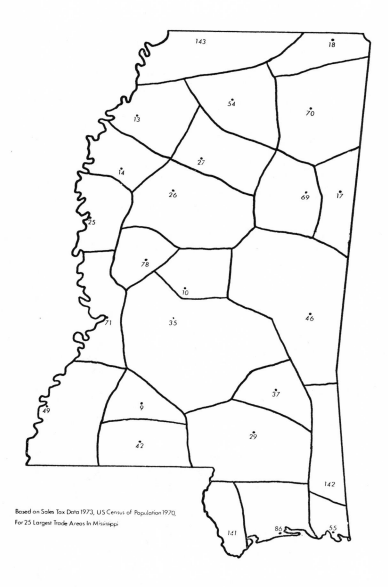

Based on Sales Tax Data 1973, US Census of Population 1970,
For 25 Largest Trade Areas In Mississippi

Figure 4: **Mississippi Trade Areas 25 Cities**

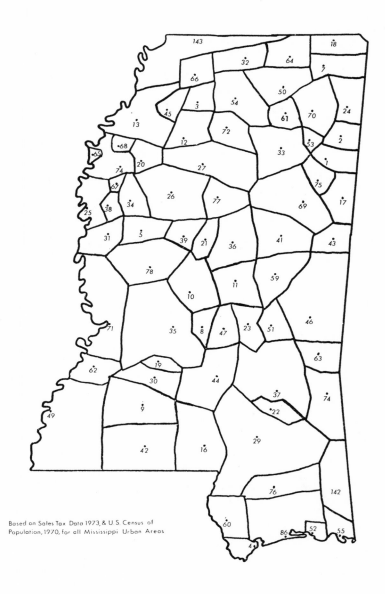

Based on Sales Tax Data 1973, & U.S. Census of
Population, 1970, for all Mississippi Urban Areas

Figure 5: **Mississippi Trade Areas 72 Cities**

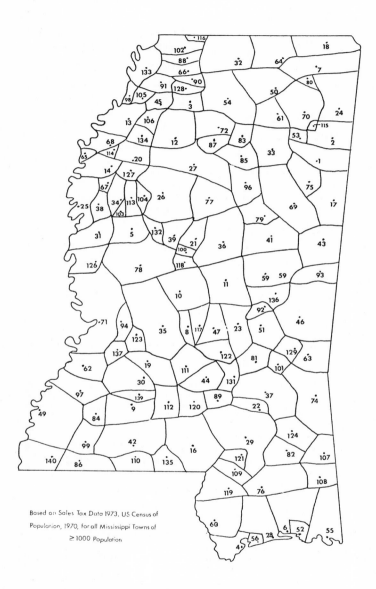

Based on Sales Tax Data 1973, US Census of
Population, 1970, for all Mississippi Towns of
≥ 1000 Population

Figure 6: **Mississippi Trade Areas 130 Cities**

course, Mississippi has become a new area for many out of state businesses. This has meant new economic opportunities for Mississippians, as products of the state flow out and needed and desired goods come in. However, the increased connectivity and economic interaction that Mississippi is now experiencing with the rest of the nation have been dependent upon spatial and economic adjustments of the agricultural sector to significant national programs such as the Agricultural Adjustment Acts (AAA) of the 1930s and subsequent land diversion programs.

National Agricultural Policies

In 1935 the per capita personal income of Mississippians averaged 37 per cent of that of the nation as a whole.[8] By 1975 Mississippi's average per capita income was 67 percent of the national average.[9] The relative increase in per capita personal income of Mississippians is related to the Agricultural Adjustment Acts beginning in 1933. These acts did not free Mississippians from dependence on agriculture; they did enable Mississippi farmers to obtain higher prices for their agricultural commodities, thereby initiating a series of events that caused profound changes both on the rural landscape and in life styles. The objectives of the Agricultural Adjustment Act of 1933 were the following:

(1) To establish . . . such balance between the production and consumption of agricultural commodities . . . as will reestablish prices to farmers at a level that will give agricultural commodities a purchasing power with respect to articles farmers buy, equivalent to the purchasing powers . . . in the base period [August 1909—July 1914].
(2) To approach such equality of purchasing power by gradual correction of present inequalities therein at as rapid a rate as is deemed feasible.[10]

The Agricultural Adjustment Act of 1933 and subsequent agricultural legislation set price support norms (parity prices) that assured in-

[8]Middle South Services, Inc., *The Changing Middle South: Basic Economic Data*, 13th ed. (New Orleans: Middle South Services, 1972).
[9]U. S. Department of Commerce, Bureau of Economic Analysis, *Survey of Current Business* (Washington, D.C.: GPO, 1976).
[10]Agricultural Adjustment Act, Public Law 10, 73rd Cong., 1st sess., Title I, Section (2) 1933, as quoted in Rainer Schickele, *Agricultural Policy, Farm Programs and National Welfare* (Lincoln: Univ. of Nebraska Press, 1954), p. 190.

creased income for producers of certain basic crops (initially cotton, wheat, tobacco, and corn for feed). The act and subsequent legislation set acreage restrictions on production and, in the case of tobacco, on quantity per acre. The net result of these acts was two-fold: (1) they increased the spendable income of farmers, and (2) they essentially froze the distributional patterns of the involved allotted crops.

The Agricultural Adjustment Acts were the first step in breaking the crop-lien system of credit that had prevented economic growth in Mississippi and the South. The crop-lien system, a product of the Reconstruction era, was a credit system based upon loans made in late winter against crops to be planted in spring and harvested in the fall. When the crops were "made" everyone from tenant to banker was repaid—if the crops were abundant. If the yields were poor, the tenants could not pay the landowner, who in turn could not pay the local banker, who could not pay his creditors. In order to continue, the landowner would have to mortgage his land—the land on which indebted tenants and sharecroppers farmed. This system placed tremendous pressure on the land, for it appeared to the landowner and tenant alike that the only way to get out of debt was to cultivate more land more intensively.

Concerning the crop-lien system, Merle C. Prunty makes the following observations: "Paradoxically, a land whose climate and soils placed few limitations on economic production of a great variety of field, forage, and tree crops, was restricted to growth of those few commodities which satisfied the monetary constraints of the crop-lien and farm tenancy systems. In no other section of the nation was it necessary to mortgage a crop or commodity that did not exist to provide for a second issue loan to individuals who possessed no capital goods with which to secure it."[11] The entire system, therefore, was based on a collective region-wide personal faith in God and man that all would survive. But the realities of the system were that the South, including Mississippi, was in debt to itself and its northern brethren.

The effects of the crop-lien system were felt by the merchants in all

[11]"The Agrarian Contribution to Recent Southern Industrialization," in *The South A Vade Mecum*, ed. James Heyl (Washington, D. C.: Association of American Geographers, 1973), pp. 107-108.

sizes of Mississippi communities, for retail sales were dependent on how much money the crops generated. Like the bankers and landowners, many merchants, particularly those in farm oriented businesses, were accustomed to selling "on loan" in the spring and collecting after harvest. Whenever the farmer suffered a crop failure, the merchant suffered also.

In establishing price supports and parity, the Agricultural Adjustment Acts provided protection for the American farmer from international competition. Prior to the AAA Mississippi cotton producers, for instance, could not pay wages any greater than those received by laborers in the cotton fields of India or Egypt, nor could the economic rents accruing to their lands regularly exceed those of landowners in other parts of the world. In other words, to stay in business the Mississippi farmer had to compete on the international market. This situation reinforced landuse patterns and tenancy practices established in the capital deficient South of the Reconstruction era. After the AAA was implemented, the Mississippi farmer did not have to compete with low wage/low cost foreign agricultural products on the international market while buying high cost consumer goods and equipment from American industries protected by tariffs.

With more money in his pocket, the Mississippi landowner could afford to modernize his farm and to buy those consumer goods that heretofore had been unavailable to him. The "extra change" in his pocket meant that he was a viable market for a host of manufacturers, thereby encouraging industrial growth in Mississippi and elsewhere in the South.

Not only did the AAA enable the landowner to accrue capital, it provided the sharecropper with increased income, income that could be used to pay debts and to secure transportation to northern industrial cities where jobs were available. The beginning of the end of the sharecropper tenancy system came with the AAA not because the acts resulted in push forces, such as mechanization, at least not initially, but because of increased income to the individual tenant, providing him with the means to pay his debts and to move to areas offering greater economic opportunity.

In retrospect, when viewed in light of U.S. farm policies prior to the AAA and in relationship with the international agricultural scene, the much maligned sharecropping system was the only agricultural production system that would have worked. The poverty experienced in the pre-World War II Mississippi agricultural community was caused not by the sharecropping system, but by competition with cheap labor found in some of the most poverty stricken areas of the world.

Landowners in Mississippi prior to World War II realized the inefficiencies of the sharecropping system. Like their forefathers immediately after the Civil War, they preferred a cash wage labor system. And like them, they did not have the capital to support this type of labor. Not only did the sharecropping system produce a debt-ridden society, it produced a distinct pattern on the landscape. The sharecropping system engendered small fields and dispersed housing; it increased mileage of farm roads, the number of fences, and the amount of wasteland; and it dispersed the cultivating power—the mule—from central managerial control. All of these attributes of the system led to inefficiencies of production. Until the mid 1930s the trend was to more farms of smaller acreage. In 1930 there were 312,663 farms in Mississippi; in 1935 there were 311,688. This downward trend has continued, and in 1974 there were only 53,620 farms in Mississippi. Concomitantly, the trend to smaller farms was reversed and average size of farms has increased from 21 acres in 1935 to 267 acres in 1974. Accompanying this post 1935 trend, accelerated after World War II and virtually completed by the early 1960s, has been the demise of the sharecropper system.[12]

The decrease in number of farms enumerated in the various years since 1935 does not necessarily mean the demise of the family farm. The reduction in numbers does indicate a decrease in sharecrop and tenant farms that traditionally have been enumerated as separate entities regardless of land ownership and management characteristics. Replacing tenant farms are farming operations characterized by consolidated landholdings having large fields, centralized management, centralized control of cultivating power, and cash wage labor. The trend towards capital intensive cropping methods using large inputs of mechanized power has replaced the labor intensive

[12]U. S. Bureau of the Census, *Census of Agriculture*, for 1935, 1940, 1945, 1950, 1954, 1959, 1964, 1969, and 1974.

systems, and since the late 1950s and early 1960s has been a "push force" encouraging people to move from the land.

The shift to mechanized farming is now well established. It is not uncommon for a single piece of equipment, such as a cotton picker or grain combine, to cost a minimum of $50,000, and few Mississippi farmers have equipment inventories of less than $25,000. To return to capital the investment made, the equipment must be used efficiently. Technology has created the means to cultivate more and more land, but the land, particularly farms having allotted crop acreage, is not readily available. This circumstance has led to reorganization of farm landholdings and managerial systems.

Aiken states that enlarging the scale of farming operations is the chief means of supporting machinery inventories.[13] However, the acreage expansion of such cash crops as cotton has been restricted by the Federal crop allotment programs. The AAA based allotments on "histories" of production on a particular landholding. Even with modifications, the allotments to individual landholdings are more suited to the labor intensive production system of pre-World War II than to the mechanized systems of the 1970s. Aiken indicates that between 50 and 250 acres of cotton are needed to justify ownership of a one-row mechanical picker, whereas the average allotment in Mississippi is less than 31 acres.[14]

In order to acquire sufficient allotment acreage to support equipment inventories, the farmer must either buy land or rent land. Since the purchase of farm land does not necessarily provide the farmer with sufficient allotment acreage, his only viable alternative is to lease allotments of several landholdings. The leasing of farms or allotments from many individuals by one operator has given rise to multiple-tenancy. Multiple-tenancy provides sufficient land for viable farming operations and allows the operator to concentrate his capital in the purchase of equipment rather than in land.

Inspection of census data reveals that the trend to multiple unit

[13]Charles S. Aiken, "The Fragmented Neo-Plantation: A New Type of Farm Operation in the Southeast," *Southeastern Geographer,*XI (April 1971), 46.
[14]Aiken, p. 47; U. S. Department of Agriculture, *Agricultural Statistics for 1976* (Washington, D.C.: GPO, 1976).

operations is increasing in Mississippi.[15] Table 1 shows operational types for 1940, 1964, and 1974. The term "part-owner" as used by the Census indicates that the individual both owns and rents land used in his operation. It is not uncommon for one farmer to control the operations on several different landholdings yet be counted as one farm by the Census. The production of cotton in Mississippi is indicative of the trend to multiple-tenancy. In 1974 the average acreage of cotton under the control of one operator was 150 acres. Based on the average allotment size for that year, this figure would mean that one operator, the multiple-tenant, would be producing cotton from allotments assigned to five different landholdings.

The phenomena of multiple-tenancy is partially a response to the unavailability of land. Between 1940 and 1974 Mississippi experienced a decline of 237,472 farms.[16] Tenant operations accounted for 79.6 percent of this decrease. However, since the tenants did not own the land, being only operators of a small portion of a larger landholding, the actual number of cadasters did not decrease significantly.

Table 1

Farm Control by Operator Type in Mississippi, 1940, 1964 and 1974

Operator Type	1940	Per Cent	1964	Per Cent	1974	Per Cent
Full-Owners	88,697	30.5	64,557	59.2	38,683	72.1
Part-Owners	8,569	2.9	18,542	17.0	11,113	20.7
Tenants	192,819	66.2	25,634	23.4	3,824	7.1
Managers	1,007	.4	408	.4	NA	—
TOTAL	291,092		109,145		53,620	

Source: U.S. Census of Agriculture, 1940, 1964, 1974.

Retirement and death of landowners do not necessarily result in the sale of farms. Heirs to rural landholdings are reluctant to part with the old "homeplace." In many cases they become "sunrise" farmers or absentee landlords.[17] In other instances, particularly in areas within

[15]U. S. Bureau of the Census, *Census of Agriculture*, for 1935, 1940, 1945, 1950, 1954, 1959, 1964, 1969, and 1974.
[16]U. S. Bureau of the Census, *Census of Agriculture*, for 1940 and 1974.
[17]Aiken, p. 46.

easy access of population centers, larger units are subdivided into "nickel and dime" tracts (five and ten acres) for sale to urbanites.

Results of changes in the operational characteristics of farms have had significant impact on crop production in Mississippi. The Agricultural Adjustment Acts, in limiting acreages of money crops, reduced pressure on the land and allowed farmers to turn to other crops with some expectation of financial success. The diversification of crops not only increased farm income and allowed exhausted, nutrient-depleted soil to rest; it also created new cropping patterns that are only now being recognized.

Cotton is no longer "king" in Mississippi, if indeed it ever was. As the following figures indicate, cotton's position as "king" was never secure, at least not in area. In 1899 it occupied 2,897,920 acres while corn was grown on 2,276,313 acres. In 1942 corn was dominant with 2,894,000 acres compared with cotton's 2,392,000 acres. In 1977 soybeans, with 3,650,000, had replaced both corn and cotton as the areally dominant crop. Cotton was produced on 1,360,000 acres and corn on 160,000 acres.[18] Feed grains and pasture lands also increased. Table 2 depicts 1977 crop land usage in the state.

Table 2
Mississippi Crop Land Usage 1977

Crop	Acres (Thousands)	Per Cent of Total Cropland	Value (Millions)
Soybean	3,650	59.7	$453
Cotton	1,360	22.2	$467
Corn	160	2.6	
Sorghum	24	.4	87
Hay	662	10.8	
Rice	111	1.8	
Wheat	105	1.7	48
Other	46	.8	
TOTAL	6,118	100	$2,203*

*From all agricultural and forest sources
Source: Mississippi Cooperative Extension Service, "Trade Secrets," No. 69, May 1978.

[18]Mississippi Cooperative Extension Service, "Trade Secrets," No. 69, May 1978, p. 48.

Although cotton acreage has declined dramatically since the 1930s, yields per acre have increased. Today the average yield is approximately 1.2 bales per acre and, regardless of soybean's areal dominance, cotton still is the more valuable crop. The 1977 crop was valued at $467 million while soybeans were valued at $453 million. Cotton's position as the state's leading crop in spite of acreage decline is attributable not only to the consolidation of small allotments into viable production units and to mechanization, but also to heavier use of fertilizers, herbicides, and pesticides.

The diversification of crops was accompanied first by a trend in reduction of harvested crop acreage from 6,952,931 harvested acres in 1940 to a low of 4,400,150 harvested acres in 1964. The trend since 1964 has been reversed, showing a slight increase to 4,793,365 harvested acres in 1974.[19]

Cotton and soybeans are dominant and spatially associated in the Yazoo Basin and the surrounding loess hills. Figures 7 and 8 indicate this association. When compared with the rest of the state, counties in the Yazoo Basin are the only ones having more than one half of their land area in harvested crops (Fig. 9). Siniard observed that between 1959 and 1969 that the Yazoo Basin counties gained more than 554,000 acres of harvested land while other counties in the state lost almost 366,000 acres of harvested cropland.[20] Figure 10 shows the per cent change in the per cent of land area in harvested crops from 1969 to 1974. Although the pattern indicates greater growth outside the Yazoo Basin, it must be remembered that many of these counties had a very low percentage of area in harvested cropland in 1969.

Woodland in Mississippi is an important source of income for many people. In 1977 the value of Mississippi woodland products was placed at $362 million from 16,891,000 acres of land.[21] Most of this acreage is in large tracts owned by paper companies, other wood products companies, and the federal government. Only 3,666,730

[19]U. S. Bureau of the Census, *Census of Agriculture*, for 1935, 1940, 1945, 1950, 1954, 1959, 1964, 1969, and 1974.

[20]L. Arnold Siniard, "Dominance of Soybean Cropping in the Lower Mississippi River Valley," *Southeastern Geographer*, XV (May 1975), 20.

[21]Mississippi Cooperative Extension Service, "Trade Secrets," No. 69, May 1978, p. 48.

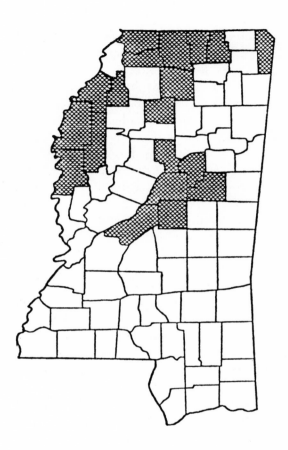

COTTON - 30 PERCENT OR MORE

Figure 7: **Harvested Cropland in Cotton, Percent by Counties 1969**

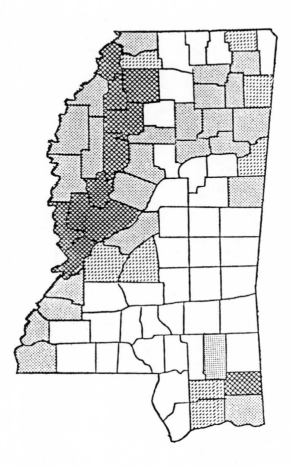

IN PER CENT OF HARVESTED CROPLAND
- 60 OR MORE
- 40 - 59
- 39 OR LESS

Figure 8: **Soybeans Leading Crop in Land Use, 1969**

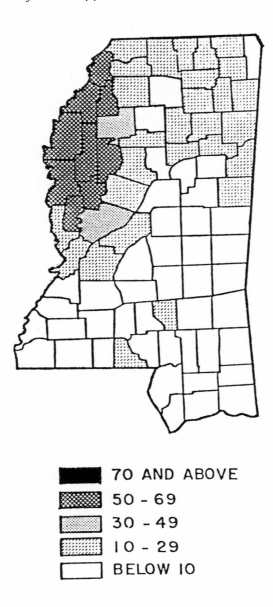

70 AND ABOVE
50 - 69
30 - 49
10 - 29
BELOW 10

Figure 9: **Percent of Land Surface in Harvested Crops 1974**

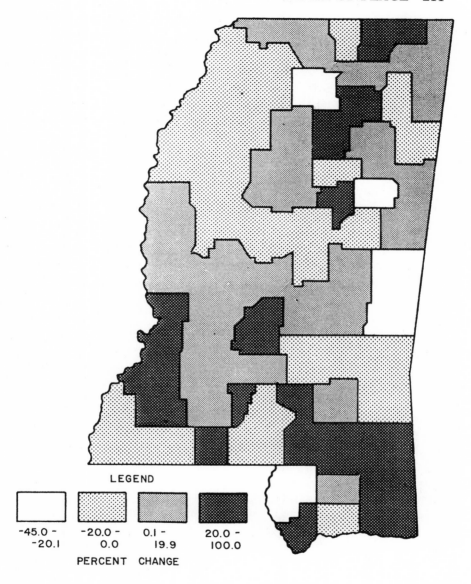

Figure 10: **Percent Change in Percent Land Area in Harvested Crops 1969-1974**

acres of woodlands were found on farms, down from a high of 8,877,148 acres in 1954.[22] Both the increase and decrease in woodlands during the last forty years have been a partial response to government land diversion programs.

Pasture land on farms has been increasing after a twenty year period of relatively little change. Cropland used for grazing or as pasture amounted to 2,477,646 acres in 1974, up more than one million acres since 1964.[23] Associated with increased pasturage is the development of the livestock industry, particularly in southern Mississippi. Cattle produced in the state (some 1.1 million in 1977) are pastured on improved and native forages prior to shipment to feedlots in the West and Mid-West.

Urbanization

A final factor causing changes in the rural Mississippi landscape is urbanization. In 1970, 44.5 percent of the state's population was classified as urban; today it is more than 50 percent. An estimated 1,165,000 acres, 3.8 percent of the state's land area, is urban. Even though Mississippi is still one of the least urbanized states in the nation, only 11.8 percent of the 1970 population was rural farm (compared with a national average of 4 per cent). One recent estimate placed the rural farm population in Mississippi at only 2.4 percent of the total population.[24] As the population of Mississippi grows, the percentage of non-farm rural residents will increase. This trend is borne out in the most recent estimates for the state. Showing the first population growth since 1940, Mississippi recorded a net increase of 1.8 percent between 1960 and 1970. More significantly, the state's population grew an additional 6.28 percent between 1970 and 1976. Whereas urban areas showed the greatest growth in the six year period (14.8 percent), rural areas also increased in population (3.4 percent).[25]

The effect of this increased growth is felt in the rural areas as land

[22]U. S. Bureau of the Census, *Census of Agriculture*, for 1935, 1940, 1945, 1950, 1954, 1959, 1964, 1969, and 1974.
[23]U. S. Bureau of the Census, *Census of Agriculture*, for 1964 and 1974.
[24]Mississippi Cooperative Extension Service, "Trade Secrets," No. 18, February 1974.
[25]Mississippi Cooperative Extension Service, "Trade Secrets," No. 68, April 1978.

near growing cities becomes transitional from agricultural to urban functions and as nonfarm rural residents, some one-third of the state's population, require additional services. Another "spin-off" of the urbanization process that is beginning to be felt in Mississippi is the development of "weekend" retreats, especially along the coast and in the vicinity of recreational areas. Self contained resort areas, featuring permanent and seasonal vacation homes as well as single and multi-family rental properties and motels, are a new type of landuse in rural Mississippi. Characteristic of these developments are a wide variety of recreational features, many having golf courses, lakes, and horse riding trails within the confines of a security patrolled area.

Challenges

As Mississippi's population grows some thought must be given to the effect upon the state's land resources. The Mississippi Cooperative Extension Service estimates that 272.91 acres of land are needed to support 100 people (Table 3). Table 4 uses 1975 figures provided by the Cooperative Extension Service to estimate the acreage of land by category available to Mississippians. Comparison of Tables 3 and 4 reveals that the average Mississippian has access to approximately five times the acreage that is needed to sustain an adequate quality of life. The challenge to Mississippians is how to utilize this land resource without destroying the quality of life that now exists. The state must not allow indiscriminate development to occur. It must strive to attract those industries that will not only provide economic opportunity but protect and conserve the environmental characteristics of the state.

Mississippi's location within the "Sun Belt," its climatic characteristics, particularly its adequate precipitation, the availability of ground water, its developed highway and rail systems, and its progressive agricultural sector provide the basis for economic growth. The economic constraints that tied Mississippians to a labor intensive and inefficient agricultural system have been broken. The land and population resources are available for increased industrialization. However, raw material oriented and capital intensive industries are unlikely to locate in Mississippi because of constraints of the existing geographic pattern of national industries and the economic and spatial relationships that exist between fuel and raw material suppliers and the primary and secondary manufacturers of the Mid-West-Mid-Atlantic region of the U.S.

Mississippi should capitalize on increasing light, consumer-oriented industries and, particularly, on the recreational and retirement potentials of its Gulf Coast. Expansion of service oriented activities will provide new opportunities for Mississippians and will attract new and talented residents to the state.

Even in looking to the challenges of the future, Mississippi will continue to rely on her viable heritage: her land resource. Particularly in the alluvial valley of the Mississippi River—the Yazoo Basin—and the Coastal Plain of central and southern Mississippi are land resources yet untapped. The potential for increased agricultural production is enormous—and the land is cheap compared with the Mid-West. The technology exists; the management expertise is there; the opportunity is there.

Table 3
Average Acreage To Support 100 Mississippians

Use		Acreage
Agricultural		144.21
Crops	43.47	
Pasture	100.74	
Forests		96.9
Recreational		20.0
Urban		11.8
Residential	5.1	
Commercial	.5	
Industrial	1.4	
Streets	2.9	
Utilities and Parks	1.9	
TOTAL		272.91

Source: Mississippi Cooperative Extension Service, "Trade Secrets,"
No. 27, Nov. 1974.

Table 4
Acreage Per 100 Mississippians*

Use	Acreage
Cropland	224
Pasture	233
Forest	714
Urban	51
Water	42
Other	25
TOTAL	1,389

*30.5 million acres of land (1975); population estimate 2,365,488
(1976).
Source: Mississippi Cooperative Extension Service, "Trade Secrets,"
No. 39, Nov. 1975 and "Trade Secrets," No. 68, April 1978.

Mississippi Music:
That Gospel Sound

JAMES DOWNEY

When cataloguing those elements by which we define a "sense of place," priority is due those that come to us through the sense of hearing, whether they be dialect, speech patterns and symbols which grow out of shared experience, or the music that entertains and inspires us and gives expression to our values and aspirations. Many of the "sounds" which we identify with Mississippi are shared by other communities in the South, but this does not in any way diminish their associations to an expatriate. Actually, their appearance in other geographic areas extends the sense of community and eases the adjustment to new surroundings.

An example of a true "Mississippi sound" is a musical style called gospel. Gospel music can be heard at any place on the dial at any hour of the day from one of the fifty-four country and western radio stations in the state. Gospel music is not unique to Mississippi: gospel music is the sound of the Bible Belt. James R. Shortridge, writing in *The Geographic Review* in October 1976, said that Jackson, Mississippi, could perhaps be called "the Buckle of the Bible Belt."[1] H. L. Mencken coined the term "Bible Belt" around 1925. He intended the term to be a title of derision, but in the ensuing years it has become, for some, a point of pride. Mencken, in his *Prejudices: Fifth Series*, said: "Where it [evangelical spirit] lingers is in far places—on the Methodist prairies of the Midwest and the Baptist backwaters of the South.

---

[1]"Patterns of Religion in the United States," *The Geographic Review*, 66 (October 1976), p. 427. A discussion of the use of media in the Bible Belt may be found in Steven W. Tweedie, "Viewing the Bible Belt," *Journal of Popular Culture* (Spring 1978), 865-76.

There it retains a little of its vitality. Their Puritanism survives not merely as a system of theology, but also as a way of life. It colors every human activity."[2]

In the first half of the nineteenth century, many communities came into being in the South and Midwest in which economic and political incentive combined with a millenarian expectation. Communities later further isolated themselves in an attempt to realize their expectations of a New Zion in the face of urbanization and industrialization. Mississippians, in the traumatic years from 1865 to 1910, saw many reasons to "withdraw" and to create their own counter culture in which fundamentalist religion would serve as a cornerstone.

The music of evangelical fundamentalism is a form called the gospel song. Prototypes first appeared in the revival campaigns of Charles G. Finney in New York in 1831, published and promoted by Joshua Leavitt, one of the editors of the religious penny press.[3] By 1875, the gospel songs were clearly defined in the publications of Ira Sankey, who, with the evangelist Dwight L. Moody, spread them throughout the world. This music, closely associated with revival preaching, came into rural areas of the United States near the end of the nineteenth century through publishers like A. J. Showalter of Dalton, Georgia, and Chattanooga, Tennessee, who took the revival songs and put them into the shaped-note style which we now call Old Harp or Sacred Harp music. In the process, these gospel songs were freed from the revivalist's pulpit and became a religious pastime. In this formative period, 1890 to 1920, country gospel was born, a hybrid product of the union of the music of urban revivalism and the shaped-note tradition of the South, which dated back to the early years of the nineteenth century.

Because of gospel music's early association with evangelical Baptists and Methodists and their influence on the rural and small town populations, it became the form of music most performed and listened to in the state. As so often happens, sacred and profane combined to produce a new form. The "bedrock" Baptists and Methodists looked

[2](New York: Alfred Knopf, 1926), p. 253.
[3]The best study of Joshua Leavitt's *Christian Lyre* is Cynthia D. Stribling's "Joshua Leavitt's *The Christian Lyre*: An Historical Evaluation," Thesis, William Carey College, 1976.

upon dancing music as evil. There is reason to believe that they did
give credence to the old folk belief that a good fiddler had made a pact
with the devil. For the lively music which they may have secretly
wanted, they substituted religious texts with music that was as lively
as any the devil's fiddlers might have played. Gospel music served
that function; it gave them worldly pleasures within a "sanctified"
form.[4]

The state can boast of its Jimmie Rodgers, Charley Pride, and Elvis
Presley; but gospel, and not country and western music, appears to
have greater appeal in the state. For example, in the twelve days from
September 16 to 28, 1978, the *Hattiesburg American* carried twenty
announcements of gospel quartet singers as compared to only two
announcements for a country and western or bluegrass group.

In many of the Mississippi counties are still to be found "fifth
Sunday gospel singing conventions," which date back forty years or
more. No comparable country and western institution exists. The
small country churches often had a male quartet or women's trio of
gospel singers. Many churches use the music exclusively in their
congregations to this day, particularly the Landmark Baptists and the
"hard-core pentecostal" groups.

We find that about the time of the merging of urban gospel with
shaped-note tradition, which produced the rural gospel sound, the
black community had developed a similar but distinct style. One form
is called the Jubilee gospel sound, patterned after the Fisk Jubilee
Singers. One can hear this in the concerts of the Heavenly Gospel
Singers of Jackson, Mississippi, a group of black men in their late
sixties who have been singing together for over forty years. Another
black gospel style is that of Sister Rosetta Tharpe, Mahalia Jackson, or
Aretha Franklin. One form, Jubilee, is oriented toward an ensemble,
the other toward a solo singer whose style is similar to that of the
secular blues singer of the 1930s. The parallels which can be drawn
between the practices indicate that black and white traditions at some
point along the way influenced each other.

Among the white communities we find two styles as well: one

[4]The relationship between the gospel songs and the secular forms in 19th century
America is treated in James C. Downey, "Revivalism, the Gospel Songs and Social
Reform," *Ethnomusicology*, 9 (March 1965).

which may be called the ensemble, or singing convention or gospel quartet style; and the gospel ballad, sometimes now incorrectly called bluegrass gospel, heard in the recordings of Jimmie Davis, former governor of Louisiana, or Cal Smith or even Kris Kristofferson when he sings, "Why Me, Lord?" One style, the singing convention, is a natural outgrowth of the shaped-note singings; the gospel ballad is a kind of complement to country and western music.

It is not possible to discuss the two styles, black and white, in one brief paper. I shall discuss only the white tradition as it appears in the gospel ballad and the singing convention styles. It is a sad commentary on Southern musical scholarship that no one has completed a satisfactory study of these forms to this time. My own studies at the University of Southern Mississippi in 1963 and later with the National Endowment for the Humanities pretty much stand alone and incomplete.[5] Mississippi scholars tend to avoid the study because of its "common" application and origin. An analytical, social or historical study of the genre would contribute little to the "magnolia myths" which we have too often projected as cultural studies. Musicologists, for the most part, have an aesthetic bias and do not consider the material worthy of their refined analytical skills.

After Showalter's publications of urban gospel songs in shaped-note form, other publishers helped to spread the practice throughout the South. James Vaughn of Lawrenceburg, Tennessee, was typical. Vaughn began by selling books and sheet music, but later, in 1924, he established WOAN, one of the earliest radio stations in Tennessee. Vaughn trained singers and sent them out to teach the shaped-note system and to sell new gospel music and records in rural areas. WOAN became the principal means of spreading the new sound in Tennessee. The recordings which he sold were advertised as the only "Southern records" on the market. He preceded the famed Ralph Peer of RCA with records aimed at a Southern market. He published 105 gospel songbooks, each of which sold an average of 117,000 copies.[6]

In the early 1930s, there appeared in Texas the Samps-Baxter Quar-

[5] James C. Downey, "The Gospel Hymn, 1875-1930," Thesis, University of Southern Mississippi, 1963.

[6] An extensive discussion of Vaughn's activities, summarized here, may be found in Charles Wolfe, *Tennessee Strings* (Knoxville: Univ. of Tennessee Press, 1977).

tet which dominated country gospel until the 1970s. Virgil O. Stamps and Fred Baxter published songbooks, owned a radio station (KRLD, Dallas) and trained singers and teachers of gospel styles. In addition to the stations already in existence, gospel music with its country and western sibling was to come into Mississippi homes through the Mexican border stations XERA, XERL, and later XERF, whose broadcasts reached into Canada when there was a good rain in the Pecos and Rio Grande valleys.

The Stamps-Baxter Quartet in 1936, singing its theme song "Give the World a Smile Each Day," became the model upon which countless gospel groups were built. In one month in that year, the Stamps Quartet received over 25,000 pieces of fan mail. They could be heard daily over KRLD from 6:45 to 11:45 A.M. The Stamps school prepared singers, pianists, and teachers to go throughout the United States. In 1957, there were some 200 different Stamps Quartets, all promoting tne gospel sound and the Stamps publications. In 1949, enrollment at the school was 1100. By 1957 it was estimated that over 5 million paperback shaped-note songbooks had been printed by the company. Virgil Stamps encouraged consumption in every form—records, music books, radio and live concerts. There was a planned obsolescence in their publications, each succeeded by a "new" and "better" series of books. According to Stamps some 5,000 new gospel songs were received each year from would-be composers, for which the company paid from $5 to $10 for exclusive rights. An estimated 600 songs found their way each year into one of the Stamps publications.[7]

There is a direct link between the Stamps-Baxter organization and the state of Mississippi. For many years, travelers along the Gulf Coast saw the sign reading "Gospel Singers of America" in front of a stately white building. Until its destruction in 1969 by Hurricane Camille, this was the site of a thriving gospel singing school for young people, operated by Videt Polk. Polk was one of the principal composers for Stamps Publications. He later became the president of the Stamps-

---

[7]The most authoritative history of the Gospel Singing Convention style is the trial transcript of a suit, AFFILIATED MUSIC ENTERPRISES, Inc. v. SESAC, United States District Court, S.E. New York, summarized by David Crawford in "Gospel Songs in Court," *Journal of Popular Culture*, II (Winter 1977), 551-567. I am indebted to him for much of the material on the Stamps-Baxter organization summarized above.

Baxter organization in Dallas and served in that position until the company was sold to Zondervan Family Publishers.

Polk first came to my attention in 1966 when some of his students appeared in my music theory classrooms. They were exceptionally good at reading music at the piano and at singing difficult vocal parts at sight. From them I learned that Polk employed music graduates from Louisiana State and other Southern universities as teachers. He even taught music history, voice, and theory as well as conducting. At my request a student recorded an interview with their former teacher.

Listening to Videt Polk talk about gospel music is an experience not easily forgotten. In 1967 when the entire nation was torn by what we call the Youth Revolution, Polk spoke highly of the kind of Mississippian who came to his school to study. At that time he saw gospel music as a force doing battle with rock music for the allegiance of the youth of the country. He believed that only gospel music could "save the country" and those old values that had made the nation great. Polk now lives in Baton Rouge, but he is still extremely active in the state.

In the years following World War II, gospel music appears to have changed to some extent. In this period, also, emphasis seems to have shifted from the singing convention tradition to that of the gospel ballad. Walley Fowler, the founder of the Oak Ridge Quartet, saw the enormous success of the Grand Ole Opry country and western troupes which toured the country. He moved into the larger Southern cities with what he called the all-night singing. He was extremely well received in what can be called the redneck ghettos, which had been filled with rural families that moved to the cities in the 1940s for "war work" and never went back to the farm. In Montgomery, Alabama, Fowler's show drew 9,000; in Winston-Salem, 10,000. The all-night singing, Fowler style, drew more paying customers in the 1950s than any other paid event except, perhaps, a crucial football or baseball game.[8]

Across the stage, in a typical Fowler show, would pass the Oak Ridge Quartet, the Statesmen, and the Blackwood Brothers, who brought national attention to the style when, in 1954, they were the

[8]Allen Rankin, "They're 'singin' all-nite' in Dixie," *Colliers*, 19 Aug. 1955, p. 27. Reprinted in Linnell Gentry, *A History and Encyclopedia of Country, Western and Gospel Music* (Nashville: Gentry, 1961), pp. 141-45.

first gospel group to win on Arthur Godfrey's Talent Scouts. There were also solo singers like Jimmie Davis, governor of Louisiana. The fans described the show as "good, wholesome entertainment." The gospel ballad style had been nurtured by Roy Acuff in the thirties with "Great Speckled Bird." In the forties, Hank Williams's greatest hit was the gospel song "I Saw the Light." Country and western, not gospel quartet, maintains that tradition. The "all-night singing" brought the singing quartet and the country gospel ballad together in the same program.

Along with Fowler's new gospel sound emerged that style which we now call bluegrass gospel, complete with banjo, dobros, and electric guitars. Instead of books sold at the old gospel singings, the fans bought records and slick souvenir albums. Instead of participating by singing, they observed and responded by stamping, clapping, and cheering.

Gospel music, which had begun as an aid to evangelical preaching but had passed into a religious "pastime" at the hands of Vaughn and Stamps, now became a form of entertainment which appealed to a shared cultural background and social position, restating the old values but recognizing and expressing some new anxieties. Gospel is the sound of the Bible Belt, the sound of Mississippi—but the sounds are changing, just as are other features that define a sense of place.

A new form of gospel is now emerging that may have as much potential for expressing the conflict and stress of the Southern contemporary white as the blues once did for the black man. From recent examples, gospel ballads now truly can be called a white man's blues. A former Ole Miss chaplain, Will D. Campbell, is the prophet of this new gospel social consciousness. To Waylon Jennings, Kris Kristofferson, Larry Gatlin, Johnny Cash and the new gospel singers, Campbell is father-confessor. Jesse Winchester, Charley Pride, and O. B. McClinton are in the advance guard. Most country and western singers have done a gospel song or album—even Willie Nelson of the Outlaws and Shel Silverstein, known as much for his Playboy cartoons as for his country and western songs. In fact, gospel is now influencing country and western in a profound way. Kristofferson's biggest hit was "Why Me, Lord?" Bill Anderson's "The Lord Knows I'm Drinking" is a story about a "high stepping good ole boy" who is going to have a "heart to heart" talk with God after just one final round at the bar.

We can discern the "creative sadness" of country music blending with the basic optimism of the older gospel in the music of Johnny Cash and of John Prine, a young Chicago gospel singer born in Appalachia, nurtured in the violence and confusion of Viet Nam and in the nation's loss of innocence in the Chicago summer of 1968. There is a new dimension in gospel. Will Campbell sings "Birds and Children Fly Away." The gospel cliches are gone, but the message of the old gospel is there, a belief that someone cares and understands and that if we will just believe, everything will be all right. Prine sings about the family of a veteran, dead of an overdose: "There's a hole in Daddy's arm / Where all the money goes / And Jesus Christ died for nothing, I suppose."

Even America's newest singing "sweetheart," Dolly Parton, born in Sevierville, Tennessee, to Church of God parents, cannot break away from the simple faith that permeates gospel music. She recently wrote about her new life in light of the moral teaching of her church and the gospel music in her home. She began her song "I'm a seeker, poor sinful creature, there is none weaker. . . ." In talking about her new song, she seemed to touch the dilemma of contemporary living in Mississippi and the nation: "I'm too good to be bad, and too bad to be good. I think God understands. I hope he does. If not, we all got a problem."[9]

[9]I am indebted to Frye Gaillard for much of the above discussion of the new gospel sound in country and western music. Not only has the author brought together for the first time much of the information about the new movement; he has done so with a trenchant prose that often rivals the lyricism of his subject. See *Watermelon Wine: The Spirit of Country Music* (New York: St. Martins Press, 1978).

Symposium Agenda

THURSDAY, OCTOBER 5

9:00-11:00	Registration
10:00- 5:00	Folklife Exhibits
11:00-11:15	Welcome: Aubrey Lucas (President, University of Southern Mississippi)
	Introduction to Conference Jesse O. McKee
	Introduction to the Speaker Peggy W. Prenshaw
11:15-12:00	Opening Address
	Sense of Place and the Americanization of Mississippi Willie Morris
12:00- 2:00	Lunch (On the Plaza)
	Entertainment Heavenly Gospel Singers, Mickey Davis, George McLeod

Session I: Exploring the Sense of Place

2:00- 3:00	Address
	Staying Home or Leaving Will D. Campbell
3:00- 3:15	Break
3:15- 4:45	Forum I
	Images and Impressions of Mississippi and the Sense of Place: Native View/Outside View
	Moderator: Charles Sallis (Millsaps College)
	Discussants:
	Roy Hudson (Mississippi Valley State)
	Thomas Daniel Young (Vanderbilt)

Neil McMillen (University of
Southern Mississippi)
Turner Catledge (New Orleans)
Reporter:
David Bodenhamer (University of
Southern Mississippi)

7:00- 9:00   Banquet
Address
Defining a Sense of Place   Peirce Lewis
(Pennsylvania State University)

9:00-11:30   Social Hour

FRIDAY, OCTOBER 6

Session II: Mississippi's Past: Historical Development of the Sense of Place

9:00-11:00   Registration

9:00- 9:15   Opening Comments   Charles Moorman (University
of Southern Mississippi)
Jesse O. McKee/Peggy W.
Prenshaw

9:00- 5:00   Folklife Exhibits

9:00- 5:00   Arts and Crafts Exhibits

9:15-10:15   Two Concurrent Sessions
Session A: Settlement Patterns
Chairperson: Arthell Kelley (University of
Southern Mississippi)
The Historical Geography of Extinct Towns in
Mississippi   Howard Adkins (Marshall
University)
From Prosperity to Poverty: Economic Growth
and Change to 1900   William K. Scarborough
(University of Southern Mississippi)
Session B: Folkways and Landscapes

Chairperson:　Paula Tadlock (Mississippi ETV)
Designing for a Sense of Place in Mississippi Small
　　Towns　James Barker (Mississippi State)
Traditional Food and Food Habits of the
　　Rural South
　　Sam Hilliard (Louisiana State)

10:15-10:30　　Break

Session III:　Mississippi and Its Sense of Place in the Twentieth Century: Images and Conflicts

10:30-12:00　　Forum II
Preserving. Creating, and Destroying the Sense of
Place:
　　Public Policy and Decision Making
Moderator:　Robert W. Wales (University of
　　Southern Mississippi)
Discussants:
　　Volney Cissna (South Mississippi Planning and
　　　　Development District)
　　Patti Black (Mississippi State Historical
　　　　Museum)
　　Frank E. Smith (Virginia Polytechnic Institute)
　　Robert Thorne (University of Mississippi)
Reporter:
　　Graham Hales (University of
　　　　Southern Mississippi)

12:00- 1:30　　Lunch
Speaker:　William "Fishbait" Miller

1:30- 3:00　　Forum III
Mississippi in the Media
Moderator:　Paul Pittman (*Tylertown Times*)
Discussants:
　　Sarah McClendon (Journalist)
　　Bert Case (WLBT-TV)
　　Rea S. Hederman (*Clarion-Ledger*)

Reporter:
Gary A. Stringer (University of
Southern Mississippi)

3:00- 3:15   Break

3:15- 4:15   Three Concurrent Sessions
Session C: The Changing Environment
Chairperson: James W. Gladden (University
of Southern Mississippi)
Economic Growth and Change in
Mississippi Since 1950   John Wade (Mississippi
Research and Development Center)
The Mississippi Landscape: Past, Present, and
Future   W. Ted Mealor (Memphis State)
Session D: Art of Living: Mississippi Style
Chairperson: Thomas Richardson (University of
Southern Mississippi)
Mississippi Music—That Gospel Sound
James Downey (William Carey College)
Putting Our Faith Into Action   John Perkins
(Voice of Calvary)
Session E: Mississippi Literature
Introduction: David Berry (University of
Southern Mississippi)
Voices of Fiction: A Reading   Jane Petty
(New Stage, Jackson)

4:15- 5:00   Address
Mississippi: A Personal View of Its Past and a Hope
for Its Future   Thomas Daniel Young
(Vanderbilt)

Notes on Contributors

HOWARD G. ADKINS is associate professor of geography at Marshall University in Huntington, West Virginia.

JAMES F. BARKER, co-author of *The Small Town as an Art Object*, is a registered architect and corporate member of the American Institute of Architects. He is currently Director of Instruction and professor of architecture at Mississippi State University.

PATTI CARR BLACK, Director of the Mississippi Historical Museum, has recently published *Mississippi Piney Woods: A Study in Folk Architecture.*

DAVID J. BODENHAMER, JR. is assistant professor of history at the University of Southern Mississippi.

WILL D. CAMPBELL, currently Director of the Committee of Southern Churchmen, is the author of *Brother to a Dragonfly.*

VOLNEY CISSNA, a member of the National Board of Examiners of the American Institute of Planners, is presently a planning consultant to the Southern Mississippi Planning and Development District.

JAMES DOWNEY is professor of music history and literature at William Carey College, Hattiesburg, Mississippi.

GRAHAM HALES is Chaplain and Coordinator of Religious Activities and assistant professor of philosophy and religion at the University of Southern Mississippi.

REA S. HEDERMAN of the *Clarion Ledger*, Jackson, Mississippi, has won several awards in journalism, including the Heyward Brown Memorial Award and the Scripps-Howard Foundation distinguished journalism citation for public service reporting.

ROY HUDSON is associate professor of English and teacher education at Mississippi Valley State University.

PEIRCE LEWIS, whose most recent book is *New Orleans: The Mak-*

ing of an Urban Landscape, is professor of geography at Pennsylvania State University.

SARAH McCLENDON, a Washington journalist and White House reporter, is the author of *My Eight Presidents*.

W. THEODORE MEALOR, JR. is chairman of the department and professor of geography at Memphis State University.

WILLIE MORRIS, a former editor of *Harper's Magazine*, is the author of *North Towards Home*, *The Last of the Southern Girls* and *Yazoo: Integration in a Deep Southern Town*.

PAUL PITTMAN, publisher and owner of the *Tylertown Times* and president of the Tylertown Broadcasting Company, writes a syndicated column published in over sixty Mississippi newspapers.

CHARLES SALLIS, professor of history at Millsaps College in Jackson, Mississippi, is co-author of *Mississippi: Conflict and Change*.

WILLIAM K. SCARBOROUGH, professor of history at the University of Southern Mississippi, is the editor of the *Diary of Edmund Ruffin* and author of *The Overseer: Plantation Management in the Old South*.

FRANK E. SMITH, a former member of Congress and a former Director of the Tennessee Valley Authority, presently teaches in the department of public administration at Virginia Polytechnic Institute. He has written numerous books including *The Yazoo River*, *The Politics of Conservation*, *Land Between the Lakes* and a chapter on land use in *You Can't Eat Magnolias*.

GARY A. STRINGER is associate professor of English at the University of Southern Mississippi.

ROBERT THORNE is associate professor of anthropology and Co-Director of the Center for Archeological Research at the University of Mississippi.

F. JOHN WADE is Director for Job and Income Development at the Mississippi Research and Development Center.

ROBERT W. WALES, associate professor of geography at the University of Southern Mississippi, is co-editor of the *Atlas of Mississippi*.

THOMAS DANIEL YOUNG, Gertrude Conaway Vanderbilt Professor of English at Vanderbilt University, is the author of numerous articles and books including *Gentleman in a Dustcoat: A Biography of John Crowe Ransom*.